LIBRARY TECHNICAL SERVICES
OPERATIONS AND MANAGEMENT

LIBRARY AND INFORMATION SCIENCE

CONSULTING EDITORS: *Harold Borko and G. Edward Evans*
GRADUATE SCHOOL OF LIBRARY SCIENCE
UNIVERSITY OF CALIFORNIA, LOS ANGELES

Thomas H. Mott, Jr., Susan Artandi, and Leny Struminger
Introduction to PL/I Programming for Library and Information Science

Karen Sparck Jones and Martin Kay
Linguistics and Information Science

Manfred Kochen (Ed.)
Information for Action: From Knowledge to Wisdom

Harold Borko and Charles L. Bernier
Abstracting Concepts and Methods

F. W. Lancaster
Toward Paperless Information Systems

H. S. Heaps
Information Retrieval: Computational and Theoretical Aspects

Harold Borko and Charles L. Bernier
Indexing Concepts and Methods

Gerald Jahoda and Judith Schiek Braunagel
The Librarian and Reference Queries: A Systematic Approach

Charles H. Busha and Stephen P. Harter
Research Methods in Librarianship: Techniques and Interpretation

Diana M. Thomas, Ann T. Hinckley, and Elizabeth R. Eisenbach
The Effective Reference Librarian

James Cabeceiras
The Multimedia Library, Second Edition: Materials Selection and Use

G. Edward Evans
Management Techniques for Librarians, Second Edition

Irene P. Godden (Ed.)
Library Technical Services: Operations and Management

LIBRARY TECHNICAL SERVICES
OPERATIONS AND MANAGEMENT

EDITED BY IRENE P. GODDEN

The Libraries
Colorado State University
Fort Collins, Colorado

ACADEMIC PRESS, INC.

(Harcourt Brace Jovanovich, Publishers)

Orlando   San Diego   San Francisco   New York   London
Toronto   Montreal   Sydney   Tokyo   São Paulo

ACADEMIC PRESS, INC.
Orlando, Florida 32887

United Kingdom Edition published by
ACADEMIC PRESS, INC. (LONDON) LTD.
24/28 Oval Road, London NW1 7DX

Library of Congress Cataloging in Publication Data

Main entry under title:

Library technical services.

(Library and information sciences series)
Includes bibliographies and index.
1. Processing (Libraries) 2. Libraries--Automation.
I. Godden, Irene P., Date   . II. Series.
Z688.5.L5 1984   025'.02'02854   83-15645
ISBN 0-12-287040-9

PRINTED IN THE UNITED STATES OF AMERICA

84 85 86 87   9 8 7 6 5 4 3 2 1

Contents

7. Circulation Functions

Leslie A. Manning

Contributors

Numbers in parentheses indicate the pages on which the authors' contributions begin.

BETTY G. BENGTSON (133), The University of Tennessee Library, Knoxville, Tennessee 37996–1000

IRENE P. GODDEN (1), The Libraries, Colorado State University, Fort Collins, Colorado 80523

KAREN L. HORNY (43), Northwestern University Library, Evanston, Illinois 60201

A. DEAN LARSEN (195), Harold B. Lee Library, Brigham Young University, Provo, Utah 84602

LESLIE A. MANNING (15, 249), Libraries, Kansas State University, Manhattan, Kansas 66506

MARION T. REID (89), Troy H. Middleton Library, Louisiana State University and Agricultural and Mechanical College, Baton Rouge, Louisiana 70803–3300

Preface

Although there is no lack of articles or books on various aspects of technical services operations, Tauber's *Technical Services in Libraries,* which appeared in 1954 and does not cover the many dramatic developments of the last 30 years, is the only comprehensive treatment of the topic intended for a professional audience. The present text is therefore intended to give an overview of current operations and techniques associated with the acquisition, organization for access, and physical processing and maintenance of collections of library materials. Typical organizational patterns and representative examples of work flow are included, but detailed procedures are not. Instead, each chapter provides published sources of further information.

The actual descriptions of technical services operations are based mainly on the practices of academic and research libraries, which for various reasons have tended to dominate change and codification in this area of library work. One of the major reasons is that the high costs of technical processing in large research libraries have generated much management interest and resultant research in order to gain efficiencies. The editor and contributors are of course aware that, given certain general objectives for technical services, organizational structures and procedures will vary from library to library, depending on size, specific internal objectives, and the nature of technical support and requirements. Nevertheless, we hope that the present volume will be useful to all library administrators, librarians, and library school students concerned with technical services, regardless of their affiliation.

Because the actual organization of technical services activities varies widely among institutions for both philosophical and administrative reasons, we had to decide which activities to cover, in what depth, and in what order. We settled on the following structure. Administration, automation, and networking provide the framework within which all other technical services activities take place; these, therefore, are discussed first and in some detail. Acquisitions and bibliographic control, or cataloging, the traditional core activities, are discussed next, and again in depth. The chapter on preservation covers materials processing and collection maintenance activities, as well as weeding, storage, and preservation microfilming.

In order to avoid repetitive treatment of general principles that are common to all library materials, discussions of specific materials are covered in each functional chapter. Thus the acquisitions of serials are covered in a separate section in the chapter on acquisition; various methods of bibliographic control of serials are discussed in a section in the chapter on bibliographic control; and there is a subsection on serials binding in the preservation and maintenance chapter. There is also a section on serials control under the heading of automated applications to individual processing operations in the chapter on automation.

We decided to include a brief chapter on circulation-related functions because the current trend seems to be to shift circulation from public services units to technical services. This development is rooted in the historical practice of grouping materials-related functions together and has been furthered by the growth of integrated systems which mandate work flows related to a single master record in a common database (see Chapters 2 and 3). We decided not to cover collection development because the trend is to move this activity to a unit of its own, separating out the selection decision—increasingly the concern of subject specialists—from the actual acquisitions process.

The editors and contributors are of course aware that current information quickly becomes dated in a rapidly changing field and have therefore tried to indicate evolving trends. We have also, at the end of each chapter, included a section suggesting how to keep up-to-date on a given topic in addition to the usual list of references and bibliography. In general, we have defined specialized terms in the text. Readers are also referred to the 1983 *ALA Glossary of Library and Information Science*, edited by H. Young.

The editor gratefully acknowledges the help and encouragement received from Dr. G. Edward Evans, Associate Dean at the University of Denver Graduate School of Librarianship and Information Management and library science series editor at Academic Press, who originally suggested this book. Very special thanks also go to Betty G. Bengtson, Karen L. Horny, A. Dean Larsen, Leslie A. Manning, and Marion T. Reid, the chapter contributors, who unfailingly met deadlines and accepted suggestions and revisions with equanimity. It was a pleasure and a privilege to work with them.

LIBRARY TECHNICAL SERVICES
OPERATIONS AND MANAGEMENT

1 Introduction

Irene P. Godden

WHAT ARE TECHNICAL SERVICES IN LIBRARIES?

Technical services in libraries have been defined as "services involving the operations and techniques for acquiring, recording, and preserving materials" (Tauber, 1954, p. 4). Tauber goes on to define *service* as all the work connected with some activity, such as acquisitions; *operations* as the steps involved in performing the service; and *techniques* as the methods used in executing the operations involved in a service. Horny (1980) more broadly defines technical services as those services that provide access to information existing in some published form. She divides access into two major components: (1) physical access, which is created through the process of acquiring, organizing, and labeling information packages; and (2) bibliographic access, which requires the creation of the descriptive and subject tags that allow the eventual users to select the information package needed. Horny concludes (p. 588) that "all other aspects of library service depend upon the efficiency and accuracy with which this work is accomplished." There are several other definitions: Some are based on separating intellectual tasks such as cataloging and collection development from materials-related "technical" tasks such as ordering and preservation activities; others are based on the concept of calling all nonpublic services technical services. Although different styles of organization based on different concepts of technical services are considered in the following chapters, Tauber's and Horny's definitions have generally been used as working definitions for this book.

DEVELOPMENT OF TECHNICAL SERVICES

History

It may be useful to remind ourselves that although "the services involving the operations and techniques for acquiring, recording, and preserving materials are among the oldest aspects of librarianship" (Tauber, 1954, p. 4), the concept of a technical services department or division and the term "technical services" are of comparatively recent origin, as Tuttle (1976) traces in her excellent article on the history of technical services in academic and research libraries from 1876 to 1976. The problems of cataloging and classification occupied the attention of such library pioneers as Cutter, whose *Rules for a Printed Dictionary Catalog*, and Dewey, whose *A Classified and Subject Index for Cataloging and Arranging the Books and Pamphlets of a Library* both appeared in 1876 and were apparently the major topic of discussion at contemporary library conferences; however, the concept of a technical services or technical processes unit including the acquisitions and processing functions was first proposed in published form in a paper by Coney (1939) at the University of Chicago. As Tuttle (1976) shows, the pros and cons of a technical services unit or division were debated at ALA conferences and in the literature in the 1940s, with proponents of the concepts winning out in the 1950s. This is evidenced by the general acceptance of the technical services divisional plan in academic libraries, the establishment of the Resources and Technical Services Division of the American Library Association (composed of the former acquisitions and cataloging divisions) in 1956, and the publication, in 1954, of Tauber's previously cited volume, which was the first comprehensive text on the topic.

Recent Issues

Since Tauber's (1954) book was published, there have been many and radical changes, not so much in what is done in technical services, but in how it is done. Most, if not all, of these changes have been caused by economic pressures, coupled with advances in automation and resulting new standards, and a renewed emphasis on the need of preservation of materials, caused by the rather dramatic evidence of shelves upon shelves of books printed in the late nineteenth century crumbling under our very eyes in the 1970s.

Some highlights taken from annual review articles on technical services, published by *Library Resources & Technical Services* (LRTS) for the last 5 years, will serve to illustrate this point.

In bibliographic control, 1977 brought "disquiet for those concerned with the future of the card catalog" (Berrisford, 1978, p. 227). Issues such as the potential and limitations of online computerized catalogs; the implications for libraries of new standards, such as the International Standard Bibliographic Description (ISBD); and the forthcoming second edition of the *Anglo-American Cataloguing Rules* (AACR2), which was written "with particular attention to developments in the machine processing of bibliographic records" (*Anglo-American Cataloguing Rules*, 1978, p. vii) were first discussed at several professional institutes and in the literature, and technical services managers realized the impact these changes would have on their operations.

1978 was the year that AACR2 was actually published, and the problems discussed in the 1979 LRTS review article on cataloging and classification (Jones, 1979) reflect the concern of technical services experts for the future of the card catalog: Should one close or freeze or begin a new catalog? And should the new catalog be a COM (computer-output microform) or an online catalog? Is an interim card catalog needed? Or is it possible and desirable to integrate the new cataloging rules with the old ones within the existing card catalog? The Library of Congress (LC) had agreed, upon the urging of larger libraries, to delay the closing of its own catalog until January 1, 1981, thus delaying the impact of having LC cataloging copy based on AACR2 arriving at libraries unprepared to handle it;[1] however, by 1979 the profession had to come to serious grips with interpreting the specific provisions of the code, training staff, and making a firm decision for at least the immediate future of the catalog, which clearly lay, according to Rinehart (1980, p. 218) in having "the bibliographic record supported in some way by computer technology," be it in card form with the cards produced by computer, computer-produced microfiche or film, printouts, or online. Net-

---

[1]As LC copy distributed by tape or in card format accounts for as much as 80% of cataloging copy for many (if not most) libraries, *not* accepting LC copy was not really a choice.

work developments and interrelations were also given extensive coverage in the 1980 review article, with questions of balance between support for a national bibliographic network, local needs, costs and benefits, and regional commitments being considered by technical services managers trying to decide whether to use one or the other of the larger networks or "bibliographic utilities," commercial vendors, local and regional networks, or a combination of these for automated technical services support.

AACR2 still dominated the literature in 1981, the year that the Library of Congress did close its card catalog. Accordingly, AACR2 interpretations, problems, and training efforts were covered in the 1982 LRTS review articles on descriptive cataloging and subject access, along with general "nagging and difficult questions for computer support of technical services procedures" (Rinehart, 1982, p. 254). These questions ranged from what forms bibliographic access and control should and would take in the near and intermediate future, to cost-effectiveness and limitations of network participation and of the whole cataloging process itself. Younger (1982, pp. 270–271), after reviewing current research into new methods of access made possible by computer capabilities, concluded that by 1985 not only will "many people . . . be service users of several online systems and multiple databases," but that "it will not be acceptable to turn card catalogs and printed indexes into online services without redesigning the cataloging and indexing procedures." Full text storage, with automatic indexing using probabilistic retrieval models containing term significance weights, and natural language processing systems were seen as some possibilities.

In acquisitions, technological and resource-sharing issues began to dominate the literature in the late 1970s. Lynden (1978, p. 330), reported that with tightening funds "libraries shifted from collection building to collection analysis . . . and there was greater emphasis put on access than on possession." By 1978, automated acquisitions systems began to receive more attention. Although still considered "in their infancy" (Lynden, 1978, p. 319) when compared with automated catalog support systems, enough interest in automated acquisitions systems had been generated by 1978 for them to become the topic of both a program meeting at the ALA 1978 annual conference and of a survey of the Association of Research Libraries, as reported by Lynden in the 1979 *LRTS* review article on resources. Better management reports and increased standardization were seen as benefits, although direct cost savings seemed elusive if not nonexistent. In that same year resource sharing on a national scale seemed a real possibility. According to Lynden (p. 213) "the most important news of 1978 was the publication of a plan to create a National Periodicals Center," which was seen as "a most welcome step toward the long-term goal of relieving libraries of the burden of maintaining extensive local periodical collections." Lynden went on to cover in approximately five pages other resource-sharing ventures that seemed to validate optimism that "the framework for a national system of interlibrary cooperation . . . has been laid" (p. 219).

The building blocks for this interlibrary cooperation were, first of all, financial constraints, or, as Magrill said in her 1980 review article on resources, "the gradual acceptance of and adjustment to restricted materials budgets as the normal situation" (p. 247), and second, rapid communication of data via computer links between cooperating libraries. Magrill (p. 255) cited the Research Libraries Group as an example of a group attempting to view its members' collections as a single distributed collection to which efficient access could be gained via online searching of requests and rapid delivery of items requested.

In serials work, as with acquisitions, the largest changes were again caused by the twin forces of budget constraints and automation. The budget crunch forced libraries to look toward resource sharing and automation forced reorganization. Glasby (1981), reviewing a work on serials in libraries that concludes that serials functions should be grouped because they are interdependent, notes that nevertheless the pendulum that had favored integration of serials work in the 1950s was now swinging the other way. She closes with the statement that "although budget restraints are sometimes given as the reason for the dispersing of serial activities among other cataloging, control, and reference functions, it would appear that the computer may be what is really behind the movement to realign organizational patterns" (p. 317).

The most exciting new developments related to serials and those with the most implications for the future of information transfer and of technical services, are the potentials of electronic journals and systems of document deliveries. Weber describes (1) ADONIS (Article Delivery Online Network Information Service), a proposal by several publishers to provide full-text storage of journal articles on optical video disk, from which hard copies of articles could be retrieved; (2) DIANE (Direct Information Access Network for Europe), a project of the Commission of the European Communities that provides online access to major bibliographic databases; and (3) its planned companion, ARTEMIS (Automatic Retrieval of Text from Europe's Multinational Information Service). Weber calls these projects "fascinating thrusts into the future of scholarly dissemination of information" (p. 290).

Although selected preservation activities have always been a part of library operations, their scope has increased tremendously in just the last 5 years, confronting library and technical services managers with new sets of policies, procedures, and resultant reorganization strategies.

Just how immensely the interest in this previously somewhat marginal activity has grown is reflected by the amount of work reviewed in the LRTS review articles between 1979 and 1981. Thus, in 1979, the review article "Resources in 1978" had one paragraph on the topic, and the statement that "preservation is an increasingly important aspect of resource management" (Lynden, 1979, p. 229). Two articles on cold storage as an antidote to bug infestation and water damage were cited.

By 1980, the review article was titled "Collection Development and Preservation in 1979," and had almost 2 pages on preservation. The author stated, "concern for preservation is clearly growing" (Magrill, 1980, p. 247). The following year, the same author concluded in a more extensive review, "local preservation activities are spreading so rapidly that it would be impossible to compile an accurate summary of them" (Magrill, 1981, p. 257). In 1982 "Preservation of Library Materials" rated its own separate review article, 17 pages long with 135 references, and its author closed as follows:

> In 1976, participants at the National Preservation Program Planning Conference identified research, educational, and cooperative efforts as critical needs if the problem of deterioration of library materials is to be resolved. Just five years later, a concentrated effort to address those needs is beginning to bear fruit. The progress made during 1981 toward developing opportunities for formal training, planning cooperative programs for conservation activities and the production and bibliographic control of microforms, increasing general awareness of the need for alkaline book paper, and sharing expertise in such areas as conservation techniques, disaster preparedness, and preservation program development augurs well for the 1980s as the decade in which an enormous problem was brought to heel. (Reprinted by permission of the American Library Association from Margaret M. Byrnes, "Preservation of Library Materials: 1981 (*Library Resources & Technical Services* 26(3):234[July/Sept. 1982]); copyright © 1982 by the American Library Association.)

Current Status

What have the changes and trends discussed in the previous section meant to the organization of technical services? New realities and ways of doing things have given the impetus to emerging new structures, and today, not quite 30 years after separate technical services divisions as such were first generally established, many questions are being raised as to whether maintaining a separate division or department for technical services is either feasible or desirable. The organization of technical services had been based originally not only on a desire to centralize like tasks, but also on the necessity to organize around central files, such as on-order files, the serials check-in record, and the card catalog and shelf list. Other organizational structures may be more appropriate when integrated system files are shared by monograph and serials acquisitions, cataloging, circulation, interlibrary loans, preservation, collection development, or reference staffs, and have in fact been adopted by several libraries. For example, the University of Illinois Library at Urbana–Champaign recently created an organization based on the concept of general- versus subject-oriented services. Gorman (1979), in an article entitled "On Doing Away with Technical Services Departments," gives some of the rationale for this change, making among others the point that the division of cataloging and reference, for example, with one person in cataloging assigning access points and another in public services interpreting them, has resulted in a disservice to the professional librarian and the library patron alike. Thus:

> One finds catalogers who have a tremendous knowledge of the subject field in which they work, yet that knowledge is seldom or never used in reference work. Again, one finds reference librarians who disavow cataloging as a process and seem almost proud of their inability to grasp the basic concepts underlying cataloging and the most important and expensive tool in the library—the catalog. (Reprinted by permission of the American Library Association from Michael Gorman, "On Doing Away with Technical Service Departments" (*American Libraries* 10[7]:435 [July/Aug. 1979]); copyright © 1979 by the American Library Association.)

One would have to agree that a specialist involved in the total process of selecting and acquiring any information packages in a given field, creating access points for them, and then interpreting those access points, would be in an ideal position to aid a searcher for that information. Certainly job satisfaction would be enhanced if such an arrangement were feasible and cost effective. However, in a complex automated environment consisting of a multiplicity of databases, indexing approaches, and command languages, such a specialist would have to be versatile indeed.

Of course, Gorman (1979) does not propose that the services now organized in the so-called technical division should or could be abandoned; rather, he believes that separating the professional functions, such as selection, collection development, reader advisory and reference services, original cataloging, and bibliographic instruction, from the more or less automated routine tasks is desirable and feasible. Such an approach has been taken by Columbia University Libraries as described by Booz, Allen, and Hamilton, Inc. (1973). In a reorganization of existing services most of the processing operations were included in the "support group," whereas professional catalogers were placed with reference specialists in the "resources group."

THE FUTURE OF TECHNICAL SERVICES

What about the future? Pratt, in *The Information of the Image* (1982, p. 80) has described information systems as "CPOD" systems, involving "the collection, preservation, organization, and dissemination (CPOD) of records." Their purpose, in whatever environment, "involves the collection of large masses of data from the external world, the retention of it for some appropriate length of time, its organization by some systematic means so that it can be located as needed, and its distribution to those who have need for it."

If we may then extend Tauber's (1954, p. 4) original definition of technical services from "those services involved in the acquisition, recording, and preserving of materials" to "those services involved in the acquisition or collection, preservation and organization of information in any form or medium for the purpose of eventual dissemination," it should be evident that there is indeed a central role for the services described in our coming information society, be it within what we call a library or some other setting. However, dangerous as it may be to make predictions through a decidedly murky crystal ball, it is this writer's belief that visions of researchers accessing databases from terminals in their own offices notwithstanding, libraries, or their successors by some other name, are here to stay. Even leaving the continuing value of the codex form to humanistic scholars aside for a moment, the social implications of commercially produced "for profit only" databases that would record and make accessible only information that can be profitably sold, keep it available only as long as it was economically rewarding, and disseminate it only to those who can pay the price is a frightening possibility. This possibility will no doubt create a demand for a counterforce, such as an agency that can provide some guarantee of permanent access to accumulated knowledge as well as information to communities of scholars and citizens. If libraries did not already exist, they probably would have to be invented, although the name *library* may well disappear and particular services, as opposed to the basic function of managing an information system in response to the needs of a group of users, shift. This scenario is forseen by Bailey in his epilogue to Chapter 1 of *Scholarly Communication: The Report of the National Enquiry* (1979):

> The boundaries between scholar–authors and publishers and the booktrade . . . and libraries and scholar–readers will shift and blur. New librarylike services will be offered by publishers and wholesalers, scholars will enter materials directly into libraries, libraries will perform publisherlike or bookstorelike functions. (p. 34)

Whatever the face of the future, it does seem safe to predict that, just as the recent past in technical services has been dominated by change, the continuing diversification of the information environment in the future will bring more and accelerated changes in how the unique and central functions now called technical services will be performed.

THE FUTURE ROLE OF THE PROFESSIONAL IN TECHNICAL SERVICES

With many technical procedures standardized and automated and with original cataloging largely centralized at the Library of Congress and other large research libraries, there has been much concern as to whether there is indeed a future for the professional in technical services, and if so, what future?

We believe that there will be a need in library and other information centers for planners and managers of technical services functions, for specialists, such as catalogers, and for intermediaries that can maximize the utility of an information system to the eventual user by interpreting the interrelationships of what will probably be multiple "information systems," all having slightly different contents, patterns of organization, and protocols for access.

New short-term future areas of responsibility that will require the attention of technical services professionals are the closing of current catalogs, the design of online catalogs, further exploration of automation potential to acquisition processes, serials control, circulation and interlibrary loan control, and the analysis of management data that can be gathered by the computer for such purposes as budget control, collection development, and design of better methods of bibliographic control. Technical services professionals will also continue to participate in setting network standards and assessing network potential for purposes of bibliographic access and technical processing requirements.

In the somewhat longer term, that is the next 25 years or so, we would, with Williamson (1982), writing about access to information in the year 2006, "assume the presence of information and a need to provide access to it" (p. 125).

The task of creating and managing a future information system capable of linking users to different sources of bibliographic data and documents contained in distant collections is a large one, demanding vision, ability, and expertise to deal with the many logical and technical details that must be worked out both in the local and larger contexts. Technology has changed how information is organized, obtained, and used and is in the process of changing technical services and the role of the technical services librarian, but technology does not work in a vacuum. Technical services professionals, as information experts, must provide the intellectual framework in which the information transfer takes place and help build the systems that will support that framework. This is indeed a vital role for the future.

FINDING OUT MORE ABOUT TECHNICAL SERVICES

There are several publications that should be reviewed by anyone with an interest in the general topic of technical services. Tauber (1954) is still a good introduction to the topic for students and practitioners, particularly administrators. Although dated, it is the only comprehensive text on the then-current philosophy and practice designed for the professional librarian. *Introduction to Technical Services for Library Technicians* (1976), a more current text by Bloomberg and Evans, is an excellent source for basic definitions and descriptions of typical workflow in technical services operations, not only for the intended audience of library technicians and other nonprofessional library personnel, but for the librarian involved with supervising and training library staff. *Technical Services: A Selected Annotated Bibliography* (Magrill & Rinehart, 1977) is also highly recommended as a guide to the recent literature of technical services and provides a convenient overview of the state of the art in the 1970s. Applebaum's (1973) *Reader in Technical Services*, a compilation of historical papers, essays, and reports, augmented by selections from contemporary research and development, is useful for getting a sense of the issues that have occupied experts in the field over the last 100 years or so.

For reviewing issues and trends in the more recent literature, the annual "This Year's Work in" reviews of various aspects of technical services published in the summer or July/September issue of *Library Resources & Technical Services* are extremely useful. Originally begun by M. F. Tauber in 1961 as a review of current and significant events and publications covering technical services in general, these now include review articles on selected areas of technical services by various experts in the field.

Although, as a brief review of *Library Literature* will show, many articles on the topic of technical services can be found in general library journals such as *American Libraries, Journal of Academic Librarianship, Library Journal, Journal of Library Administration,* and *Information Technology and Libraries,* to give but a few examples, *Library Resources & Technical Services* is probably still *the* journal to read regularly for anyone interested in the topic. Two promising recent entries, *Technicalities* and *Technical Services Quarterly* are also worth reviewing regularly. There are also many periodicals devoted to particular aspects of technical services, such as *Cataloging & Classification Quarterly, Library Acquisitions: Practice and Theory, Serials Librarian,* and so on. References to the more basic titles can be found in the appropriate chapters by topic.

For novice and seasoned practitioner alike, there is probably no better way to get a feeling for what is or soon will be happening in technical services than to attend the program and committee meetings sponsored by the ALA Resources and Technical Services Division at the midwinter and summer conferences. Discussion groups sponsored by the technical services administrators of large research libraries, medium-sized research libraries, smaller research libraries, and large public libraries are particularly recommended. Not only does one get a chance to hear about issues of current concern before they ever appear in the literature, but the opportunity to meet and speak informally to others in the field is invaluable.

There are also many state and regional technical services interest groups. Sometimes these are a part of the state library association; other times they may be independent. Checking with someone in the field is the best way to find out.

REFERENCES

American libraries (Vols. 1–). Chicago: American Library Association, 1970–.
Anglo-American cataloguing rules (2nd ed.). M. Gorman & P. W. Winkler (Eds.). Chicago: American Library Association, 1978.

Applebaum, E. L. *Reader in technical services.* Washington, D.C.: NCR Microcard Editions, 1973.

Bailey, H. S. Epilogue: A longer view. In *Scholarly communication: The report of the National Enquiry.* Baltimore: Johns Hopkins University Press, 1979.

Berrisford, P. D. Year's work in cataloging and classification: 1977. *Library Resources & Technical Services,* 1978, *22,* 227–262.

Bloomberg, M., & Evans, G. E. *Introduction to technical services for library technicians* (3rd ed.). Littleton, Co.: Libraries Unlimited, 1976.

Booz, Allen, & Hamilton, Inc. *Organization and staffing of the libraries of Columbia University: A case study.* Westport, Conn.: Redgrave Information Resources, 1973.

Byrnes, M. M. Preservation of library materials: 1981. *Library Resources & Technical Services,* 1982, *26,* 223–239.

Cataloging & Classification Quarterly (Vols. 1–). New York: Haworth Press, 1980–.

Coney, D. The administration of technical processes. In C. B. Joeckel (Ed.), *Current issues in library administration: Papers presented before the Library Institute at the University of Chicago, August 1–12, 1938.* Chicago: University of Chicago Press, 1939.

Cutter, C. A. *Rules for a printed dictionary catalogue* (Public libraries in the United States of America, their history, conditions and management, Part II). Washington, D.C.: Government Printing Office, 1876.

Dewey, M. *A classification and subject index for cataloging and arranging the books and pamphlets of a library.* Amherst, Mass.: N.p., 1876.

Glasby, D. J. The year's work in serials: 1980. *Library Resources & Technical Services,* 1981, *25,* 310–318.

Gorman, M. On doing away with technical services departments. *American Libraries,* 1979, *10,* 435–437.

Horny, K. L. Technical services librarians a vanishing species? *Illinois Libraries,* 1980, *62,* 587–588.

Information Technology and Libraries (Vols. 1–). Chicago: American Library Association, 1982–.

Jones, M. H. Year's work in cataloging and classification: 1978. *Library Resources & Technical Services,* 1979, *23,* 246–288.

Journal of Academic Librarianship (Vols. 1–). Ann Arbor, Mich.: Mountainside Publishing, 1975–.

Journal of Library Administration (Vols. 1–). New York: Haworth Press, 1980–.

Library Acquisitions: Practice and Theory (Vols. 1–). New York: Pergamon Press, 1977–.

Library Journal (Vols. 1–). New York: R. R. Bowker, 1876–.

Library Literature (Vols. 1–). New York: H. W. Wilson, 1936–.

Library Resources & Technical Services (Vols. 1–). Chicago: ALA Resources and Technical Services Division, 1957–.

Lynden, F. C. Resources in 1977. *Library Resources & Technical Services,* 1978, *22,* 310–333.

Lynden, F. C. Resources in 1978. *Library Resources & Technical Services,* 1979, *23,* 213–245.

Magrill, R. M. Collection development and preservation in 1979. *Library Resources & Technical Services* 1980, *24,* 247–273.

Magrill, R. M. Collection development and preservation in 1980. *Library Resources & Technical Services,* 1981, *25,* 244–266.

Magrill, R. M., & Rinehart, C. *Technical services: A selected, annotated bibliography.* Westport, Conn.: Greenwood Press, 1977.

Pratt, A. D. *The information of the image.* Norwood, N.J.: Ablex Publishing, 1982.

Rinehart, C. Descriptive cataloging in 1981. *Library Resources & Technical Services,* 1982, *26,* 254–262.

Rinehart, C. Year's work in descriptive cataloging: 1979. *Library Resources & Technical Services,* 1980, *24,* 217–234.

Serials Librarian (Vols. 1–). New York: Haworth Press, 1976–.

Tauber, M. F. (Ed.) *Technical services in libraries.* New York: Columbia University Press, 1954.

Technical Services Quarterly (Vols. 1–). New York: Haworth Press, 1983–.

Technicalities (Vols. 1–). Phoenix: Oryx Press, 1980–.

Tuttle, H. W. From Cutter to computer: Technical services in academic and research libraries, 1876–1976. *College & Research Libraries,* 1976, *37,* 421–51.

Younger, J. A. Year's work in subject analysis: 1981. *Library Resources & Technical Services,* 1982, *26,* 264–276.

Weber, B. M. The year's work in serials: 1981. *Library Resources & Technical Services,* 1982, *26,* 277–293.

Williamson, N. J. Is there a catalog in your future? Access to information in the year 2006. *Library Resources & Technical Services,* 1982, *26,* 122–136.

2 Technical Services Administration

Leslie A. Manning

INTRODUCTION

A technical services unit provides for the administration of similar library functions, usually under the coordination of a single manager. The purpose of this chapter is to present the reader with a discussion of three fundamental areas of technical services administration. The first section outlines the basic management and organization of technical services. This is followed by a discussion of personnel management concepts that are specific to the technical services environment. The final section describes some of the measurements and statistical procedures that are inherent to successful operations. Before proceeding directly into these subjects, it is helpful to first examine the definitions and purposes of technical services.

Tauber (1954) defines *technical services* as comprising the functions of acquiring, recording, preserving, and circulating materials. A more modern definition identifies technical services with the functions of acquisition, cataloging, processing, inventory, circulation control, and patron registration (Rochell, 1981) and the library operations that provide the acquisition, organization, and preparation of materials (Lynch & Eckard, 1981). These differences in definition are reflected in variations in the organizational structure of technical services from library to library.

LIBRARY TECHNICAL SERVICES   15   Copyright © 1984 by Academic Press, Inc.

The purpose of a technical services department is to improve efficiency by grouping similar functions together. The similarities of technical services functions can be seen in the repetitive procedures that are basically production and materials oriented. Most of these activities are consecutive, and thus dependent on the completion of the first before the beginning of the next. The sequence of activities is performed repeatedly, resulting in the final product: a collection of materials, collocated on the shelves and accessible through a catalog. Grouping similar functions into a technical services department has improved efficiency by providing increased coordination, allowing for greater staff flexibility, and allowing for the assimilation of larger amounts of materials (Dougherty, Wadsworth, & Axman, 1967).

MANAGEMENT

The successful operation of a technical services unit is dependent upon the application of sound management principles and philosophy. A good manager of technical services has the same attributes as other good library administrators as well as specialized knowledge and experience with acquisitions, cataloging, and/or automation and must be capable of planning, organizing, communicating, and coordinating the activities within the division. Further, he or she must coordinate the technical services functions with the activities of the rest of the library through participation in library-wide planning, budgeting, and policy formulation.

Planning

Planning is the most critical single management activity because it prepares for the future. Effective planning is the cornerstone of other management activities. The planning process involves setting goals, establishing long and short range plans, and evaluating the attainment of the goals. Through proper planning, managers identify what must be accomplished today in order to be prepared for tomorrow (Stueart & Eastlick, 1981).

The initial step in the planning process is the identification of the mission and goals of the library. The mission is a broad statement of organizational purpose; although the manager of technical services makes contributions to the formulation of the mission statement, the responsibility for the statement rests with the director and library governance group. A typical statement might indicate that the mission of the university library is to acquire, organize, and make readily available a collection of recorded knowledge that supports the instructional, research, and service goals of the university's faculty, students, and staff.

Goals are general statements that identify aspirations for the library and provide direction for the planning process. Goals are action oriented and serve as a general measure of success. An example of a library's goal might be to maximize access to information and the use of collections so that the greatest number of patrons can be served.

Once goals are set, the next step is the development of objectives and activity statements for technical service operations. Objectives are specific statements that relate to a particular goal and state what is to be done with resources. Objectives are often departmental and short-range in scope, and their success is readily measurable or definable. An example of an objective for the goal in the preceding paragraph would be to implement an automated circulation system by June 1, 1984.

Activities describe specific actions, operations, or events that are necessary to accomplish a given objective. Activities are shorter-term and measurable. An activity statement for the preceding objective might be to link the item records via bar codes to the 150,000 bibliographic records in the circulation database by January 1, 1984.

The mission, goals, objectives, and activity statements result in a hierarchical pattern (see Figure 2.1). With this pattern each goal interacts with every other goal, each objective with every other objective, and each activity with all the activities. The goals and objectives deal not only with the desirable, but also the obtainable; and they should expand and challenge the organization. Further, these statements provide the library staff with direction as well as explain why a task is necessary. Such a sense of direction can improve both morale and productivity.

The second phase of planning establishes a course of action by identifying short-range and long-range plans. Long-range plans should cover a 5–10-year period and connect the plans of individual departments into one overall program. Long-range planning, also called strategic planning, identifies policies for obtaining and using resources in the accomplishment of goals. It is necessary for long-range plans to undergo periodic review because they do not incorporate strategies for dealing with funding reductions or failures and

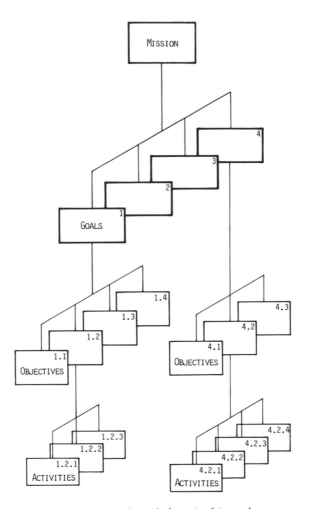

Figure 2.1   Goals and objective hierarchy.

because they are based on assumptions about the future that may not occur. Short-range plans describe action that covers a year or less, and these operational plans are more detailed and should not reflect the uncertainty of the more general long-range plans. Like long-range plans, however, they must undergo periodic review to accommodate change and philosophical redirections of the parent institution.

The final phase of the planning process is to evaluate organizational performance by determining how well it has met its goals and objectives. Measurement is a difficult part of the planning process.

Fortunately, the quantifiable, task-oriented nature of technical services operations makes measurement somewhat simpler than in other administrative units of the library. Subjects for measurement include accuracy, financial effectiveness, operational effectiveness, productivity, timeliness, and staff morale (Lynch & Eckard, 1981). Performance measurements relate to the degree of accomplishment of a particular goal and, to some extent, the level of accomplishment is specified within the goal.

The success of all three phases of the planning process is dependent on staff involvement. The greater the staff involvement in this process, the greater their commitment to the accomplishment of the plans. If total staff involvement is not possible due to size, time, or expense, certainly all supervisors should be involved in the planning process.

Budgeting

Budgeting is a continuous activity involving the entire staff and dependent upon planning. The library budget is a plan for the coordination of resources and expenditures over a specified period of time. Further, the budget provides managerial control when comparisons are made between the budget and the accomplishments of the library. The technical services administrator and staff play a critical role in the budgeting process, although the major budget responsibilities rest with the library director.

The budget process contains eight basic steps which may vary somewhat from library to library, depending upon the requirements and funding source. These eight steps include planning the request, formulating the request, reviewing the request, defending the request, approving the request, monitoring the budget, modifying the budget, and closing out the books. This process actually takes from 3 to 4 years to complete for any given budget, assuming that the period covered by each budget is only 1 year. Consequently, a minimum of three budgets are usually in various stages at any given time. More than three budgets may be in process if the budget period varies from 1 year, or if closing out the books is extended beyond the budget year.

The whole library staff is involved in planning the budget request by developing cost estimates based on past expenditures. First-line supervisors identify needs and formulate estimates, which are passed up the chain of command. Each successive level of management compiles and expands upon the requests and estimates. The next step is to take each of these requests and, based upon overall goals and objectives, formulate the total budget request. The preparation of the complete request is usually the responsibility of the director, or in larger libraries a budget staff.

Once formulated, the request needs to be reviewed both internally and externally. The library staff needs to review the total request to be aware of the library's direction. Others, such as friends of the library groups, trustees, faculty advisory committees, and other interested support groups need to be familiar with the total request. Such groups may be called upon to provide valuable support in the next phase of the budget process: the budget defense.

When the budget request is finalized, it is presented to the funding source for consideration and approval. The funding source generally provides a timetable and a format for submission of the request. The timetable may include a hearing at which the request is explained to those who will determine the extent to which the request will be approved. The library director may or may not be the individual that defends the budget request at the hearing. If not, the earlier review process takes on the added dimension of preparing whoever is responsible for presenting the budget to the funding source.

The funding source approves the budget request, with or without modifications. Once approved, funds are allocated to the library to cover the budget period. Upon receiving the funds, the library becomes responsible for the next step in the process: monitoring encumbrances, expenditures, and balances. The monitoring process provides for the comparison of actual expenditures against the budgeted estimates. The budget is modified as necessary, based upon these comparisons. These comparisons also provide improved cost figures for future estimates and budget requests. Upon the completion of a budget period, the books are closed out so that the dollars allocated and the dollars expended are equal and the balance remaining is zero.

The funding source often determines the format of the budget request. There are several basic formats which may be used. In fact, most library budgets will represent a combination of these basic formats. The formats include the line item budget, lump sum budget, program budget, performance budget, and the zero-based budget. In many cases a library will submit a line item budget to the funding authority, but it uses one of the programmatic budgets internally to develop the request.

The line item budget format lists estimated costs by general type and amount for the budget period. The general types may include a line for professional salaries, library materials or supplies, and equipment, etc. The line item is often calculated on the basis of a formula, institutional percentage, or multilibrary comparison. The line item is an incremental budget, with each new budget request representing a percentage increase (or decrease) over the preceding estimates. Frequently funds allocated for one line of the budget cannot be transferred or expended for units within another line of the budget. This format provides the funding authority control over expenditures to ensure that allocations are used for intended purposes. The line item budget does not directly represent the programs or goals of the library. This disadvantage to the line item approach has led to the development and adoption of several additional programmatic budget formats (Stueart & Eastlick, 1981).

The lump sum budget is similar to the line item approach with the added advantage that the dollars are allocated in total to the library, and the library director decides how the sum is divided into categories. The lump sum provides greater flexibility within the library and can allow allocation of funds based upon goals and objectives. Control of expenditures with the lump sum budget rests with the library rather than the funding authority.

Program budget formats base the budget request directly upon the activities performed by the library. Funds are allocated to programs. This approach is often carried one step further to the performance budget approach of Program Planning Budgeting Systems (PPBS). Performance budgeting relates library goals to specific programs, resource requirements, and achievements by relating costs to work performed and services provided. The use of PPBS is dependent upon the accurate identification of the unit of work and unit of time as well as extensive data collection over a period of time (Evans, 1976).

Zero-based budgeting, a more recently developed format, requires the rejustification of every budget request, as if each activity and program were new to the organization, and has grown out of the increased need for accountability for nonprofit and government agencies. As with other programmatic approaches, extensive cost information is needed for budget estimates.

A major portion of any library's budget request is for library materials. Frequently the materials budget is allocated in a lump sum to be further allocated by the librarian or collection development officer. The allocation of the materials budget is a critical, and sometimes a political, question particularly in the academic library setting. Allocations are frequently formula based and include the three major classes of monographs, serials, and binding, which are further divided into subject funds. The formula used may be developed internally or adapted from a state or national standard. Book allocation formulas reflect the institution's needs, programs, and users. The formula must be flexible and continually analyzed. Items that might be considered in a materials formula include inflation rate by type of material and subject; collection strengths and weaknesses; curriculum and program changes; numbers of titles published in a given field; numbers of students, faculty, and courses; educational level of programs; and necessary duplications. Clearly some of these factors are objective and measurable, whereas others are subjective and require judgmental evaluations. Because of the subjective factors, a given formula may include weighting factors (Martin, 1978).

The serials allocation is one of the most crucial questions to resolve in the materials budgeting process and represents a continuing commitment of funds into future years if the library expects to maintain current subscriptions. When this continuing commitment is coupled with high inflation and minimal budget increases, the results can be an unbalanced allocation or extensive serials cancellations. As a rule of thumb, serials allocations should not exceed 60–70 % of the academic library materials budget (Martin, 1978).

Organizational Structure

An organizational structure is the assignment of personnel into units under a manager who has the authority to accomplish assigned responsibilities. The organizational structure facilitates coordination and outlines channels of formal communication. The library's organizational structure reflects its goals and changes as the goals change.

The determination of an organizational structure to accomplish these aims is a two-part process. The first part involves an analysis of the operations, including a study of workflow, decision patterns, communications, and personnel interactions. The result of this analysis is the determination of the major functional divisions of the library. The second part of the process is to divide these major functions into units and departments. The resulting structure of units and departments should facilitate materials flow, communication, production, and teamwork.

The determination of which functions will be collected together to form technical services depends on an analysis of each library's goals, activities, and resources. Obviously, the analysis can result in a variety of structures. An examination of the relationships of the programmatic functions of a library will aid in the identification of an appropriate structure. Lynch and Eckard (1981, p. 98) developed a graphic representation (see Figure 2.2) that clearly identifies these relationships. In Figure 2.2, technical services are defined as acquisitions and cataloging functions. Resource distribution services are defined as circulation and interlibrary loan. Administrative services are personnel and budget activities.

Tauber (1954), Rochell (1981), and Sinclair (1965) associated all the materials-related functions together in their definitions of technical services. In practice, however, many libraries have not always included circulation in the organization of technical services. This has more often been true in academic libraries than in public libraries. The placement of circulation within technical services is becoming more common in libraries that use automated systems providing a single database for circulation, acquisitions, and cataloging (see Figure 2.3).

Another traditional technical services organization includes the functions associated with indirect user services, thus placing book selection within the structure of technical services. Changing goals for collection development have caused many libraries to move it from technical services into public services or into a division of its

	CONTENT RELATED	MATERIALS RELATED
DIRECT USER SERVICES	INFORMATIONAL, EDUCATIONAL, CULTURAL, AND RECREATIONAL SERVICES	RESOURCE DISTRIBUTION SERVICES
INDIRECT USER SERVICES	COLLECTION DEVELOPMENT SERVICES	TECHNICAL SERVICES
SUPPORT ACTIVITIES	ADMINISTRATIVE SERVICES	

Figure 2.2   Relationships of programmatic functions. (From Lynch & Eckard, 1981, p. 98.)

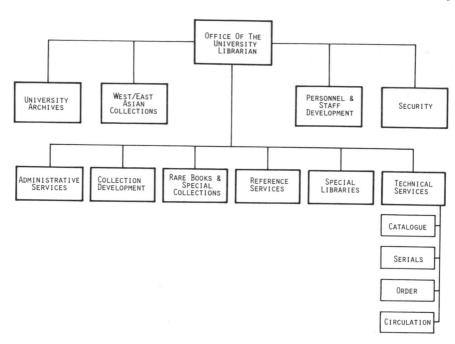

Figure 2.3 Organizational chart, Princeton University Library.

own (see Figures 2.3 and 2.4). Numerous other variations can occur, as seen by Figure 2.4, in which binding is not included in technical services. Obviously, no single organizational structure seems appropriate for every library. Each library, after assessing its needs, goals, and resources, must develop its own organizational structure.

After the functional divisions are identified, tasks are assigned to units. This represents the second step of the organizational process. There are several basic patterns for departmentalization that include grouping tasks by number of staff such as a moving crew, by function such as circulation, by geographic territory such as a branch, by product such as a print shop, by patron such as a childrens' division, and by process such as binding. Two other patterns that are specific to libraries include grouping tasks by subject such as genealogy and by format such as a government documents department. Departments within a given library may represent a combination of any of these patterns.

A number of organizational principles must be applied to the departmentalization process. The first is the *scalar* principle, which states that authority is delegated downward from an ultimate authority to subordinate positions through a hierarchical structure of

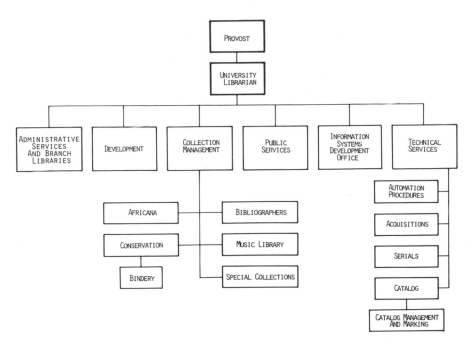

Figure 2.4   Organizational chart, Northwestern University Libraries.

supervisors and subordinates. Every employee must clearly understand where he or she is in the line of authority, to whom he or she is responsible, and what his or her relationship is to the other employees.

Another principle of organizational structure is *unity of command*, which ensures that an employee has only one supervisor who assigns duties and evaluates his or her performance. Adhering to this principle protects the employee from multiple supervisors and the organization from an environment of contradiction and conflict.

The principle of *span of control* plays an important role in the development of an organization. Span of control refers to the maximum number of employees that a manager can effectively supervise. This number changes according to the variety and complexity of responsibilities of the subordinates. The span of control also depends on the amount of time required for communication with each individual. Although the principle does not seem to dictate a specific number, it is generally found that most managers cannot directly supervise more than five to nine employees effectively.

Once an organizational structure is identified, a graphic representation or chart of the organization can be drawn and distributed to the staff. An organizational chart can help each employee to identify his assignment within the organization. The same chart also identifies the span of control, lines of communication, and the flow of authority. If there are inconsistencies within the organizational structure, in assignment of activities, in lines of authority, or in unity of command, the chart can make these problems immediately evident.

An examination of the application of these processes and principles to technical services organizational structures is helpful. The American Library Association published two studies (Shachtman, 1955; Dougherty *et al.*, 1967) that examined the organization, processes, and policies of technical services in American libraries. The results of both studies are still the most comprehensive examination of technical services organizations available. The basic structures identified 3 decades ago are essentially the same as those in use today. The structure that was evident before the development of a technical services division is still seen in some libraries (see Figure 2.5). With this pattern, department heads report directly to the head librarian with no intervening coordinator for technical services. Although on paper this design resembles older patterns, its actual operation has been greatly influenced by the procedures developed

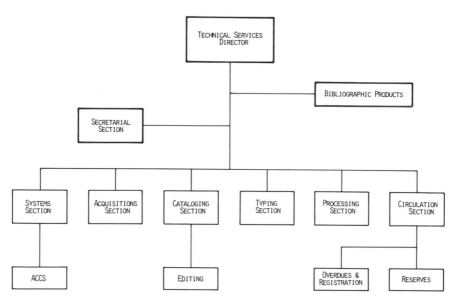

Figure 2.5 Organizational chart, Hennepin County Library. ACCS stands for Automated Circulation Control System.

within coordinated technical services divisions (Dougherty *et al.*, 1967).

The most common organizational structure for technical services utilizes a single administrator who is responsible for supervision and coordination of the divisional activities. This technical services administrator reports either to the director or to an associate director. The composition of the division then seems to follow two basic patterns. The first organizes the division into the major units of acquisition, serials, cataloging, and circulation. The second organizes the division into more specific activity units, such as order, gifts, binding, cataloging, serials, processing, etc. This second approach was labeled the "true" technical services organization by the investigators in 1967 (Dougherty *et al.*) because it recognized the interdependence of the different activities. Many combinations of these patterns are currently in practice (see Figures 2.6 and 2.7).

Another structure found in smaller libraries consists of a small, highly cohesive staff that is responsible for accomplishment of all technical services activities. This situation, of course, has the potential for a fully coordinated effort because the same few people are performing all tasks. The same idea, taken one step further, results in a technical services unit that consists of a single individual.

Commercial and Cooperative Processing

In the very smallest libraries and in many school libraries yet, a different pattern emerges when these institutions purchase the services of a commercial processing firm or of a cooperative centralized processing center. This is done because the libraries do not have the staff to perform the functions locally. Larger libraries have also used this approach to save time and money, as well as to supplement in-house processing. The use of commercial processing does not preclude the need for a technical services specialist on site to ensure the consistent assimilation of the commercial product.

The concept of commercial and cooperative processing began as early as 1876 (Applebaum, 1973) when the idea of sharing cataloging information was first mentioned in library literature. The dream was realized in 1901 when the Library of Congress began offering cards for sale. By 1938, the Wilson Company entered the market with the sale of catalog cards. The processing of books to accompany the cards is a more recent adaptation that appeared in 1958. By 1968, over 50 firms were selling both processed books and catalog cards (Westby, 1969).

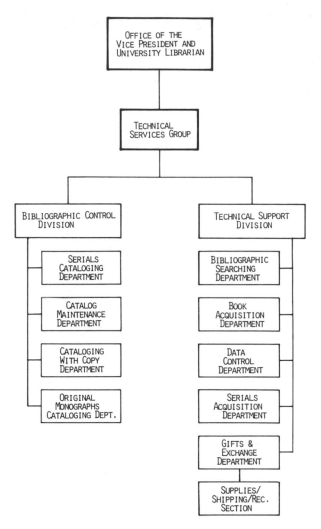

Figure 2.6 Administrative structure, Columbia University Libraries.

The growth of commercial processing paralleled the growth of the nation's school systems and the availability of federal funds for library materials. The 1960s found many new schools in need of fully processed opening day collections. The federal funds that became plentiful were only for materials and not for the staff required to process them. The book vendor who could supply cards and pro- cessed books soon found his or her business thriving. This same dilemma of funds for materials, but not for staff, also forced the larger libraries to seek the same type of assistance (Westby, 1969).

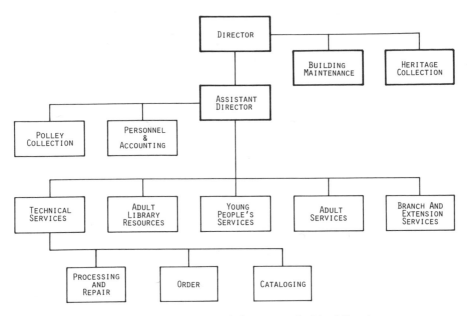

Figure 2.7   Organizational chart, Lincoln City Libraries.

The use of commercial processing served to point out the lack of standardization. Each firm provided cataloging that was different from its competitors and the library's existing catalog. It was evident that commercial processing reduced only some of the workload associated with technical services. The libraries still had to perform all of the acquisition functions of selecting, ordering, and receiving materials as well as integrating the commercially produced cataloging into the existing card catalogs.

The growth of cooperative processing is most evident in the development of the bibliographic utilities of the Online Computer Library Center (OCLC), the Research Libraries Group Information Network (RLIN), the Washington Library Network (WLN), and the University of Toronto Library Automated Systems (UTLAS). Thousands of American libraries are currently inputting their cataloging into the databases maintained by the utilities, either directly or indirectly through local processing centers. As output, the libraries receive catalog cards and/or magnetic tapes. Unlike libraries using commercial processing vendors, libraries using bibliographic utilities receive unprocessed materials from publishers and vendors. The physical labeling of the materials occurs in the library. Of course those libraries using utilities through intermediary processing centers may have arrangements with the center for the physical labeling of the materials. The development of bibliographic utilities is covered in more detail in Chapter 3, "Automation: The Context and the Potential."

Coordination

The manager of the technical services division is responsible for coordination in several ways: (1) he or she is responsible for coordinating efforts within the departments that compose technical services; (2) the manager is responsible for coordination of technical services with the rest of the library's operations; and (3) the manager of technical services is often responsible for various types of coordination between the library and other libraries or networks. This coordination is accomplished through the identification of objectives, planning, organization, and communication.

Earlier studies (Shachtman, 1955; Dougherty et al., 1967; Tuttle, 1975) identified specific topics for coordination within technical services. These topics include workflow, utilization of forms, use of common files, elimination of duplicate functions, and the implementation of automation. The development of the multipurpose order form is an excellent example of the benefits of coordination among technical services units. The current trends in automation are also increasing the requirements for coordination within technical service operations.

The manager of technical services must also work closely with the managers of other divisions in the library to improve coordination. This type of coordination is the result of library-wide planning and policy formulation. Clearly defined goals as well as precisely specified areas of responsibility are essential for this type of coordination. Examples of such intralibrary coordination include the development of an automated serials list, the establishment of circulation policy, and feedback on patterns of catalog utilization.

The coordination of technical services with other libraries (interlibrary coordination) often involves the exchange of cataloging data through bibliographic utilities that have been established for this purpose. Also, the broadening scope of the utilities, from the single purpose of shared cataloging to the additional purposes of interlibrary loan, acquisitions, union lists of serials, etc., necessitates more extensive coordination between the technical services operations of member libraries. These libraries are learning that sharing bibliographic information requires the acceptance of, and compliance with, strict bibliographic standards. The technical services manager plays a key role in the coordination and implementation of such standards.

Effective communication is an essential factor for coordination. Communication is the exchange of information requiring a sender, a receiver, a message, and a means of transmission. Good communication requires constant effort on the part of managers. Meetings and individual conferences are examples of formal communication. A good meeting requires careful planning, including an agenda, individual preparation, and accurate minutes. Most importantly, a good meeting must involve two-way communication in which the sender and receiver of messages are interchangeable. Written communications such as annual reports, procedure manuals, policy statements, letters, and memoranda are also essential means of formal communication.

PERSONNEL MANAGEMENT

Personnel management is concerned with the effective utilization and development of a library's most valuable resource—its staff. Human resource management in technical services can be divided into three basic topics: (1) staffing patterns, which examines the levels of staffing required to perform various functions, (2) job analysis and performance evaluation, and (3) staff development.

Staffing Patterns

A staffing pattern can be viewed as a system by which individuals are assigned to different positions within the organization. It involves the matching of skills, knowledge, and experience to a specific set of tasks. The staffing patterns that result from the application of this system reflect a library's goals, size, resources, governance, organizational structure, applications of automation, service requirements, etc.

As throughout the library, the technical services staff can be divided into two categories: the professional staff and the support staff. In many libraries the support staff is further divided into technicians and clerical employees. The differences between the duties of employees at the two levels are not always clear. The duties of the professional librarian are basically those that require the graduate library degree. Further, professional staff must demonstrate abilities in the areas of problem analysis and in integrating theory with practice. Independent judgment, decision making, and rule interpretation are additional capabilities of the professional librarian. Generally speaking, the duties of the support staff are more clerical in nature. However, some libraries may assign tasks that require judgment and specialized training to the intermediate level of technician. Such a technician normally has extensive on-the-job experience or a 2-year community college degree.

Duties once considered to be professional in nature are now being assigned to support staff. This trend can be seen in the changing ratio of professional to nonprofessional staff. In the 1930s approximately 50–60% of a library's staff was employed at the professional level, but by the 1970s this percentage had decreased to only 33% (Creth & Duda, 1981). This trend is particularly apparent in the staffing patterns of technical services. The once professional duties of filing revision and bibliographic searching were being delegated to nonprofessional staff members in some libraries as early as 1955 (Shachtman) and were completely transferred by the late 1960s (Dougherty *et al.*, 1967; Rosenthal, 1969). With the advent of cooperative cataloging via automated bibliographic utilities, many libraries have delegated copy cataloging and even some original cataloging to technicians (Holley, 1981).

Currently, professional librarians in technical services are performing supervisory functions, formulating policy, establishing procedure and/or resolving difficult bibliographic problems. The growing use of automation and increasing demands for reference staff will continue the trend of decreasing numbers of professionals in technical services. Only in the larger libraries that perform significant amounts of original cataloging will the need continue to exist for large numbers of professional librarians in nonsupervisory technical services positions.

Job Analysis and Performance Evaluation

As previously described, jobs are developed by grouping related tasks. The assigned tasks comprising the job should be at the same level and require comparable experience, education, and skills. The requisite tasks should also carry comparable responsibility and similar levels of supervision.

Each position should have a written job description that cogently defines all duties and responsibilities. The job description is used for recruitment and performance evaluation and identifies qualifications in terms of experience, education, and job-related skills. In addition, the written job description contains the title of the supervisor, the purpose and scope of the job, and a place to indicate that the job description has been carefully discussed with the employee. These descriptions need continuing review and revision in order to reflect the dynamic nature of the positions.

A performance evaluation is a formal, systematic program of employee evaluation by supervisors and provides the supervisor with a comprehensive picture of the employee's performance. In turn, the employee is then able to use the evaluation to improve performance and further develop his or her own potential. The system of performance evaluation in general is used as a means of organizational goal attainment; and more specifically, it is a measure of individual performance towards attaining the stated goals.

It is important that good performance be recognized and reinforced. All employees have a strong need for personal accomplishment, for growing, and for being challenged. Feedback produces some of this motivation and subsequent job satisfaction and includes immediate knowledge of the results of one's work, both from the recognition of the supervisor and peers. Providing the employee with a sense of accomplishment is one of the purposes of evaluations.

Evaluation procedures are generally defined by the library or its parent institution. Evaluations are commonly scheduled on an annual basis, with more frequent evaluations for newer employees and others who seem to require more follow-up. Evaluation procedures often include both a written evaluation and a performance interview. The written evaluation usually follows a prescribed format and is made available to the employee well ahead of the interview. The interview atmosphere needs to be conducive to a private, unhurried discussion in which both parties can concentrate on the employee's performance. The interview stresses the problem-solving approach rather than a judgmental perspective. The supervisor guides the interviewing, keeping it on the topic of performance. During the interview, problems are identified and both parties plan how to resolve them. Also, future expectations and plans of both the supervisor and the employee are outlined (Creth & Duda, 1981).

Many detailed studies of the job analysis and evaluation process are available. Familiarity with the theory of the process as well as the specific system used by the given institution is essential.

Staff Development

Staff development is a broad range of activities designed to provide job-related knowledge and skills necessary to improve performance. Improved staff performance results in increased library effectiveness by improving the quality and increasing the quantity of work, reducing the need for supervision, improving morale, and increasing flexibility. Staff development requires supervisory and managerial encouragement at all levels. A successful program is an integral part of the library's operations.

Staff development activities can be divided into three main types. The first, orientation activities, introduces new employees to the job, the department, the library, and the parent institution. Orientation activities can also introduce current staff to new library programs, departments, branches, etc. and familiarize new employees with basic information about personnel rules, policies, and procedures. They introduce employees to co-workers and the physical surroundings. Finally, orientation includes an explanation of the library's goals and organizational structure. A checklist of people, locations, policies, rules, etc. can ensure that items are not overlooked in the orientation process. Supervisors may ask the co-workers of the new employee to assist in this process.

Training activities comprise the second and usually the largest group of staff development activities. These activities provide the employee with the specific knowledge and skills necessary to perform a task and are developed by supervisors for new employees, employees performing new tasks, and employees requiring retraining. Training activities require careful preparation on the part of the supervisor. Each task should be identified and divided into basic components. Components can then be explained in sequence, followed by a practice period that is observed and revised. Repetition and practice are essential to the mastery of many tasks. The supervisor should also explain why a task is performed and how it fits into the overall operations. The ability to perform a task and to understand its relationship to other tasks will provide employees with the knowledge to act independently and to assume greater responsibilities.

Finally, the third group of staff development activities consists of continuing education and developmental activities. Developmental activities deal with broad concepts such as management training or supervisory techniques, rather than specific operational skills. These activities will often introduce employees to different management techniques or approaches to a situation. Professional reading and research are also developmental activities. Continuing education includes workshops, conferences, and related course work. The purpose of continuing education and developmental activities is to encourage employees to seek new approaches and new solutions.

In summary, staff development is a necessary part of the library's personnel program. Its purpose is to train employees, improve performance, and increase production. To be effective it requires the support and commitment of managers at all levels. The final result of an effective staff development program is a motivated staff offering improved library services.

MEASUREMENT AND EVALUATION

The following discussion of measurement in technical services brings together many of the concepts mentioned earlier in this chapter. Good measurement is the key to effective administration of technical services. Measurements help the manager identify the availability of resources in terms of time, money, or personnel and also indicate how the resources are allocated and expended. Without accurate, timely measurement, the technical services operation is essentially uncontrolled. The purposes of measurement and the subsequent evaluation are to document historical performance, to identify the present operational configuration, and to assist in arriving at meaningful decisions affecting the future.

Standards

At the outset, measurements have to be designed so that the technical services staff and management can evaluate the information obtained. The evaluation consists of a comparison of the new measurement against existing standards. This is the case whether one is considering the number of volumes purchased, the number of items bound, the number of items cataloged, or virtually any other technical service measurement. There are two general sources of standards: shared data from comparable environments, such as other libraries with similar demographic features, services, etc.; or data from the same institution collected over time. Within certain limits, shared data is readily available from professional and governmental organizations such as the American Library Association, Association of Research Libraries, and U.S. Department of Education and from direct inquiry between libraries. Unfortunately, no two situations are completely identical. Measurement techniques, unit definitions, and time periods may differ with each institution. Although efforts for standardization of measurement and terminology exist (Lynch & Eckard, 1981), they have not yet been widely adopted. Thus comparisons between libraries may require modifications.

The second source of standards is measurement made at different times in the same library, which establishes a baseline for comparison. For example, a library may elect to make a careful measurement of its shelving requirements once every 2 years or it may record cataloging production with monthly cumulations. After a period of time, these types of measurements yield a characteristic pattern that can be used for evaluative purposes of the shelving requirements or cataloging productions. Assuming that these measurements are consistently obtained, the standards will tend to incorporate many of the local characteristics. The effect of changes in operations, personnel, and resources will be reflected in the measurements.

Techniques

The possibilities for obtaining and evaluating technical services data are almost unlimited. Historically, some of the more popular techniques have been time studies, cost studies, and diary methods. In addition, cost–benefit analysis and operations analysis have been used to evaluate the data (Dougherty & Leonard, 1970).

The application of scientific management techniques is a five-part process that includes defining the problem to be studied, gathering the data, analyzing the current operation, developing an improved operation, and implementing the improved operation. Defining the problem involves determining the operations to be studied and the objectives of the study. For example, a manager may decide to study the book-labeling process in order to eliminate bottlenecks in workflow. Once the study has been defined, the data gathering procedure consists of two steps. In the first step each activity and production unit of the operation must be distinctly identified. Secondly the manager determines which data gathering technique to use, based on the purpose of the study and the activity to be measured.

One of the most frequently used methods of data collection is the time and motion study. The concept of time and motion studies originated in the late nineteenth century with the work of Taylor (1947). A time study consists of an observation of the number of times some activity is completed in a given period. It attempts to identify all the significant components of a function, to determine the rate at which these components are accomplished, and then to see if there is a more efficient alternative. The purpose is to recognize the tasks, or at least to balance them so that there is a smooth continuous flow of production. As a result, the manager obtains accurate data that are observed by a trained analyst, measured with a stop watch, and systematically recorded. This important advantage has to be weighed against certain disadvantages: the necessary intervention and disruption of the normal work place, even by the most subtle and sensitive observer; the inherent volume and complexity of the data received; and the constant possibility of misinterpretation of data.

The diary method is another commonly used technique in library management studies. With this method, workers record the task, the amount of time expended performing the task, and the number of units produced. Another technique that often uses the diary method is the cost study, which measures units of production and costs in terms of salaries, overhead expenses, and materials costs. A unit cost is then determined by dividing the total costs by the number of units produced.

Analysis of the data and of the operations are the next steps in the process. Collected data may be compared with other studies or past situations. The operation is studied step-by-step using such methods as operations analysis, flow charting, decision analysis, or cost analysis (Dougherty & Heinritz, 1982). The purpose of analysis is to answer the questions of why, what, where, when, who, and how; and the result is to develop an improved method of operation. Operations may be improved by eliminating unnecessary routines, combining routines or files, changing the sequence of activities, changing staff, simplifying the operation, or introducing an innovation such as automation. The final step in the application of scientific management techniques to technical services involves implementing change. This is often the most difficult phase and requires careful communication, training, testing, and refining. Greater staff involvement throughout the study process ensures smoother implementation.

Statistics

Reports and statistics are used in several ways: (1) reports are used as support for budget requests and revenue generation; (2) reports and statistics are used for resource allocation; (3) statistics are used for descriptive purposes, to compare and contrast various libraries or operations; and (4) perhaps most importantly, statistics are used for management and forecasting (Lynch & Eckard, 1981).

Library materials collections have been traditionally a favorite topic for statistical analysis. Public libraries, for example, often relate the size of collections in specific subject areas to the needs of their service clientele. Academic library collections are constantly evaluated for accreditation purposes. The importance of a timely, accurate, physical description of each library's collections is obvious. The quantitative description of collections is not the whole story. The qualitative dimension, such as collection holdings measured against standard subject bibliographies, is another major consideration. Qualitative statistics are difficult to define and time consuming to collect. As is always the case with statistics, the objective evidence must be tempered with the more subjective evaluation of the experienced librarian.

Collection statistics and reports can be designed in a variety of formats. Librarians can develop systems that take into account various branches, time periods, media types, subject areas, etc. Also, collection statistics can indicate the dynamic character of the environment. For example, statistics can reflect additions, deletions, net growth, and relative-size estimates.

A logical extension of the collection statistics and reports concept is collection utilization. Libraries with automated circulation systems might obtain reports directly from the computer. Libraries with manual systems can often get similar information using sampling techniques. Collection utilization information might identify the number of items circulated after a specific date, the average number of circulations for a specific subject or branch location, or the heavily used items (for purchasing copies). A library's need for management information will determine which of the wide variety of collection statistics available will be gathered. Lynch and Eckard (1981) provide a format for reporting statistics as well as a comprehensive listing of areas for measurement.

Production statistics focus on the outputs of a technical services division. They represent an attempt to identify all of the work that is accomplished in a specific period of time or a specific department. For example, circulation, acquisition, bindery, and cataloging statistics are all common production topics. The importance of production statistics is clear. They indicate what resources (time, personnel, and money) have been used to produce services and facilitate rational decision making through the systematic identification of these resources. Further, they serve to provide realistic forecasts for future activities in technical services.

Documentation

Clearly the results of measurement and evaluation efforts are to direct improvements in technical service activity. These improvements are incorporated into revised policy and procedure documents. These manuals usually consist of very detailed descriptions of appropriate activities under various conditions. It is imperative for technical service employees to have consistent instructions to which they can easily refer. It is also important for the supervisor to have documentation available for training and evaluation.

Policy and procedure manuals should consist of an introduction defining the scope of the activities, a body describing all normal conditions with appropriate responses, and a summary directing the employees to the appropriate supervisor for further clarification. At a minimum each department or unit needs a manual; and ideally, each employee needs a manual for his or her specific position. Another important group of manuals are those for files and forms. The manual for files defines the purpose, scope, and content of each file as well as its use and maintenance. The forms manual contains copies of each form for each department or unit and describes who completes the form, how it is completed, and how it is used.

Manuals ensure continuity of the operations over time, especially when several employees may be working on different stages of the same project, assist the supervisor during the training process, and guide the employee in the performance of daily activities. Because manuals cannot cover all possible situations, they cannot substitute for the thorough training by the supervisor or the good judgement of the well-trained employee and need to be revised regularly to assure that they are current with changes in policies and procedures.

THE LITERATURE OF TECHNICAL SERVICES ADMINISTRATION

Library managers draw on the knowledge, opinions, and insights of others by reading widely in library and in management literature. The list of references and the bibliography at the end of this chapter contain monographic titles and journal articles that provide a basic background for technical services administrators. Journal articles in both fields cover the theory, application, and evaluation of various management techniques. Business management journal literature is accessed through the *Business Periodical Index*. *Library Literature* and *Information Science Abstracts* provide access to journal articles, theses, research reports, and monographs. *Library Resources & Technical Services* is the basic technical services journal and contains research articles on all aspects of technical services. The *Jour-*

nal of Academic Librarianship contains articles on academic library management and reviews of current publications on a variety of subjects of interest to librarians in all types of libraries. The *SPEC Kits and Flyers* (1973–) provide information on the practical application of management techniques in the research library setting, however, this information is transferrable to most technical services situations. (The acronym, SPEC, stands for Systems and Procedures Exchange Center.)

SUMMARY

The effective administration of a technical services division is dependent upon the application of sound management practices including planning, organization, and communication. A comprehensive personnel management program is especially important in the management of technical services. Finally, the measurement and evaluation of the overall operation is essential to the administrative process.

Several considerations are now evident to the critical reader. The management of a technical services organization is a dynamic, rather than a static process. It represents an ongoing struggle to impose good judgment, logic, organization, and structure on a dynamic environment while improving library services. These considerations reside within the division itself, throughout the library, and across the whole context of library services in the community. Finally, the management of technical services borrows heavily from disciplines such as psychology, management, computer science, accounting, and industrial engineering. Thus, a key element to the effective management of technical services is a broad knowledge of management and library practices.

REFERENCES

Applebaum, E. L. (Ed.). *Reader in technical services.* Washington, D. C.: NCR/Microcard Editions, 1973.

Creth, S., & Duda, F. (Eds.). *Personnel administration in libraries.* New York: Neal-Schuman Publishers, Inc., 1981.

Dougherty, R. M., & Heinritz, F. J. *Scientific management of library operations* (2nd ed.). New York: Scarecrow Press, Inc., 1982.

Dougherty, R. M., & Leonard, L. E. *Management and costs of technical processes: A bibliographic review* 1876–1969. Metuchen, N. Y.: Scarecrow Press, 1970.

Dougherty, R. M., Wadsworth, R. W., & Axman, D. H. Policies and programs designed to improve cooperation and coordination among technical services operating units. *University of Illinois Graduate School of Library Science Occasional Papers*, 1967, No. 86.

Evans, G. E. *Management techniques for librarians*. New York: Academic Press, 1976.

Holley, R. P. The future of catalogers and cataloging. *Journal of Academic Librarianship*, 1981, 7 (2), 90–93.

Lynch, M. J., & Eckard, H. M. (Eds.). *Library data collection handbook*. Chicago: American Library Association, 1981.

Martin, M. S. *Budgetary control in academic libraries*. Greenwich, Conn.: JAI Press, 1978.

Rochell, C. *Wheeler and Goldhor's practical administration of public libraries* (Rev. ed.). New York: Harper and Row, 1981.

Rosenthal, J. A. Nonprofessionals and cataloging: A survey of five libraries. *Library Resources & Technical Services*, 1969, *13*, 321–331.

Shachtman, B. E. Technical services: Policy, organization and coordination. *Journal of Cataloging and Classification*, 1955, *11* (2), 59–114.

Sinclair, D. *Administration of the small public library*. Chicago: American Library Association, 1965.

Stueart, R. D., & Eastlick, J. T. *Library management* (2nd ed.). Littleton, Col.: Libraries Unlimited, 1981.

Tauber, M. F. *Technical services in libraries*. New York: Columbia University Press, 1954.

Taylor, Frederick W. *Scientific management, comprising shop management, the principles of scientific management, testimony before the Special House Committee*. New York: Harper, 1947.

Tuttle, H. W. Coordination of the technical services. *Advances in Librarianship*, 1975, *5*, 123–146.

Westby, B. M. Commercial processing firms: A directory. *Library Resources & Technical Services*, 1969, *13*, 209–286.

BIBLIOGRAPHY

Auld, L. Functional organization plan for technical services. *Library Resources & Technical Services*, 1970, *14*, 458–462.

Berkner, D. S. Library staff development through performance appraisal. *College & Research Libraries*, 1979, *40*, 335–344.

Bernhardt, F. S. *Introduction to library technical services*. New York: H. W. Wilson Company, 1979.

Bloomberg, M., & Evans, G. E. *Introduction to technical services for library technicians* (4th ed.). Littleton, Col.: Libraries Unlimited, 1979.

Business Periodical Index (Vols. 1–). New York: H. W. Wilson Company, 1958–.

Ducker, P. *Management: Tasks, responsibilities, practices*. New York: Harper, 1974.

Heinritz, F. J. Optimum allocation of technical services personnel. *Library Resources & Technical Services*, 1969, *13*, 99–101.

Information Science Abstracts (Vols. 1–). New York: Documentation Abstracts, Inc., 1969–.

Jenkins, H. *Management of a public library*. Greenwich, Conn.: JAI Press, Inc., 1980.

Journal of Academic Librarianship (Vols. 1–). Ann Arbor, Mich.: Mountainside Publishing, 1975–.

Lancaster, F. W., & Joncich, M. J. *The measurement and evaluation of library services.* Washington, D. C.: Information Resources Press, 1977.

Lee, S. H. (Ed.). *Emerging trends in library organization: What influences change.* Ann Arbor: Pierian Press, 1978.

Library Literature (Vols. 1–). New York: H. W. Wilson Company, 1933–.

Library Resources & Technical Services (Vols. 1–). Chicago: Resources and Technical Services Division of the American Library Association, 1957–.

Magrill, R. M., & Rinehart, C. *Library technical services: A selected, annotated bibliography.* Westport, Conn.: Greenwood Press, 1977.

Martin, M. S. *Issues in personnel management in academic libraries.* Greenwich, Conn.: JAI Press, 1981.

Mitchell, B. J., Tanis, N. E., & Jaffe, J. *Cost analysis of library functions: A total system approach.* Greenwich, Conn.: JAI Press, Inc., 1978.

Ricking, M., & Booth, R. E. *Personnel utilization in libraries: A system approach.* Chicago: American Library Association, 1974.

Rizzo, J. R. *Management for librarians: Fundamentals and issues.* Westport, Conn.: Greenwood Press, 1980.

Rogers, R. D., & Weber, D. C. *University library administration.* New York: H. W. Wilson Company, 1971.

SPEC Kits and Flyers (Vols. 1–). Washington, D.C.: Association of Research Libraries, 1973–.

Tuttle, H. W. From Cutter to computer: Technical services in academic and research libraries, 1876–1976. *College & Research Libraries,* 1976, *37,* 421–451.

Tuttle, H. W. Standards for technical service cost studies. *Advances in librarianship,* 1970, *1,* 95–112.

Welch, H. Technical services costs, statistics and standards. *Library Resources & Technical Services,* 1967, *11,* 436–442.

Wiederkehr, R. R. V. *Alternatives for future library catalogs: A cost model.* Rockville, Md.: King Research, Inc., 1980.

3 Automation: The Context and the Potential

Karen L. Horny

THE INTEGRATED SYSTEM IDEAL

The challenge for any discussion of library automation is that the state of the art is continuously and rapidly advancing. A tremendous acceleration in the planning and application of computer-support service has occurred since the middle of the 1960s, and it is now astonishing to recall that the applicability of computer resources to library service was a matter of heated debate and considerable skepticism through the early years of the 1970s (Clinic, 1972). Increased recognition of automation's capability for improving service has combined with shifting economic circumstances to establish the computer as an essential element in library operations within a few short years.

In the library context, the minimum aim of automation must be to improve the means of accomplishing work already being done manually. A computer system requires a transformation of procedures to ensure that the system is not merely "superimposed" on previous, possibly now inappropriate, methods of operation. Ideally, machine applications should enhance services while allowing more efficient utilization of staff. Cost benefits derived from sharing the results and thereby avoiding duplication of the labor-intensive work of bibli-

LIBRARY TECHNICAL SERVICES

43

ographic control are especially important, although they are only the beginning of potential savings. As equipment prices have declined while personnel costs have continued to rise, a shift of routine operations to machine processing has become increasingly attractive.

Most librarians have some contact with automated systems in the current library environment and, although few libraries have totally integrated systems, such systems are clearly the aim and the ideal. Proposed "integrated systems" encompass a wide variety of library functions, with the most generally accepted description including computer applications for all the major support services of acquisitions, serials control, cataloging, authority control, and circulation. An online public access catalog completes the ideal basic system. An economical and effective balance between convenient access to a national, and eventually to an international bibliographic network, and the efficient maintenance of local applications is a high priority for most types of libraries in the 1980s.

The nature of bibliographic files is such that individual records have many data elements, generally of variable length and often requiring special characters, which must be maintained by a variety of processing techniques, for varying purposes, and accessed by a number of approaches. An integrated automated system provides access to data at every stage of processing and eventual circulation activity because the system modules are linked in recognition that the library is one complex, interrelated, interconnected, multifa eted operation. An additional advantage of an integrated system that supports a full range of library operations, from acquisitions and serials control through circulation and the public access online catalog, is that costs for the system are spread over the whole array of high transaction activity tasks, making the per unit cost correspondingly low.

It is possible to contemplate the eventual linkage of a library's online public access catalog with the commercially available online abstracting and indexing reference databases as one of the next logical extensions of service. The ability of a local computer system, perhaps shared by several regional libraries, to interface with computers hosting larger files of bibliographic or textual information is under development. The anticipated link will allow machine-to-machine transfer of data and make it possible for a user of one system to retrieve and locally manipulate data from another system, whether for processing activities or for the creation of individualized bibliographies. Even when local system computer command languages vary, the programs that handle the machine linkage will do appropriate translation internally without the user needing to be aware of the differences.

As smaller, less expensive computers become more powerful and readily available, an increasing number of libraries are likely to have access to suitable equipment, either in-house or within the parent institution, to handle the kinds of transactions best done locally. The costs of long distance communication and of maintaining and manipulating information in immense combined databases are apt to prohibit performing such high volume activities as an individual library's circulation transactions, serials subscription issue receipt and claiming operations, and all local catalog public inquiry, via the bibliographic utilities such as the Online Computer Library Center (OCLC) or the Research Libraries Information Network (RLIN). Many libraries have partially solved this problem by using a network utility for cataloging and interlibrary loan transactions and an in-house commercially supplied automated circulation system which they hope to be able to expand into a local full service online public access catalog. Rapid developments have been occurring in this area of system enhancement.

From the point of view of avoiding duplication of data entry, the ideal system is one that provides access to a large central file of bibliographic records as a source of cataloging copy and resource-sharing location information while allowing the computer transaction load costs and telecommunication charges to be reduced by doing most library processing and information inquiry locally. This is the "distributed processing" approach to library automation.

AUTOMATION AND THE CHANGING CONCEPT OF TECHNICAL SERVICES LIBRARIANSHIP

The application of computer support to basic processing operations has done much to alter the traditional concept of technical services librarianship. Access to consistent and authoritative cataloging copy in machine-readable form, both from the Library of Congress via its MARC (Machine-Readable Cataloging) Distribution Service and from cooperating members of the large bibliographic networks to which so many libraries now belong, has led to a more efficient use of staff. Much duplication of cataloging effort has been eliminated by more rapid access to information formulated by others according to accepted standards. Although staff reductions have occurred, professional librarians remain necessary and have, perhaps, increased in importance in several automation-related ways: As original catalogers, they contribute records to the shared database and, as administrators, they plan for the most cost-effective use of computer applications. In addition, they supervise the assistants who handle the items for which bibliographic records are already available in automated systems.

Management and Administration of Automated Services

The introduction of any automated system is a challenge to the basic administrative skills of the librarians who must make the decisions, facilitate smooth implementation, and achieve maximum benefits from the capabilities of a computer-based system. The initiation process itself is discussed in the section "Transitions, Training, and New Standards." When a system is in operation, careful attention is necessary to ensure that procedures are fully adjusted for efficient use of available features. Enlisting the assistance of staff using the system to suggest alterations in processing methods is one useful way of improving both operations and morale.

The administrative skills and specialized expertise that have long characterized professional work in technical services will undoubtedly remain essential in coping with the new possibilities that have become available as automation has developed. New organizational patterns and shifts in the physical location of the staff performing various assignments related to online systems have become common. A frequent development has been the shifting of circulation, often including reserve functions, into the library's technical services division. This organizational change has generally reflected a decision to develop a full-record public access online catalog from a computer-based brief record circulation system. The required interface between the system used for cataloging and the system serving circulation and public online catalog needs has resulted in an organizational tie between the processing operations and departments often designated as "public services" for administrative purposes.

Access to an online system from remote locations has made it possible to perform tasks such as serials check in and cataloging in a more consistent manner in branches as well as in centralized locations. With an effective quality control system, including methods of conflict resolution, communication of changes in standards, and appropriate personnel training, locally dispersed processing can be far more effective than was previously possible in large systems where it often was found.

New Interrelationships

The increased flexibility permitted by remote access to a centralized database offers one of the most positive challenges in any reassessment of libary organizational patterns. Within technical services, departmental lines have shifted from traditional groupings, and new departments have been created while others have merged. As a library comes closer to achieving the integrated system ideal, conventional organizational and staffing lines blur to the point at which criteria other than simple division by major function (e.g., acquisitions and cataloging) or type of material (e.g., serials) may be the determining factors in deciding administrative structure. Recent trends have included having copy cataloging performed by acquisitions staff upon receipt of items or establishing a separate department for "automated processing" as a substitute for the traditional copy cataloging unit. For the professional, it is no longer desirable or perhaps even possible to specialize in either acquisitions work or cataloging without a considerable understanding of automation's applications to the other end of the processing flow. In integrated systems, the same computer record is used from the preacquisition stage through cataloging to circulation, with public access possible to at least portions of the information contained at any point after initial input.

Even when the historical pattern of organization remains, interrelationships between departments become more clearly evident than was often true in preautomation days. Of course all competent librarians in technical services positions should always have been conscious of the ultimate purpose in those activities: acquiring and making available *to users* the information needed, regardless of format. Fortunately, automation reinforces that aim and accomplishment in numerous ways, making acquisition status information for both serials issues and monographs immediately available to the public as well as to the staff assisting them directly, and allowing access to the catalog in areas in which duplicate card catalogs would have been impossible—to name only two of the major benefits. Public service is, at long last, an *obvious* result of the work being performed within technical services.

TRANSITIONS, TRAINING, AND NEW STANDARDS

Planning and Implementing

Although so many libraries now have at least some portions of their operations supported by automated systems that experience with planning and implementation of computer support is quite commonplace, several basic points are worth repeating. The first step in any planning process is to clearly define the goals in terms of a library's institutional objectives. With a specific definition of what is to be accomplished, it is next possible to identify alternative ways of meeting the goals. Before alternatives can be assessed, however, it is necessary to have a detailed understanding both of the operations that will be affected and of the system that will be substituted for or added to the current methods of doing the job. Flow charting and task analysis, as explained in many standard texts, are usual aids in this process, and it is useful for all technical services librarians to have a basic understanding of these techniques.

Although it is undeniably true that organizational and technical changes need to be made in combination with a reasonable estimate of costs and benefits, difficulties are often encountered in meeting this ideal. A classic problem is the frequent absence of cost information for existing systems. It is also difficult to attribute a value to potential service improvements and to compare costs across multiple functions such as those included in the spread of library applications covered by an integrated system. Another factor that is hard to assess is the potential for avoiding cost increases for processing by shifting support funds from escalating salary accounts to less inflationary equipment charges. Consultants can sometimes be of assistance with cost–benefit analysis, and some helpful techniques can be found in texts such as Matthews (1980).

Definition of the library's requirements will usually result in either of two types of formal documents. One, termed a *request for quotation* (RFQ), is a set of detailed specifications to be presented to vendors for direct price bids. The second is a more general *request for proposal* (RFP), which includes functional specifications for both mandatory and desirable features, to be offered to the marketplace for competitive proposals in response. The latter approach, which elicits detailed system feature descriptions from dealers, is likely to be a somewhat safer technique although the resulting proposals can be quite difficult to evaluate comparatively.

Having chosen to adopt a particular automation application and negotiated a contract (a process discussed in more detail in the section "Networks, Commercial Services, and Local Solutions: Goals and Accomplishments"), the library must prepare to implement the new system. Documentation of system features along with a training plan should be adapted or developed and made available to staff at the earliest possible time. Every effort should be made to anticipate, plan for, and document the necessary revisions in policies and procedures. During the earlier system selection process, staff should have been kept involved with and informed of major developments to ensure they have a basic grasp of the positive factors that led to the eventual choice of a particular system. In most cases the result will be a nonthreatening atmosphere and favorable attitude on the part of staff and administrators alike, facilitating the adjustment to new methods and equipment. Allowing sufficient training time for staff to develop confidence in and with new procedures and machines, and encouraging personnel to ask questions and to report problems at every stage of planning, training, and implementation are likely to reap benefits in a successful accommodation to the new system.

Human Factors, New Standards, and Managerial Accountability

A discovery made by a number of libraries that have introduced automated systems is that many of their long-time employees are among the most enthusiastic advocates of the new system. Because these staff members are thoroughly familiar with the drudgery and limitations associated with the previous manual operations, they often have a keen appreciation of the benefits of the new system for improved procedures and service. For most library personnel, the challenge and interest generated by the introduction of new methods will be basically positive. Perhaps the most likely cause of staff uneasiness will become apparent only after the initial adjustment: Although use of terminals and new basic procedures may be quite simple, the system, particularly when part of a network configuration, may require adherence to new, usually more stringent, performance standards than had formerly been enforced. For example, the level of accuracy required by the intricate MARC formats adds another layer of complexity to the already complicated process of original cataloging. Authority work also takes on additional importance when data must be formulated to conform to usage in a network file. In local integrated systems, consistency between headings in on-order or in-process records and headings established for items already cataloged is essential for both staff searching and public online access because variant headings mislead users who, finding one entry, believe they have retrieved all the relevant information.

One benefit of the necessity for adherence to new standards is that it provides a new opportunity for objective assessment of individual performance. Because staff in each library have the responsibility to meet standards that are recognized beyond their own department, and often are reviewed by users of not only their local system but of a wider network as well, the importance of quality is emphasized and lapses are more evident. From a managerial point of view, this new level of accountability can be very helpful both in setting performance requirements and in reinforcing, in a very positive way, the contributions made by technical services personnel.

The File Conversion Challenge

Transitions to new modes of operation, unfortunately, are seldom simply a matter of installing equipment and training staff. Even after procedures are developed to deal with materials newly entering the system, coping with files in several incompatible forms remains a major challenge. Because it is generally necessary to continue dual file access for "pipeline" materials, advance planning of procedures to correlate access and accomplish necessary conversion is essential. Regrettably, in some cases a complete file conversion is either not possible or may only be achieved over a considerable period of time. Whereas active monographic order files can make a reasonably rapid transition to automated form as normal order fulfillment continues, serials Kardex conversion is a much more substantial project, often requiring a data gathering process in several other files such as the library's shelflist. Beyond the problems of converting acquisitions records, conversion of the card catalog to machine-readable form at a large library will require a major commitment of time and money. Any conversion project should be carefully planned to assure that the benefits outweigh the costs, especially when the library must forego offering other services to finance the conversion.

Promising possibilities for retrospective conversion (often referred to as recon) of catalog print data include techniques such as optical character recognition (OCR), which uses a device to "read" print materials and transcribe each character into machine-readable form. To provide appropriate computer identification for the transcribed data, OCR may be combined with programming that supplies standard internal data coding, often referred to as automatic format recognition (AFR). As yet, however, these methods have not proven feasible for large-scale use at individual libraries because of problems concerning bibliographic information that has been formulated according to changing cataloging rules over many years of varying local practices. Nevertheless, with the advent of large-scale projects such as the Library of Congress REMARC conversion contracted with Carrollton Press (discussed in the section "National and International Formats and Standards"), many libraries, including some research libraries with sizeable collections, have been able to accomplish complete transfers of catalog information from card format to online catalog files.

Analytical Data: Traditional Statistics and Beyond

One of the potential benefits of an automated system is the enhanced availability of statistical data coupled with the greatly improved facility for analysis of that data by use of the computer. There are numerous potential applications; for example, vendor performance can be compared by examining time intervals between order and receipt of items, discounts can be reviewed, acquisitions price increases for materials can be analyzed according to subject by using information about the requesting department or other criteria, and processing times from receipt to cataloging can be monitored. In some systems it is possible to have the computer keep a count of items cataloged by each staff member. As with any statistics, the manner in which available data are extracted and used is a matter for professional judgment and will vary according to institutional needs and priorities.

In addition to mere counts of items in various categories defined by selected parameters, a computer can be programmed to generate listings of specific titles according to predetermined criteria. For example, the donor of a book fund endowment may wish to know which titles were purchased during the past year with that money or an acquisitions librarian may want to review orders outstanding with a particular dealer. Another interesting possibility is correlation of circulation activity with acquisitions patterns. The possibilities are almost infinite.

NATIONAL AND INTERNATIONAL FORMATS AND STANDARDS

Several basic types of standards have been established to facilitate comprehension and transfer of bibliographic data between institutions within the United States and with other countries. Although considerable standards development preceded the inauguration of automation, cooperative efforts facilitated by use of computer-based systems have encouraged increased activity in the area of standardization. There are currently standards addressing the format and content of machine-readable records and methods of data transfer. A variety of national and international bodies are involved with the formulation and review of automation-related standards; these include the Library of Congress (LC) and other national libraries; the American Library Association (ALA); the Book Industry Systems Advisory Committee (BISAC); the Council on Library Resources (CLR), which supports the Bibliographic Services Development Program (BSDP) and the Network Advisory Committee (NAC); the American National Standards Institute (ANSI); the International Standards Organization (ISO); the United Nations Educational, Scientific, and Cultural Organization (UNESCO); and the International Federation of Library Associations (IFLA) with its Office for Universal Bibliographic Control (UBC). This wide variety of institutions, governmental bodies, and nonprofit organizations, with their wealth of acronyms, all share an interest in facilitating the exchange of information, now recognized worldwide as an essential commodity. The standards that have been developed for this purpose include the MARC (Machine-Readable Cataloging) Formats, the ANSI standard for bibliographic information interchange on magnetic tape, the *Anglo-American Cataloguing Rules*, ALA and LC Filing Rules, and the International Standard Bibliographic Descriptions.

Machine-Readable Cataloging (MARC) Formats

Consistent record format and content designation make both exchange and analysis of data feasible in ways not previously in the realm of possibility. The MARC formats are the key to the surge in automated support for libraries since the mid-1960s. By the early 1980s development was nearly complete for eight U.S./MARC formats for bibliographic data: Books (monographs), Serials, Maps, Films, Music, Analytics, Manuscripts, and Machine-Readable Data

Files. A MARC format for authorities was nearing completion and one for holdings/locations was also being designed.

Although each country's applications of the International Standards Organization's standard ISO 2709: "Documentation–Format for Bibliographic Information Interchange on Magnetic Tape" are intended to be internationally compatible, on the national level variations in the implementation of the MARC formats exist. There are several mechanisms for the development and review of each country's MARC formats. Within the United States, ALA's interdivisional MARBI (Machine-Readable Bibliographic Information) Committee brings together, for review of proposals for changes to the U.S./MARC formats, representatives of the general professional community and those from LC and the largest of the "bibliographic utilities": the Online Computer Library Center (OCLC), the Research Libraries Group (RLG), and the Washington Library Network (WLN).

During the early stages of their development, the U.S./MARC Formats were frequently criticized for being "LC-centric," a circumstance that arose quite naturally from LC's pivotal role in their development. In 1965 the original MARC Pilot Project for the development of a standard format was begun at the Library of Congress. With the cooperation of 16 libraries of various types, including research, public, school, special, and government, an initial experiment in the production and distribution of machine-readable records on magnetic tape was carried out over a 2-year period. Experience with the early version of the Machine-Readable Cataloging format led to a revision in 1967 when MARC II became operational. LC/MARC tapes became available on a subscription basis via LC's MARC Distribution Service in 1969, and by 1973 the English-language-only record content was expanded to include non-English materials. Meanwhile, Cataloging in Publication (CIP) provisional records, based on prepublication data provided by most U.S. publishers, began to appear in 1971, and records in nonbook formats were distributed starting the following year.

Efforts to add records to the pool of machine-readable data in MARC format have taken several directions. In 1969 the Council on Library Resources (CLR) made a grant to LC to fund a feasibility study on the possibility of doing retrospective record conversion. The subsequent 24-month "recon project" tested various conversion techniques, including computer-programmed "format recognition" of data fields, while converting LC's English language cataloging records for 1968–1969 as well as some 5000 miscellaneous records of various ages and languages. By 1974, when involvement with automation had reached the point at which a number of libraries could participate with LC in a cooperative project to contribute machine-readable cataloging to the MARC Distribution Service, COMARC (Cooperative MARC Pilot Project) was born.

Initially funded by the Council on Library Resources, COMARC was conceived to explore the feasibility of having cooperating libraries supply records for monographic cataloging to LC for verification against its *Official Catalog* and for distribution through the MARC Distribution Service. Initially, these machine-readable records were to be based on pre-MARC LC source data, such as the printed cards or LC entries in the *National Union Catalog* (NUC). Some dozen libraries participated in this experiment, which was discontinued for lack of funds in 1978. One result of the project was the testing of a program whereby machine-readable data could be used to update the NUC and its *Register of Additional Locations* (RAL).

Since the demise of COMARC, the database of MARC records at the Library of Congress has been substantially increased by another cooperative project, CONSER (Conversion of Serials), discussed in the section "Automation-Based Cooperation: Shared Databases and Resource Sharing." In addition, the Library contracted with Carrollton Press for conversion of cataloging copy for the over 5 million records produced prior to full implementation of the MARC program at the Library of Congress. Because of the contractual arrangement, however, LC restricts use of its copies of the MARC format records produced by Carrollton, redistributing only those (less than 15,000 per year) that LC has subsequently altered. In a number of cases, however, use of Carrollton's REMARC database by other libraries, singly or cooperatively, has been negotiated directly with the producer. The data may also be accessed via the DIALOG Information Services reference search service.

The production of catalog cards was, of necessity, a significant consideration in the early developmental stages of MARC and played a major part in shaping the formats as they exist today. Once established and applied, especially when related to traditional bibliographic methods and formats, the standards became increasingly difficult to modify on a large scale, and the original card relationship has been essentially preserved. Even the development of UNIMARC (Universal MARC) as an international exchange format between national agencies has tended to solidify the local applications already in place.

A MARC record consists of bibliographic or authority data with content designation accomplished via codes and conventions for each data element. There are three major sections in each record: the leader, the directory and the variable fields. The leader carries the codes that determine the manner in which the record is processed. The directory contains information on the "tag" (field identifier), starting location, and length of each variable field in the record, allowing transfer of data into local processing formats. The tags identifying each variable field are composed of three numeric characters, the first of which usually indicates the traditional bibliographic designation of the data contained. Although some local systems, including that at the Library of Congress, have substituted mnemonic three-character alphabetic tags for ease in human interpretation, for computer processing the alphabetic tags are directly equivalent to their numeric counterparts. In very general terms, for bibliographic records the numeric groups are designated as follows: 0XX, variable control fields; 1XX, main entry; 2XX, titles (including edition and imprint); 3XX, physical description; 4XX, series statements; 5XX, notes; 6XX, subject added entries; 7XX, added entries other than subject or series; 8XX, series added entries; and 9XX, local data.

The Authorities Format tagging differs because the record content is so different, but structural similarity is preserved across the MARC bibliographic data formats wherever possible. The second numeric character, designating a subgroup of the main catagory, is used in the same generally consistent manner as the first character in order to facilitate both human and machine manipulation.

In addition to the three-character tag, each variable field contains "indicators" that supplement the basic identification of the data. Within the variable fields, subfield codes further distinguish the data elements to allow separate manipulation of discrete pieces of information. In 1978 the Library of Congress joined with the staff of Stanford University's BALLOTS (Bibliographic Automation of Large Library Operations using a Time-sharing System) Project to develop a machine-readable database that contains a description of each element within the U.S./MARC formats. This database is currently used to publish loose-leaf hardcopy editions of LC's *MARC Formats for Bibliographic Data* for sale to institutions using these formats.

National Level Bibliographic Records

As standards for the format and content designation of machine-readable records have developed, there has been increasing discussion about the actual data elements that must be included, both at a minimum and to meet full expectations for exchange of data. When records are to be shared by multiple organizations or contributed to a national database, agreement is needed concerning basic standards for record content. In the United States the *National Level Bibliographic Record* (NLBR) was developed, as a companion to the MARC formats, to define such standards. As with MARC, the NLBR is further differentiated according to the type of material to which it specifically applies. The *National Level Bibliographic Record—Books* addresses the requirements both for records that can be designated as full level cataloging and for those to be identified as minimal level cataloging. The NLBR also deals with the problems of transcription of LC copy from manual records into machine-readable form, a topic that has grown in importance as retrospective conversion projects have become increasingly common.

The question of acceptable "minimal level cataloging," suitable for shared use and possible future enhancement to full level, became pressing as budgets dwindled while publishing expanded. As the result of growing acquisitions funding that far outpaced processing staff allocations in the 1970s, followed by personnel budget reductions at the turn of that decade, many of the larger libraries have found themselves with substantial cataloging backlogs. In a budget-conscious networking environment, consistency of records has become increasingly important. In this context, when staff availability does not allow all cataloging to be done at the fullest level, it is essential that whatever abbreviated records are created contain the appropriate minimum of data, complete with correct content designation. The NLBR defines the specific data elements necessary for effective sharing of machine-readable records.

International Standard Bibliographic Description and Cataloging Codes

The International Standard Bibliographic Description (ISBD) is a set of standardized patterns for the physical description of bibliographic items in various formats. Development of the ISBD began in 1971 with publication of the first provisional edition of the ISBD(M), the description for monographs. Soon description standards were being proposed and drafted for materials in various media, and it became apparent that a generalized format that could be used to establish consistency for all ISBDs was necessary. As a result, the ISBD(G) was promulgated in 1977. Since that time, the first "official" edition of the monographic standard for description has appeared and ISBDs have also been prepared for serials (S), nonbook materials (NBM), cartographic materials (CM), printed music (PM), antiquarian materials (A), and component parts (CP). Although the International Federation of Library Associations (IFLA), which holds responsibility for these standards, has agreed upon a quinquennial review for each, there has been no basic dispute with the original principle that physical description of an item should transcribe details in the order and form in which they appear, using prescribed punctuation to distinguish between the separate elements and areas of the description.

The ISBD conventions have been widely accepted because they facilitate both machine manipulation of the data and human recognition of the various elements, especially when the bibliographic information is in an unfamiliar language. As cataloging codes have been developed or revised, the ISBD standard has been incorporated. Chapter 6 of the first edition of the *Anglo-American Cataloguing Rules* (AACR) was revised to allow ISBD implementation, and AACR2 (discussed at length in Chapter 5) reflects this decision even more fully.

International Standard Book Number and International Standard Serials Number

Many standards, such as the ISBD, although useful for machine processing, are of equal importance in manual contexts. Among these are the numbering identification schemes for both monographs and serials. Of increasing importance in the order process, both the International Standard Book Number (ISBN) and the International Standard Serials Number (ISSN) offer new methods of item verification by visual checking as well as machine identification. As acquisitions operations become ever more widely computer supported, the numeric tie to items in vendor inventories will grow in importance and should aid in the accuracy and efficiency of procurement. The U.S. Postal Service already requires the ISSN as identification for serials issues in order for these publications to receive the advantageous postage rate that applies to periodicals, and computer supported check-in systems can also make efficient use of this unique access mechanism.

The ISBN–ISSN standard numbering systems, administered by the R. R. Bowker Company as the designated agency for monographs in the U.S. and by the National Serials Data Program (NSDP) of the Library of Congress under the auspices of the International Serials Data System (ISDS) for serials, assign blocks of authorized numbers to publishers for use on their individual titles. These numbers are formulated to include a "check digit" as the last character, its value mathematically determined by the composition of the number proper so as to be readily validated by computer systems. The ISBN consists of 10 digits divided into four functional segments. The first segment of one or more characters identifies the country or group of countries where the item was published. The second group of digits is a prefix assigned to a specific publisher, and the following segment represents the specific title. The final character is the check digit. The ISSN consists of only 8 digits, with the final character also used for automated validity checking. Despite the unfortunate prevalence of misprints of these numbers either on the publications themselves or in advertisements, the use and usefulness of the ISBN and ISSN are steadily increasing.

Standard Address Number

Another device for the improvement of ordering processes is the Standard Address Number (SAN). This unique seven-digit number is also assigned by the ISBN Agency at the R. R. Bowker Company. A standard developed under the auspices of the American National Standards Institute, the SAN is intended to improve communication between libraries, vendors, and publishers. The SAN is one of a number of standards promoted with the active assistance of commercial representatives working through the Book Industry Systems Advisory Committee (BISAC), which has become a permanent committee of the Book Industry Study Group, Inc. (BISG).

The SAN system number assigned to a specific library or vendor address provides a positive means of identification in circumstances in which confusion has frequently arisen over both shipping and billing locations. Each library is asked to have its SAN printed on letterheads, purchase orders, and checks. Individual library SANs appear in the *American Library Directory*, and publisher SANs are listed in *Publishers, Distributors, & Wholesalers of the United States*. In 1980, SANs were assigned to all of the wholesalers and retail dealers listed in the *American Book Trade Directory*.

American National Standards Institute Z39 Standards

Facilitating the acquisitions process for libraries is only one of many interests of the American National Standards Institute's (ANSI) Committee on Library and Information Sciences and Related Practices (Z39). Librarians join with staff from commercial ventures in a wide variety of Z39 subcommittees, frequently addressing questions relating to the development of automated support for library operations. Among these concerns, a recent standard has been established for the "Order Form for Single Titles of Library Materials"; this standard includes three versions, one of which is the "Basic Computer-Generated Form." A standard format for computerized ordering of books through direct electronic methods is also under development, as are standards for a computer-to-computer invoice format and claims for missing issues of serials. Other automation-related standards include "Serials Holding Statements at the Summary and Detailed Levels." The ANSI developments are directly linked to standardization activities on the international level through affiliation with the International Standards Organization.

NETWORKS, COMMERCIAL SERVICES, AND LOCAL SOLUTIONS: GOALS AND ACCOMPLISHMENTS

Development of standards is closely related to the environment in which they will be applied. Because of recently identified and compelling needs for resource sharing, optimal use of limited staff, efficiency of processing, and improved access for the public, libraries have turned to cooperative networks to assist in supplying vital services. In a network context, consistency is essential and standards are the sine qua non for joint operations.

The Role of the National Libraries

The Library of Congress, as a de facto national library for the United States, has played a leadership role in the development of automation throughout the country. Its dual aims are to improve its own services to its constituency as a research library and to enhance the services it offers to other libraries. Computer applications for control of and access to bibliographic data have been a special focus of attention at LC since the early 1960s, and its pioneering efforts in the development of the MARC formats and introduction of the MARC Tape Distribution Service have been discussed in the section "National and International Formats and Standards." Bibliographic utilities, commercial vendors, and a number of individual libraries operating automated systems subscribe to the LC/MARC service to obtain authoritative cataloging data. Because the Library of Congress produces more bibliographic records than any other single library in the United States, these machine-readable data form the basis for most other library automation services. In addition to the distribution of records on magnetic tape, LC has made available, on a very limited basis, dial-up access to its own online files for use by other libraries participating in cooperative projects (discussed in the section "Automation-Based Cooperation: Shared Databases and Resource Sharing").

The Library of Congress is joined by both the National Library of Medicine (NLM) and the National Agricultural Library (NAL) in contributing records to the pool of machine-readable data that is forming the base for an evolving countrywide network. In addition to providing bibliographic records themselves, both NLM and NAL offer sophisticated online reference searching services, and NLM has developed a processing system package, called the Integrated Library System, which includes circulation and acquisitions components and is targeted for use by smaller libraries. Another national contributor of machine-readable bibliographic information, the Government Printing Office (GPO), has been cataloging using the OCLC (Online Computer Library Center) system and providing copies of these records for inclusion in the LC/MARC Distribution Service.

The expanding focus on automation at the Library of Congress is evidenced by the evolution of the offices headed by the LC automation pioneer Henriette D. Avram. Her work on the MARC Pilot Project in the 1960s led to her appointment in 1970 as chief of the MARC Development Office. In the mid-1970s she was named head of the newly established Network Development Office, and in 1980 she became LC's first Director for Processing Systems, Networks, and Automation Planning.

In 1976 LC established the Network Advisory Group (now Committee), chaired by Avram and including members from a variety of nongovernmental libraries, to made recommendations concerning the Library's role in the Library Bibliographic Component of the National Library and Information Service Network as proposed by the National Commission on Libraries and Information Science (NCLIS). The NAC (Network Advisory Committee) also addresses issues of proposed governance for a nationwide network and the ownership and distribution of bibliographic data produced by a variety of sources. The Network Advisory Group also spawned a task force, the Network Technical Architecture Group (NTAG) to make cooperative plans for hardware, software, and communication configurations for the development of a national network system.

Within LC, computer-based services are by no means limited to the basic technical processing operations that are the focus of MUMS, the Multiple-Use MARC System. The Library's SCORPIO (Subject-Content-Oriented Retriever for Processing Information Online) reference service system facilities are used widely for consultation in departments such as the Congressional Research Service, congressional offices, and numerous government agencies. Data input is done by several agencies, including the Copyright Office and the Division for the Blind and Physically Handicapped. One of LC's major cooperative services, the production of the *National Union Catalog* and its *Register of Additional Locations* was transformed to COM (Computer Output Microform) index-register format early in 1983.

Automation activities at the Library of Congress now include participation in cooperative programs with the national libraries of other countries. ABACUS (Association of Bibliographic Agencies of Britain, Australia, Canada, and the United States) meets regularly to discuss issues of international cooperation in cataloging and mutual exchange of machine-readable bibliographic data. Although exchange agreements have already resulted in the receipt of tapes from several foreign libraries, as of the early 1980s LC was redistributing only Canadian records via the MARC Distribution Service. Various problems, such as those involving potential royalty payments, have forestalled the inclusion of certain foreign records.

Major North American Bibliographic Utilities and Their Services

During the 1970s, four major "bibliographic utilities" evolved: the Online Computer Library Center (OCLC), the Research Libraries Information Network (RLIN), the Washington Library Network (WLN), and the University of Toronto Library Automation Systems (UTLAS). The history of each is considerably different from that of the others, reflecting the varied approaches attempted during the initial decade of operational computer support for library processes. Each system is a network that supports a not-for-profit online shared cataloging service. A basic aim common to all four networks is to reduce both the rate of per-unit processing cost increase and the quantity of labor-intensive, repetitive manual tasks in library processing activities. Because this goal demands database services as a primary focus, these organizations have come to be referred to as bibliographic utilities. Naturally other goals have also developed as networking activities have expanded and each of the four networks regards its role as reaching beyond the initial aspects encompassed by the bibliographic utility terminology. As the number of member–customers has increased and aspirations for new services have grown, each network has confronted various problems of goal interference: Added terminals have slowed system response time, and the need to maintain existing service at acceptable levels for a growing constituency has hindered implementation of system enhancements. Yet, as membership has stabilized and union cataloging services have become routine, prospects for additional service developments have improved, and discussions about linking databases have raised hopes for the formation of a truly national network.

Online Computer Library Center (OCLC)

The first established and largest of the networks is the Online Computer Library Center (OCLC). Headquartered in Dublin, Ohio, just outside Columbus, OCLC began its existence in 1967 as the Ohio College Library Center, formed by the Ohio College Association. Under the dynamic leadership of library automation pioneer Frederick Kilgour, its online shared cataloging system first became available within the state in 1971. Rapid success resulted in a decision to expand beyond the boundaries of Ohio 2 years later and to offer services outside the United States in the late 1970s. By the early 1980s OCLC's name had become the Online Computer Library Center, and its membership, mainly via regional network affiliation, had expanded to include over 2500 public, special, and academic libraries in the United States, Mexico, Canada, and Great Britain. OCLC libraries were cataloging some 14 million books and other materials, leading to a database growth rate of about 1 million records each year. The OCLC database, including both member cataloging input and records from the LC MARC Distribution Service, had grown to approximately 6 million records. By the turn of the decade, as location listings surpassed 100 million, members were accomplishing a remarkable quantity of retrospective catalog record conversion, accounting for close to half of the database input activity. OCLC is also host to the CONSER (Conversion of Serials) Project (discussed in the section "Automation-Based Cooperation: Shared Databases and Resource Sharing").

Although OCLC's major operation remains the production of catalog cards, system-facilitated interlibrary loan, available since 1979, has become a very significant aspect of its services. Central automated support of acquisitions and serials check-in activities has also grown in importance. In the early 1980s, OCLC began experiments with prototype home information sytems such as the Channel 2000 connection, whereby a television set and a telephone can serve as means of communication with a computer database. The first trial system provided library catalog information along with access to the online *Academic American Encyclopedia* and local banking services to residences in the Columbus area. OCLC is currently developing its own videotex system.

During the early years of OCLC's operation many members believed that additional access capabilities in the machine environment would decrease the importance of consistency in the form of entry used for items in the online database. As the database grew rapidly in size, searching problems, especially with the constraints of OCLC's "search key" access formulas (using specific characters from author and/or title), became severe, and recognition of the continued need for adherence to traditional cataloging rule standards spread throughout the membership. Eventually, the special concerns for record quality and consistency of the academic and research library component within OCLC resulted in formation of the Research Libraries Advisory Committee. The issue of database heading consistency became especially pressing with the revision of the *Anglo-American Cataloguing Rules.* Membership concern was taken very seriously, and by the time AACR2 was ready for implementation in January 1981, OCLC central staff were prepared to do the major changes required to switch from old to new forms of headings within the database of nearly 8 million records—a remarkable accomplishment in automated service. As an aid in maintaining heading consistency, OCLC users have had "display only" heading verification access to the name authority records produced and distributed by the Library of Congress since that file was installed online in January 1980.

OCLC has announced plans for development and integration of various local system modules, with circulation and the individual library online catalog having high priority. Although a specially designed local library system for single library or cluster use is under development, OCLC has also obtained rights to market and enhance the Claremont Colleges (California) Total Library System and to offer a version of the Integrated Library System (ILS) originally developed by NLM. The idea of using a "building block" approach to provide a full range of automated support services has grown in popularity as the network board has recognized that central database interaction cannot readily supply all library services to the more than 6000 libraries affiliated with the network by 1982.

Research Libraries Group and Research Libraries Information Network

The Research Libraries Group (RLG) is a corporation owned by some two dozen universities and research insititutions whose libraries participate in its information resource management programs. In addition to the owner–members, a number of specialized research libraries, such as those of several art institutes and law schools, maintain affiliation. Founded in 1974 by Harvard, Yale, Columbia, and the New York Public Library, RLG identified the development or adoption of a computer-based bibliographic system as a major means to the accomplishment of its full range of goals for both information processing and scholarly access. In 1978, the original members, minus Harvard, decided to acquire the BALLOTS (Bibliographic Automation of Large Library Operations using a Timesharing System) computer support system developed for Stanford University. With this agreement, Stanford joined the partnership and became the host institution for RLG's machine facility and central staff, and BALLOTS expanded to become RLIN (Research Libraries Information Network). In addition to the RLG member–owners, RLIN serves a number of other client libraries, primarily on the West Coast, which were participants in the Stanford BALLOTS system prior to its adoption by the Research Libraries Group.

As the RLG membership grew, the RLIN system became the base for each of RLG's four principal programs: Collection Management and Development, Shared Resources, Preservation, and Technical Services and Bibliographic Control. Authority control of bibliographic records has received special emphasis since the inception of the RLG, particularly because one of the original members, the New York Public Library, had been relying on a local automation-based system with full authority control for production of the book catalog which had already replaced its card file. Database quality and observance of national standards have been emphasized by all RLG members from the time of the original agreement. Another special focus of the partnership has been the development of sophisticated information access and retrieval techniques. RLIN does not rely upon "search key" formulas and provides a wide range of data access methods, including Boolean searching combinations using "and," "or," and "not" to retrieve subject information as well as author and title combinations.

Some members of the Research Libraries Group are also affiliated with OCLC and participate via direct input into the OCLC system in CONSER, a cooperative program for machine conversion of serials records. Until a link is established between the online databases of the Library of Congress, the several bibliographic utilities, and local systems, exchange of records on tape remains the only practical large-scale method of conveying machine-readable data from one system to another. The RLG libraries that earlier did all their cataloging on the OCLC system, as well as those having in-house computer-based operations, provide these bibliographic records on "archival tapes" for loading into RLIN. The RLIN database grew rapidly during the early 1980s and, due to the cataloging volume of the large research libraries in the partnership, can be expected to continue its high rate of expansion. In addition to member input and the LC MARC, GPO, and NLM records in the shared cataloging union database, RLIN supports several specialized databases, including the Avery Index to Architectural Periodicals, an index to art sales catalogs (SCIPIO), and the Eighteenth-century Short Title Catalog (ESTC).

The Research Libraries Information Network is intended to provide the technical means for achievement of RLG's general goals, all of which relate to facilitating access to information for research purposes. The Collection Management and Development Program aims for the reduction of expensive duplicative purchases of specialized materials while assuring that all materials of scholarly value will be represented within the collections of member institutions unless suitably available from another agreed-upon source such as LC or the Center for Research Libraries. In support of this program, RLG members are doing in-depth studies of their holdings and collection development practices and policies on a subject-specific basis, then agreeing upon acquisition responsibilities for each area. Closely linked to the agreements reached in the Collection Management and Development Program are the interlibrary loan and on-site access policies implemented in the Shared Resources Program. More liberal rules and special priorities for RLG partners support the decision to rely upon each other's specialized purchases while building in a library's own area of distinction. RLIN can be used to identify items to be considered as cooperative acquisitions, allowing one member's decision to purchase to permit another's use of funds for other materials. Another vital part of the cooperative collection development effort is the Preservation Program, for which RLIN provides an effective way to monitor preservation activity in each library. Records in the database can contain information about the availability of microform as well as about items identified for future filming by a member. Encouraging cooperative projects and avoiding duplicative filming are major goals.

The fourth RLG program, which essentially supports the other three, is the Technical Systems and Bibliographic Control Program. This program comprises the operation of acquisition and cataloging information-processing activities. RLIN's acquisitions component and shared cataloging services are the focus of this program. Because collection development decisions, interlibrary loan and preservation-related activities are all dependent upon the availability of information for shared decision making, RLIN is the mainstay of each RLG program. In spite of the importance of the centralized union database, however, Research Library Group members are strongly interested in distributed processing arrangements in which locally economical applications for such operations as serials check in and circulation can be maintained in an efficient relationship with the shared file.

Washington Library Network

The Washington Library Network (WLN), owned and operated by the Washington State Library, is a regional network serving state, public, and academic libraries in the Pacific Northwest. Although its own database is the smallest among the North American networks and direct services have been limited to the Northwestern United States and Western Canada, the WLN software has been purchased for replication and modification by individual libraries and regional groups elsewhere. The Australian National Library, the University of Illinois Library, and the Southeastern Library Network (SOLINET) are among those who have acquired the WLN computer-support programs for their own use.

WLN itself supports an online shared catalog with the first fully developed network authority control system. The network was formed in 1967 and implemented an initial union catalog project in 1972. Programmed by the Boeing Computer Services Corporation, the current bibliographic system has been operational since 1977. An acquisitions subsystem and a distributed circulation installation are also available. Individually tailored packages, including local online public catalog access modules, are marketed commercially by Biblio-Techniques as its Library and Information System (BLIS). Although WLN has not chosen to compete for nationwide membership, it has been eager to cooperate with the other networks in projects leading to expanded services for all.

University of Toronto Library Automation Systems

The University of Toronto Library Automation Systems (UTLAS) was in the early stages of development in the late 1960s and began offering online services and related products in both English and French to Canadian libraries in 1973. Since the inauguration of the Catalogue Support System (CATSS), service has been expanded to include contracts with libraries in the United States and Japan as well. By the early 1980s, over 600 libraries of all types were receiving services from UTLAS, and the database had grown to include over 15 million records with a broad range of access methods, including subject searching. Minicomputer-based distributed processing arrangements for such local operations as acquisitions, serials control, public online catalog access, and circulation are offered under the name Library Collection Management System (LCMS). An authority control file was established in 1978, and both the LC Name Authority Service tapes and Canadian MARC (CANMARC) Authority Files are available within the UTLAS CATSS Authority System. Source files for bibliographic information in the CATSS database include not only records from the National Library of Canada and the Bibliothèque Nationale du Québec but also those from the Library of Congress and the National Library of Medicine.

One of the early features of UTLAS was a flexible file management system that permitted individual library participants or consortia to maintain separate files with limited access rights or to agree upon sharing arrangements, especially for production of joint products such as computer-output microform (COM) catalogs. UTLAS, as a member of the Videotex Information Service Providers Association of Canada (VISPAC), is also exploring videotex applications for possible new services.

Network Cooperation

Following the individual network development of the 1970s, various cooperative projects were begun by the established bibliographic utilities. Utilizing a grant from the Council on Library Resources as part of its Bibliographic Services Development Program, WLN, RLG, and the Library of Congress started work on a project to establish a computer-telecommunications system link to enable joint creation and maintenance of shared online authority files in a nationwide Name Authority File Service (NAFS). Because the initial agreement between RLG and WLN was intended to be the first step in the creation of a multinetwork database, the Linked Authority Systems Project (LASP) soon had its aim broadened to include more general intersystem search and retrieval of not only authority records, but also full catalog records, location and holdings data, and eventually transmittal of interlibrary loan requests between systems. The expanded phase of development was renamed the Linked Systems Project (LSP), and its major objective became the design and implementation of a standard network interconnection (SNI). The Online Computer Library Center (OCLC) eventually became a participant on a technical consultancy basis. Intersystem standards and local system modifications are under development to resolve technical barriers to network linkage.

Another cooperative agreement has been reached between the RLG and UTLAS. A memorandum of understanding specifies sharing of databases and collaboration on system development projects and programs as priority goals. An initial plan proposes the production by UTLAS of page-form catalogs for the RLG member libraries based on machine-readable records supplied from RLIN. The UTLAS–RLG plans are an indication of the feasibility of eventual international as well as national networking. Within the United States, the Network Advisory Committee, which serves as an advisory group to the Library of Congress, the Council on Library Resources, and the Council on Computerized Library Networks, is working toward a functional connection among the bibliographic utilities.

Although by the end of the 1970s less than 10% of North American libraries were utilizing a bibliographic utility, the impact of networks upon library operations and services was already substantial. Most of the larger libraries were participants, which meant that a high percentage of current acquisitions by American libraries were represented in the four major databases. Retrospective catalog conversion efforts by member libraries also added significantly to the pool of machine-readable records.

Whereas early networking efforts had been aimed at increasing technical services access to an expanding database of bibliographic records, the focus of development was shifting by the end of the 1970s. Notable among trends were those toward providing a "user-friendly" public access method to the online database and developing local applications for the individual library's catalog records, circulation transactions, and acquisitions activities, including serials control. Although interlibrary cooperation via contribution and access to shared databases was undeniably advantageous, considerations of telecommunication costs and activity load on a central system resulted in strategies being devised for efficient distributed-processing methods.

An undertaking of interest to every network has been the improvement of video terminals used for record input and display. Work on equipment that will allow input and display of diacritical marks and non-Roman alphabets has proceeded quite rapidly. Within networks, special interest groups have formed to address such areas of concern in the context of automation's ever increasing possibilities.

Regional Networks

Cooperative trends furthering efficient use of automated systems have been closely tied to regional networking efforts. Across the United States, single- and multistate, same-type-of-library, and multitype cooperative organizations of almost endless variety have evolved and become involved in automation. Many of these networks provide, as one of their major services, a contractual connection with a bibliographic utility for individual members. Frequently they also broker database access to commercial reference search services, and in some cases, network members utilize a common type of circulation system with shared access to facilitate interlibrary loan.

A representative sample of networks that cover several states includes the New England Library Network (NELINET), the Southeastern Library Network (SOLINET), and the AMIGOS (a name that is not an acronym, for a change!) Bibliographic Council serving the South Central area of the country. Large states with extensive library services have sometimes formed in-state cooperative networks, frequently headquartered at and supported at least in part by the state library agency. The Washington Library Network (WLN), as a bibliographic utility, is an expansion of such a basic state-focused organization. MINITEX (Minnesota Interlibrary Telecommunications Exchange, previously Minnesota Interlibrary Teletype Exchange) has also extended services beyond its state boundaries by contractual agreements with North and South Dakota for access to shared resources. In contrast, ILLINET (Illinois Library and Information Network) and INCOLSA (Indiana Cooperative Library Services Authority) continue to direct their major efforts toward improving services within their respective states. Most regional and state networks put a heavy emphasis on facilitating interlibrary loan, a goal significantly aided by access to shared online databases with extensive holdings information. Many of the regional and state networks broker the services of a bibliographic utility. Providing a union serials list capability is also a frequent service, as is contracting for access to the major online reference search services such as the System Development Corporation's (SDC) ORBIT (Online Retrieval of Bibliographic Information Timshared), DIALOG Information Services, Bibliographic Retrieval Service, and the New York Times Information Bank.

The other major variety of localized network is organized by libraries of identical types. Both the Research Libraries Group, which began with five research institutions in the Northeast, and the Online Computer Library Center, which started its existence as the Ohio College Library Center, are essentially expansions of this type of cooperative. The Midwest Health Science Library Network, the Five Associated University Libraries (FAUL) in upstate New York, the Cooperative College Library Center (CCLC) at Atlanta, which serves institutions in 12 states and Puerto Rico, and the numerous systems linking public libraries are thriving examples of special focus networking.

Commercial Developments

By the early 1980s, a number of commercial vendors were offering computer-based systems for a wide variety of library applications. Because these developments are so extensive and rapidly evolving, this chapter will not attempt to describe individual commercially marketed systems, but rather identify some of the trends. Many of the earliest efforts were in the area of minicomputer-based circulation control. Several of these vendors enjoyed considerable success and were soon pressured by customers to broaden the brief-record circulation control database and software to serve as a local public access online catalog.

Another significant development has been in the area of online ordering through a direct link to the databases of major booksellers, who can also supply invoicing in machine-readable form for processing on the library's local institutional computer. Available serials applications include an arrangement with a major subscription agency for online ordering, problem solving, and claiming of missing issues. In addition, commercial vendors have designed interface systems that allow a library to transfer data from a terminal connected to its bibliographic utility into an in-house system. Even binderies have begun using automated record systems that integrate with the procedures of their client libraries.

Faced with the numerous possibilities for commercially vended systems, a librarian's responsibility is to determine which, if any, will enhance current library operations and to be sure that any contract will truly meet the needs and expectations of the library for the service to be provided. After the planning process and definition of requirements (discussed in the section "Transitions, Training, and New Standards"), the actual contract with the vendor must be drawn up and agreed to by both parties. Although some librarians are under the mistaken impression that a "standard contract" is the only possibility, there is considerable latitude for re-drafting to tailor the agreement to the library's special circumstances. The assistance of a lawyer already familiar with general aspects of the library's operation can be invaluable.

In any contract, special attention should be paid to provisions for delivery time, installation, test standards for acceptability, criteria for evaluation of continued successful performance, and upgrading arrangements for system expansion and enhancements. Acceptable computer response time needs to be defined, especially on a full transaction load basis, and penalties for nonperformance must be agreed upon in advance. A schedule for partial payments may be successfully linked to acceptance tests. The rights of the purchasing or leasing library vis-à-vis both records created and the system itself should be clear to all parties. Suggestions about negotiations in the library environment can be found in a number of publications and a useful starting point would be Dyer's article (*Clinic*, 1977).

Locally Developed Systems

As the bibliographic utilities were just beginning to plan and design their systems, a number of individual libraries identified automation as an essential support for their future operations. Some early, ambitious experiments, such as that at Florida Atlantic University in the late 1960s, were before their time and beyond the operational technology then available to libraries. Several pioneering efforts did, however, result in functioning systems. Three of the most elaborate and widely publicized plans were developed by Stanford University, the University of Chicago, and Northwestern University.

At Stanford, work on BALLOTS (Bibliographic Automation of Large Library Operations using a Time-sharing System) began with a prototype system designed with the help of a U.S. Office of Education grant received in 1967. From the beginning, BALLOTS was intended to be an integrated online technical-processing system with linked modules for acquisitions and cataloging. With the aid of additional grant monies from several sources, the online catalog function of the system became operational in 1972, and the in-process file for order activities was implemented the following year. The system then supported a full range of processing activities: preorder searching, ordering, receipt recording, claiming/cancelling, in-process control, cataloging, and record maintenance. In 1975 operations were expanded to permit seven public libraries in California access to BALLOTS for cataloging. This group, known as PLAN (Public Library Automation Network), formed the nucleus of a pre-RLIN Stanford-based bibliographic utility that grew to include over 100 participants. When the Research Libraries Group reached its agreement with Stanford in 1978 to adopt BALLOTS as the basis for RLIN, services were continued for those libraries already utilizing the system, although new affiliates among nonresearch institutions were no longer solicited.

At the University of Chicago, similar basic service support aims produced a distinctly different development history. Between 1966 and 1971 grants from the National Science Foundation enabled the university's Library Systems Development Office to design an integrated bibliographic data processing system. This system began with keyboarding of data to papertape which was then fed into a computer on a batch basis. In 1971, with additional funding from the Council on Library Resources and the National Endowment for the Humanities, the Library Data Management System was launched and by the mid-1970s planning was underway for a quadraplanar bibliographic item data structure. The four record levels were to include the "universal," which would contain information such as the ISBD data, which would be identical for any copy of an item; the "multi-institution" level, which would include information common to those libraries sharing authority files (e.g., choice and form of entry); the "institution" level; and the "copy" (e.g., physical piece) level. This ambitious program did not reach fruition, and by 1978 the direction of development was changed, with the inauguration of the Network Library System project. The University of Chicago reached an agreement with the University of Wisconsin—Madison and the IBM Corporation for joint development of a system that could be used for distributed processing by individual larger libraries or a cooperating group of institutions in a networking environment.

Northwestern University Library hired a systems analyst in 1967 and began the design of NOTIS (Northwestern Online Total Integrated System). In contrast to the Stanford and University of Chicago projects, all of Northwestern's system development was financed by the university on the premise that any in-house computer-based system would need to be economical enough to continue to operate within the library's budget. As the title of the system indicates, the aim from the beginning was to develop a fully integrated automated system. The first module, a circulation system that included self-service check-out terminals, was implemented in 1970, and the technical services support system went into operation the following year. An unusual feature of NOTIS is that, from the beginning, it has included serials check-in, a capability not initially shared by the other large library automated systems. By 1979 Northwestern had acquired a small mainframe computer that was dedicated to library operations and located in the main library building. In addition to support for the full range of acquisition and processing activities, in 1980 NOTIS functions were expanded to include public online catalog access.

The NOTIS software was adopted by the National Library of Venezuela at the completion of a database creation project, headquartered at Northwestern University, that produced machine-readable records for bibliographic materials by Venezuelans and about that country. NOTIS has also been made available to other institutions, and the University of Florida was the first of a number of libraries in the United States to purchase the system. Northwestern joined the Research Libraries Group in 1980 with the aim of eventually utilizing a computer-to-computer link for transfer of records to and from the RLIN union database, thereby allowing a distributed processing arrangement.

A number of other libraries launched in-house automation systems during the 1970s. These frequently had a special focus, such as Ohio State's circulation system and New York Public Library's book catalog project. In addition to projects planned for large public library systems and central university libraries, sophisticated automated support systems were developed at special libraries, such as those of Bell Laboratories and the IBM Advanced System Development Division, as well as specialized subunits at universities, such as the University of California at Los Angeles (UCLA) Biomedical Library. Each project has had an interesting and varied history.

Because a substantial number of libraries have several unconnected automated support systems for different purposes, many efforts are underway to integrate limited-function systems. Loading records received on "archival tapes" from a utility into local online catalog and/or circulation systems has been common, and libraries

with in-house processing systems have been impatiently awaiting fi-
nalization of the machine-to-machine standard network interconnection linkage. Various "black box" devices and programs to transfer
data from the screen of a terminal connected to a bibliographic utility into a local file have been developed. Among these, an early commercial effort designed by Innovative Interfaces linked OCLC terminals to CLSI (CL Systems, Inc.) circulation systems. Pennsylvania
State University developed its own "black box" technique to transfer
data from RLIN into its locally developed Library Information Access System (LIAS), and Oklahoma's Central State University designed a method for the transfer of its cataloging records from OCLC
into its local NOTIS operation.

AUTOMATION-BASED COOPERATION:
SHARED DATABASES AND RESOURCE SHARING

Shared Cataloging

As noted earlier, the basis for the development of the bibliographic
utilities is recognition of the value to each library in utilizing the
work of catalogers at other institutions, following mutually agreed
upon standards. Cataloging for any item need be done only once,
with the resulting copy available for use by other catalogers subsequently handling the same title. Although LC/MARC copy continues
to be regarded as the most authoritative data, libraries participating
in the shared cataloging activities of the bibliographic utilities benefit from the work of catalogers at other member institutions, and
much effort has been made by the respective users' councils of each
network to assure that all libraries adhere to the same standards for
input to the shared system. Recognition that inadequate funding has
made it impossible for almost any library to do original cataloging
for most items acquired has been a significant motivating factor pro-
pelling libraries into cooperative arrangements. Beyond basic participation in a bibliographic utility, shared cataloging interests have
produced several large-scale cooperative projects, among them Conversion of Serials (CONSER) and Name Authority Cooperation
(NACO).

The CONSER project for cooperative conversion of a comprehensive, retrospective bibliographic database of serials began with a
meeting of the Ad Hoc Discussion Group on Serials Databases at the
1973 ALA Annual Conference. Subsequently the Council on Library

Resources offered financial and managerial assistance, and OCLC was chosen as a vehicle for the joint effort. The Minnesota Union List of Serials (MULS) was selected to serve as a base file, to which would be added the limited number of LC and Canadian MARC serials records already produced. Ten institutions became initial participants: LC, NLM, NAL, the National Library of Canada, the University of Minnesota, Yale, Cornell, the State University of New York, the New York State Library, and the University of California at Berkeley's Library Automation Project. Each institution was to input records for serial titles from an assigned range of the alphabet. Agreement was reached that the database would contain location information but not specific holdings data and that, after a verifying process of "authentication" of contributed records by either LC or the National Library of Canada as "centers of responsibility", the records would be made available to non-OCLC institutions via the MARC Distribution Service.

By 1980, eight more libraries had become participants, Higher Education Act Title II-C grants had assisted serials conversion efforts, and pressure was mounting to establish an electronic interconnection between the bibliographic utilities in order to provide participants with dynamic access to each serials database. When the Library of Congress made available the first CONSER "snapshot file," which consisted of a magnetic tape copy of all the approximately 250,000 serial records in the CONSER database at OCLC as of December 1979, less than 100,000 of these records had completed the authentication process. By the end of 1981 a second CONSER snapshot file had been produced, containing approximately 339,000 records, and the Association of Research Libraries (ARL) and the National Federation of Abstracting and Indexing Services had joined with LC, OCLC, and CLR to add records for all serial titles currently abstracted or indexed by the major U.S. and Canadian abstracting and indexing services. CONSER records also had become the basis for the production of *New Serial Titles*. Discussion was underway about the delegation of authentication responsibility from LC to other participants, partially as a result of the success of the second major cooperative project, NACO (Name Authority Cooperation).

Late in 1979, the Library of Congress invited representatives from Northwestern University, the University of Texas, and the University of Wisconsin to join in planning to contribute headings from local cataloging to a cooperative automated name authority file. From this meeting the NACO program was born. Prior to NACO, LC was already cooperating with the Government Printing Office and the Texas State Library. Additional contributors to the shared authority file were initially sought on the basis of a broad representation of cataloging specialties. Important to the exploration of multi-institution heading formulation in the project's early phases was recognition that the University of Texas catalogs for a strong Latin American collection, Northwestern supports a distinguished Africana library, and the University of Wisconsin could offer data for Slavic materials and a variety of headings from European acquisitions. Newly established headings were to be sent by mail or telecopier to LC where they would be verified and entered into the machine-readable Name Authority File. By the end of 1983, 28 libraries had received the intensive LC training necessary for NACO participation, records from a number of early participants were being accepted by LC without further verification, and several libraries were using search-only access to LC's online files for up-to-the-minute information about headings already established. Several special arrangements had been made in which the Library of Congress was also beginning to accept full bibliographic records for original cataloging from other institutions for addition to the LC/MARC database.

Another cooperative effort that has resulted from online database availability is a project for joint cataloging of items in major microform sets. Sponsored by the Association of Research Libraries (ARL), provision of full title-by-title access to such materials became feasible when it became possible to share cataloging and already available data could be identified and "claimed" by network participants on a set-by-set basis. The ARL program staff have worked with the bibliographic utilities and micropublishers to establish mechanisms by which records for each title in a particular microform set may be assigned holdings information for an individual library that has acquired the set. Libraries have applied for grant funds to catalog titles in microform sets, and micropublishers have been encouraged to create machine-readable records for their offerings. Efforts are also underway toward establishment of a cooperative North American database of records for microform masters, to be related to nationwide preservation activities.

Cooperative Acquisitions and Interlibrary Loan

An online union catalog database provides the foundation for library services that reach well beyond shared cataloging activities. In cases such as the RLG Shared Resources Program, libraries have agreed to serve as centers of responsibility for collection development in specific subject areas with the understanding that in-depth efforts of each will support the cooperating membership as a whole. The logical corollary is that it is not necessary for every library to develop *all* subject areas with the same intensity. A set of conspectuses formulated by RLG libraries for the individual assessment of both existing collection strength and current level of acquisition is maintained in an online file accessed by subject words and phrases, institutions, and LC classification number via RLIN. Order and in-process information in the system also aids in cooperative purchasing decisions.

A popular form of resource-sharing support for participants in bibliographic utilities is the use of a union listing arrangement for serials holdings. In 1981 OCLC began offering an online union listing capability as a feature of its developing serials control system. Local holdings data, entered in summary form consistent with the ANSI serial summary holdings representation standard, may be displayed online by all libraries using the OCLC serials module. Although list production by automated systems is a vast improvement over previous compilation methods, this is an area in which online systems offer a significant untapped potential. When detailed serial holdings information for individual libraries becomes generally available in network databases, resource sharing will be greatly improved—a blessing in times of tight budgets and strict copyright limitations.

Certainly, the most obvious resource-sharing benefit of automation is the location information conveyed in the holdings symbols for participating libraries in the bibliographic utility databases. Interlibrary loan has been positively transformed by access to the large network databases, especially with the aid of electronic request transmission. Although limitations due to the lack of linkage between the bibliographic utilities leave room for improvement, the impact upon service is already enormous. In addition, exploratory projects are underway for electronic delivery of the full text of documents. In one of these, the American Chemical Society has begun to offer most of its journals online via Bibliographic Retrieval Services (BRS). The implications for both speed of delivery and preservation are substantial.

Preservation

Beyond the resource access improvements of both telefacsimile document transmission and direct electronic publishing, new technology offers the promise of significant improvements in dealing with preservation problems. In 1982 the Library of Congress announced an experimental program for the preservation of deteriorating materials by transfer to optical disks. This program is closely associated with the major project launched by the Association of Research Libraries that focuses on shared cataloging in machine-readable form for items in large microform sets. Both ARL and the Research Libraries Group have been promoting efforts to systematically microfilm deteriorating materials of research value. A key part of this program depends upon the input of information into automated databases to allow each member of the network to know what work has already been done and also which items have been identified to be filmed in the near future.

AUTOMATION APPLICATIONS TO INDIVIDUAL PROCESSING OPERATIONS

Although automation's wide-ranging benefits for interlibrary cooperation are most attractive, the major impact of participation in any computer-based system will be seen directly in a library's in-house operations. Functions such as circulation and technical processing, which are routine and yet filled with the complexities of the "exceptions that prove the rule," became the first targets for automated support. In some libraries almost all activities and services are now maintained with the aid of a computer. Looking at the full range of library functions, it is difficult to identify a single one that has not been the subject of an automation effort in some institution. Although no single library has every application, and considerable variation exists in the automation options chosen, even by similar institutions, the composite picture is impressive. Integrated systems come closest to offering the entire array of computer-assisted functions, and this approach to library automation provides a pattern for closer examination.

Acquisitions

Automation's impact may begin at the earliest stages of the acquisitions process when collection development staff are assisted by new publication review slips or lists generated from data on the weekly LC/MARC subscription tapes. Starting with the decision to acquire an item, a selector is frequently able to check the library's holdings in either a local online database or network file; ideally, access to both will be available from a single terminal. Based on the search results, a request to purchase is made, and acquisitions department staff may be able to use an existing record in the machine-readable database for production of an accurate purchase order. When no record is available, a provisional record, often with the form of the main entry verified from data in an online authority file, can be entered into the system and ordering completed—either by production done locally or at a utility—of a hard-copy purchase order; or it can also be completed by electronic transmission of the order request through an arrangement established with one or more vendors. With either method of order placement, no hard-copy files need be maintained.

Reminders to the staff to decide whether making a claim is appropriate can be programmed to be produced after an appropriate time interval has elapsed. Alternatively, the computer system could generate claims at predetermined intervals without staff review, although experience in some institutions has found complete reliance upon the system to be rather risky, because the computer lacks data about certain situations, such as shipping strikes, that affect decisions to claim. Automated systems can be used to produce a wide variety of specially tailored messages rather than only one "standard claim notice." This capability is essential for serials subscription problems and is also useful for cases in which foreign acquisitions efforts may be facilitated by communication in the language of the vendor's country.

Cancellation of individual orders, communication with suppliers about incorrect or damaged items, maintenance of "desiderata" files, and monitoring of vendor performance are other aspects of acquisitions work aided by automation. The computer record may be used both to generate correspondence and to note dealer communications about the status of an order, such as "out of stock" or "back ordered." Codes are often used to facilitate recording of these data and to generate full-text communications when appropriate. The system will accommodate receipt recording, not only for single items supplied on firm orders but also for approval plan receipts, gifts, and subscription items. The ordering and receiving process generates fund accounting records, with encumbrances and debits automatically tallied following entry of order placement price estimates and invoice payment data. Appropriate fund assignment for new orders can be assisted by system prompting based upon the location designated as the order is input.

From the time the acquisition record is first created, even at the preorder stage, this status information may be available to both staff and the public via terminals located throughout the library and in other facilities. After the item is received, its status becomes "in-process," and arrangements may be made for the public to request rush processing. The computer can also produce receipt notices if desired by requesters, SDI (selective dissemination of information) service printouts, and routing slips for new periodicals issues. Upon item receipt, the acquisitions record in an integrated system becomes the base for cataloging, needing only those additions or corrections that will bring it to *National Level Bibliographic Record* standard and the library's own location call number.

Serials Control

One of the most impressive features of the few automated serials control modules currently in operation is the instantaneous access to issue arrival information from any terminal attached to the system. For the integrated system with an online public catalog, users have vastly improved access to up-to-the-moment information about serials holdings. The computer system can also supply messages to suit such special circumstances as titles whose current issues are in the periodicals room while the bound volumes are shelved in the stacks or the latest volume is kept at a reference desk.

When an issue fails to arrive before the expiration of the number of days in an automatically set claiming interval, the lack of action in the computer record triggers a claim "prompt" for a staff member to assess. (He or she will allow for the usual array of unusual circumstances, such as postal strikes or political upheavals, that may disrupt publication service in various countries.) If a claim seems appropriate, brief coded input can instruct the computer to formulate a variety of messages, including issue-specific data where necessary, to draw the publisher or vendor address from an online file, and to either dispatch the information electronically or print a letter in a format suitable for insertion in a window envelope for mailing. In some cases, in addition to online ordering and claiming services, serials subscription agencies will now supply machine-readable check-in and subscription invoicing records for use in local systems.

When serials issues are ready for binding, in-house processing operations may interface with the automated system of a commercial firm. Eventually the type of information usually found in "sample back" files regarding the color, type of binding, and data to appear on the spine will undoubtedly be transmitted to binderies in machine-readable form.

Cataloging

Shared cataloging developments have already been discussed at considerable length, but the methods used by the individual cataloger in an automated system context have not yet been addressed. In an integrated system, an original cataloger may find more authoritative data in the provisional record established for acquisitions than would have been found on the copy of a purchase order produced manually. Whatever information the online authority file may provide will be used to assure consistency between a new record input at the order stage and full bibliographic records for cataloged items. The "shelflisting" process of call number formulation for an item can be completed online using a call-number browsing approach when a full inventory database is available. It is possible to complete the intellectual process of cataloging while sitting at a terminal, although when full bibliographic copy is not available in the system, a more common practice is for the cataloger to update information on a worksheet containing provisional data and to have actual input performed by a clerical assistant. One complication that can be expected to hinder the process of online cataloging until retrospective conversion of manual catalog records is completed is the frequent need to be concerned with two files, the old card catalog and the computer database.

One cataloging aid that may be offered by an automated system is facilitation of the creation of cross-references. In addition to the references that have been routinely furnished in the past, an online catalog also offers the opportunity to determine the need for other references by consulting the actual public-use search strategies that can be recorded by the system for analysis. Professional time freed by having copy already available for more materials, thereby allowing them to be handled by assistants, may permit additional analysis of user needs and resulting improvements in service. It may even be possible to devote more time to providing analytics for items in specially emphasized collections. In the context of the integrated system with an online catalog, the work of technical services staff in all departments is more visibly related than in previous manual multiple file systems, and the work of all, at every stage, is seen by the public at the online catalog display.

Circulation and Inventory Control

Circulation systems have utilized a wide variety of devices for recording and reading item identification. Among the most prominent methods are bar code labels, punched cards, and OCR (optical character recognition) labels. The choice of circulation system affects item-processing procedures and inventory control methods as well as the public service tie to a current or planned online catalog. At a number of libraries this increased interrelationship has led to a shift of the circulation department's administrative reporting line from public services into the technical services division.

Automation provides new capabilities for public display of current status information along with call number location data for items searched in the online catalog. A computer-support system will accomodate up-to-the-minute information on various routine changes of location for cataloged items, including movement on and off reserve and shipment to a bindery. In addition, the records that a computer-based system can readily provide for hold requests and circulation activity can be of significant aid in collection management decision making. Inventory control is also greatly assisted by the easily updated records of public requests and staff searches for missing items. Certainly, much user frustration generated by fruitless trips to the stacks can be prevented by immediate information about the current physical location of items.

DOWNTIME AND BACKUP

A library that is taking advantage of many of the wide variety of automated system possibilities has reached the point at which, if the system malfunctions (is "down"), both the basic workflow and the ability to meet public service requirements come to a halt. Computer equipment is becoming highly reliable but, for the staff as well as the public using the online catalog, system reliability is crucial and backup methods deserve serious consideration. A number of backup methods have been used for automated systems, the most complete and generally most expensive of which is computer redundancy. Having a second central processing unit, or multiples in the case of the large bibliographic utilities, is naturally the best insurance for continuous system availability. The old card catalog, if not discarded, can provide a substantial amount of backup for the online catalog. In that context, it is worth remembering that, for the manual catalog, card production, "overhead" typing, and actual filing were seldom entirely up-to-date and, for large libraries, often months behind. Other backup methods include periodic computer-generated listings, often in microform, plus some type of mini circulation system to collect charge data for future entry into the main system when it is again available.

The amount of downtime that can be considered tolerable requires close analysis because it will vary according to the combination of usage and public relations factors that make each library's situation unique. The decision whether to back up all aspects of the system in some manner or only the portions judged as having the most significant impact in the specific library's circumstances will demand both initial careful consideration and periodic review when circumstances inevitably change. If some kind of computer-produced hardcopy file is maintained, the frequency of COM or other backup list production or cumulation will depend upon cost as well as the individual library's perception both of its system reliability and the service needs of its clientele.

SERVICE IMPROVEMENTS

As has already been emphasized among the advantages of automated systems, a major improvement in public service results from the availability of information that could not previously be supplied in the conventional card catalog. The evolving online public access catalog (often termed the OPAC), when part of an integrated system that includes acquisitions and circulation, is able to furnish status information for materials that are on order, in process, or circulating. The availability of up-to-the-moment serials issue check-in data as part of public catalog access has seldom been possible prior to automation. The ability to ascertain status information for an item sought at the time of catalog inquiry and perhaps to request that it be recalled and/or held upon return from a current circulation must also rank as a major service improvement. Another interesting service aspect for libraries with some backlog of materials to be processed is that user requests for uncataloged materials located via the OPAC can become a type of demand-regulated priority system that helps to assure that the most needed items are processed first.

Another significant access improvement offered by automated systems is the ability to place terminals in locations where a duplicate card catalog could not be provided or to dial up from equipment primarily used for other services. Public use of the online catalog is feasible in numerous areas, from stacks and offices to dormitories and homes. It is also possible to provide printers to enable users to make hard copies of self-tailored bibliographies.

Because the purpose of cataloging is to make information available to those who need it by assigning appropriate access devices to materials acquired, the computer-based catalog has opened new possibilities. Because the OPAC must be at least as effective as traditional methods of access, its goal is clearly to improve upon them while maintaining the existing strengths. Catalog "structure," assured by adoption of a standard subject access system such as the *Library of Congress Subject Headings* (LCSH), adherence to the latest edition of the *Anglo-American Cataloguing Rules* for choice of entry, and provision of authority control over headings used and cross-references provided, permits the necessary comprehensiveness of information retrieval. Beyond those essential conventions and associated access methods by specific author, title, or subject heading, the computer can search for and display items using techniques not feasible in a manual context. In addition to searches by the various identification number systems such as the ISBN, ISSN, and LC card number, which can be invaluable to staff, an automated system can provide searching methods that vastly expand public catalog access capabilities. One technique already implemented in various systems is Boolean searching, in which the logical operators "and," "or," and "not" are used to expand or limit queries. Other options include search limitation by variables such as language, publisher, country of publication, cost (greater or less than a stated amount), year or years of publication, or kind of material (music score, film, etc.). Computer programming can also make possible free-form searching using natural language, access to keywords in title and subject fields, and retrieval of a specified combination of author and title. It is often possible to truncate search terms to retrieve and review records found in the proximity of the requested term; sometimes a system will provide the closest alternative match when no exact match for a search request is found. In most cases the filing order problems of hard-copy catalogs disappear, and with some search options, word order is not significant. A type of shelflisting browsing capability by call number and, for some searches in a bibliographic utility database, a display of results by location of holdings within a particular state or region, further extend options.

The OPAC has been evolving rapidly, with the introduction in the early 1980s of varying systems offered by bibliographic utilities and commercial vendors, in addition to those locally designed by individual libraries. Prompted by these developments, a number of comparative projects, including a major assessment of early options sponsored by the Council on Library Resources, have been attempting to clarify the directions that are being and should be taken in OPAC development. A major concern of recent studies has been to determine how to assure effective access to desired information while offering a readily learned and easily used self-service public searching method. Claims of user friendliness abound, although actual screen formats and access techniques vary widely from system to system. Some catalogs even allow a searcher to choose the degree of friendliness desired or required by offering different searching modes for the beginner and the more experienced. Major variations include providing a fixed "menu" of choices or requiring the user to input commands with the search request data. The importance of determining whether the diversity of search mechanisms proves a handicap for users of more than one library's system has also been recognized. If a significant negative impact is perceived, a gradual movement toward standardization by using the most effective aspects of each system is probable. Meanwhile, librarians are busy attempting to identify optimal methods of access to data, appropriate content, and display formats for information retrieved by user searches.

The possibility of improving access to materials by means of subject approach has received considerable attention, particularly because subject searches without a thesaurus that links variant terms for the topic can result in incomplete retrieval of relevant materials. Discussions concerning possible enhancement of subject access through adding table of contents information or by adopting alternative indexing systems such as PRECIS (Preserved Context Index System), used by the *British National Bibliography*, have been held repeatedly. As yet these possibilities have not been widely adopted due to the highly labor-intensive and, therefore, costly nature of such efforts. It seems most unlikely that PRECIS will be added to or substituted for LCSH in many U.S. libraries in the near future.

At present no single online catalog incorporates all of the machine-enhanced searching techniques named above, nor does any plan to do so. Even with their current limitations, however, online catalogs have been enthusiastically received by the public wherever they have been introduced. The potential for service improvement is immense and already beginning to be applied. As further developments occur in electronic publishing and item delivery technology, as well as linkage to the vast and rapidly expanding reference service databases, a major transformation in library operation is sure to take place.

TRENDS AND PROSPECTS

The surge in automation applications has made recent years particularly interesting for technical services librarianship. One trend is certainly toward distributed processing with the local integrated system interfacing with a national or international database. Bibliographic information may soon be linked with indexing, abstracting, and electronic transmission of full texts, which will undoubtedly change the nature of library processing and data retrieval operations. As both the processing operation requirements and the ultimate use and usefulness of cataloging data become more obvious to all library staff using an integrated system, ties between the conventional technical and public services will continue to strengthen, blurring traditional divisions and offering stimulating new possibilities for professional librarians while the online public access catalog continues to evolve. Managerial skills in particular will be challenged in this era of rapid change as planning, training, and providing leadership to staff for the most effective utilization of computer-support systems demand special focus. Development and application of standards will retain a high level of significance, especially in the resource-sharing network context. Automation is clearly prompting a careful review and transformation of librarianship in this century.

THE LITERATURE OF TECHNICAL
SERVICES AUTOMATION

The rapidity of change in library automation has resulted in many journal articles on the topic. During the late 1960s and early 1970s, many descriptions of planned, but not yet implemented, systems appeared, followed by a shift to articles on specific, often narrowly focused, accomplishments. Through the years, developments in automated support systems have frequently been reported in the *Journal of Library Automation* (which became *Information Technology and Libraries* in 1982). This publication of ALA's Library and Information Technology Association, along with the *LITA Newsletter*, the publications of ALA's Resources and Technical Services Division, *Library Systems Newsletter, Online, Computerworld* and the newsletters of the bibliographic utilities are major sources of current information as well as fascinating records of system evolution. Very few full scale up-to-date texts are available, undoubtedly because of the field's extremely rapid changes. This area of publication is, however, characterized by a large number of state-of-the-art volumes comparing what is currently available for specific functional applications such as circulation and acquisitions systems. Several prominent library consultants, among them Richard Boss and Joseph Matthews, are authors of a number of these practical but quickly obsolete volumes. Since up-dated texts appear as changes warrant, these items are not included in the brief bibliography for this chapter.

REFERENCES

Academic American encyclopedia (Full Text Online Database). Danbury, Conn.: Grolier, Inc., Available through Bibliographic Retrieval Service and Dow Jones & Company, Inc.

American book trade directory. New York: R. R. Bowker, 1915–.

American Library Association. Library and Information Technology Association. *LITA newsletter* (Vols. 1–). Chicago: Author, Winter 1980–.

American library directory. New York: R. R. Bowker, 1923–.

American National Standards Institute. Standards Committee Z39 on Library Work, Documentation, and Related Publishing Practices. Standards published individually. Available from American National Standards Institute, 1430 Broadway, New York, NY 10018.

Anglo-American cataloguing rules (2nd ed.). M. Gorman & P. W. Winkler (Eds.). Chicago: American Library Association, 1978.

British national bibliography. London: The British Library, 1950–.

Clinic on Library Applications of Data Processing. University of Illinois. Proceedings (Vols. 1–). Champaign, Ill.: Graduate School of Library Science, 1963–.

Computerworld (Vols 1–). Framingham, Mass.: CW Communications, 1967–.

Dyer, Charles. Data processing contracts: A tutorial. In J. L. Divilbiss (Ed.), *Proceedings of the 1977 clinic on library applications of data processing: Negotiating for computer services.* Urbana–Champaign: University of Illinois Graduate School of Library Science, 1977.

Information technology and libraries (Vols. 1–). Chicago: American Library Association, 1982–.

International Organization for Standardization. Documentation—Format for bibliographic information interchange on magnetic tape (ISO 2709-1973 (E). In *Information transfer: Handbook on international standards governing information transfer (texts of ISO standards)* (1st ed.). Geneva, Switzerland: International Organization for Standardization, 1977.

Journal of library automation (Vols. 1–14). Chicago: Library and Information Technology Association, American Library Association, 1968–1981.

Library of Congress. Automated Systems Office. *MARC formats for bibliographic data.* Washington, D.C.: Author, 1980.

Library of Congress. Subject Cataloging Division. *Library of Congress subject headings* (9th ed.). Washington, D.C.: Author, 1980.

Library systems newsletter (Vols. 1–). Chicago: Library Technology Reports, American Library Association, 1981–.

Matthews, J. R. *Choosing an automated library system: A planning guide.* Chicago: American Library Association, 1980.

National level bibliographic record—books. Washington, D.C.: Library of Congress, 1980. (Distributed by Cataloging Distribution Service).

The national union catalog. Washington, D.C.: Library of Congress, 1953/1957–.

The national union catalog: Register of additional locations. Washington, D.C.: Library of Congress, 1963/1967–.

New serial titles. Washington, D.C.: Library of Congress. New York: R. R. Bowker, 1950–.

Online (Vols. 1–). Weston, Conn.: Online, Inc., 1977–.

Publishers, distributors, & wholesalers of the United States. New York: R. R. Bowker, 1981–.

BIBLIOGRAPHY

Annual review of information science and technology (Vols. 1–). Washington, D.C.: American Society for Information Science, 1966–.

Clinic on Library Applications of Data Processing. University of Illinois. Proceedings (Vols. 1–). Champaign, Ill.: Graduate School of Library Science, 1963–.

Corbin. J. B. *Developing computer-based library systems.* Phoenix: Oryx Press, 1981.

Fosdick, H. *Computer basics for librarians and information scientists.* Arlington, Va.: Information Resources Press, 1981.

Hayes, R. M., & Becker, J. *Handbook of data processing for libraries* (2nd ed.). Los Angeles: Melville Publishing Co., 1974.

Lancaster, F. W. *Libraries and librarians in an age of electronics.* Arlington, Va.: Information Resources Press, 1982.

Malinconico, S. M., & Fasana, P. J. *The future of the catalog: The library's choices.* White Plains, N.Y.: Knowledge Industry Publications, 1979.

Martin, S. K. *Library networks, 1981-1982.* White Plains, N.Y.: Knowledge Industry Publications, 1981.

Matthews, J. R. *Choosing an automated library system: A planning guide.* Chicago: American Library Association, 1980.

Networks for networkers: Critical issues in cooperative library development. B. E. Markuson and B. Woolls (Eds.). New York: Neal–Schuman, 1980.

Salton, G. *Dynamic information and library processing.* Englewood Cliffs, N.J.: Prentice–Hall, 1975.

4 Acquisitions

Marion T. Reid

TYPICAL ORGANIZATION

Within the library, the functions related to acquiring materials customarily fall within the technical realm, placed in a division called "technical services," "technical processing," or "processing services." The scope of the acquisitions unit depends upon the needs of the institution that the library serves, the amount of staff, and the size of the library materials budget.

Scope of Acquisitions

In its broadest sense, acquisitions includes *all* tasks related to obtaining *all* library materials. The scope of such a task is most easily understood in a small library in which these functions make up a portion of the tasks for one person. The minimal volume of ordering and lack of organizational hierarchy simplify procedures. However, in larger libraries the scope of acquisitions becomes more complex and some functions are frequently found in other areas. For example:

1. Selection may be the responsibility of a collection management staff, subject specialists in other areas of the library, and/or

other members of the institution served by the library (e.g., faculty in a university library).

2. Accounting functions may be handled by the library business office.

3. Acquisitions of special classes of materials may be done by another section of the library—or even by another part of the institution—that provides other services related to that type of material (e.g., serials department, government documents division, audiovisual center).

4. Preorder search routines may be performed by staff in collection management or within a cataloging unit that also performs precataloging searching.

Although all staff within an acquisitions department may be trained to handle most daily procedures in order to cope with uneven workloads, acquisitions tasks are most easily divided by centering them around two operations: ordering and receiving. Ordering encompasses searching and verification, generating and sending orders, claiming, recording vendors' reports, and handling cancellations. Receiving includes unpacking shipments, matching the piece received against the invoice and the purchase order, communicating with the vendor to solve problems, approving invoices for payment, recording receipt of series and sets in the proper files, and resolving vendors' statements.

Within this chapter, the term *acquisitions* refers to the process of obtaining library materials *after* they have been selected. For information on selection and other aspects of the function of librarianship known as collection management, consult the items under that heading in the chapter bibliography. Except where specifically noted, acquisitions refers to procedures to purchase in-print monographs within the context of a large library. Readers who deal with libraries in smaller settings will find pertinent citations in both the references and the bibliography.

Working Relationships

As G. E. Evans (1979, p. 197) points out, it is important for acquisitions personnel to "develop close, friendly working relationships both with other library units and with vendors."

The duties of the acquisitions staff are shown in Table 4.1. In order to achieve successful interaction with all of the groups shown in Table 4.1, acquisitions staff should strive to conduct each transac-

TABLE 4.1

Communication between Acquisitions and Other Library Divisions

Group	Purpose
Collection management staff	Receive orders in the proper format with accurate library holdings information, if any is required
	Regulate the flow of orders to make sure all funds will be expended by the end of the fiscal year
	Return orders not filled because the item is no longer available, because the title is already in the collection, or because the order is not complete
	Provide input for budget allocation by estimating ongoing purchase needs such as standing orders, approval plans, serials, continuations
Other library staff with acquisitions functions (e.g., in separate serials department)	Coordinate efforts to prevent unnecessary duplication
Catalog department staff	Provide accurate information concerning bibliographic information, searching and verification done, location, and special handling.
Bindery staff	Initiate gathering of parts of serials and standing orders to be bound
	Claim missing parts or issues
	Record the fact that a volume has been bound
	Determine whether new material received in disrepair should be retained or replaced
Business office staff	Monitor monthly statement and question funds that seem to have dropped too much or too little for the amount of work put through
	Resolve payment queries from vendors
Other library staff	Help solve miscellaneous problems, such as obtaining replacement pages for a defective book
	Provide bibliographic information
Patrons	Quickly obtain titles for which there is immediate need
	Provide bibliographic information
Vendors	Acquire as rapidly as possible the highest possible percentage of materials ordered

tion with sincerity and directness. When a change that is within the
aegis of acquisitions is pending, the acquisitions librarian should
consult all contacts who may be affected prior to initiating that
change.

RELATIONSHIPS WITH VENDORS

Definition of Vendor

Vendor is defined here as the wholesaler or middleman through
which library materials are purchased. It encompasses such terms
as "bookdealer," "book store," "jobber," and "subscription agent."

Why Use a Vendor?

Some librarians send rush orders to the publisher on the theory
that going directly to the source is faster. Gregory (1972) presents an
amusing anecdote on how slow and frustrating this method can be.
Other librarians order from the publisher to net a higher discount.
Murray's survey indicated that dealing direct was "neither efficient
nor economical" for the University of Michigan Library ("Library
Survey on Direct Ordering," 1978). Of course, going directly to the
publisher is occasionally the most reasonable thing to do, but a library with any volume of orders for multiple publishers lacks the
staff to order direct for everything. The prime reason to use a vendor
is that he or she provides one source for titles originating from many
sources. This automatically eliminates the necessity of finding and
recording addresses for all sources and reduces the number of boxes
to open, invoices to process, checks to issue, and people to contact
about problem receipts.

Choosing a Vendor: Examining Services Offered

Which vendor to use depends upon the library's priorities. One
vendor may provide the best discount possible. Another may stock
more of the kinds of titles the library orders and thus supply more
orders immediately. Yet another may fill a higher percentage of
orders in a 6-month period or go to great lengths to provide the more
elusive items.
Vendors can be identified by checking the "Book Dealers" section

of *Library Resrouces Market Place;* through advertisements via direct mailings, in library literature, or conference exhibits; and by their sales representatives who visit the library.

In the initial contact with the potential vendor, find out what services are provided. Ask what publishers he or she supplies and which publishers are stocked. Find out the services for which there are additional charges and how well the services and stock mesh with the library's order needs. Decide whether his or her geographic location is a factor that may affect service.

North American vendors currently offer the following services, although no single vendor provides them all (indeed, some are mutually exclusive):

1. Scope of stock and discounts: (a) maintains a stock of a certain quantity of titles from a certain number of publishers, designed to serve certain types of libraries or to fulfill orders for specific subjects and (b) offers discounts for various categories of materials.

2. Ordering aids: (a) offers free order-typing service; (b) supplies the library with slips or lists of new titles available, which may be used as the library's order; and (c) provides postage-free, self-addressed envelopes for orders.

3. Special ordering procedures: (a) handles rush orders immediately; (b) covers prepayments required by the publisher without asking the library to prepay; (c) automatically back-orders titles found to be not yet published; (d) automatically searches for titles found to be out of print; (e) forwards to a foreign vendor orders for titles not distributed in North America; and (f) supplies foreign imprint titles.

4. Customer service: (a) assigns to one person all aspects of handling a library's account in order to provide continuity of service; (b) makes a toll-free telephone line available; (c) allows automatic return of books if they are unmarked; (d) provides free credit-memo forms.

5. Billing: (a) customizes invoices according to the library's requirements; (b) accepts deposit accounts on which interest may accrue; and (c) pays shipping costs.

6. Products providing management data or other information: (a) provides management data in paper or magnetic tape format, such as titles shipped by categorized subject, with fund and cost information and (b) supplies catalogs, guides, or newsletters pertinent to the type of materials supplied (e.g., selection aids, title change information).

7. Processing services: (a) processes books by affixing customized book pocket, affixing call number on spine, placing protective cover

on book, and supplying catalog cards; (b) offers processing kits with protective book cover, spine label, customized book pocket, and catalog cards; (c) offers any portion of items (a) or (b) desired; and (d) inserts strips or plates for theft detection systems.

8. Special ordering plans: (a) leases books for which library has a short-term need; (b) automatically provides best sellers; (c) supplies standing orders for continuations; and (d) provides books through an approval plan.

9. Other services: (a) offers an automated acquisitions system; (b) manufacturers computer-output microform (COM) catalogs; and (c) sells library furniture and/or library supplies.

10. Special services offered by subscription agents: (a) annually provides a renewal list so that the library can either revise it or automatically continue receiving the same quantities of titles and subscriptions; (b) offers various ordering schedules designed to take advantage of publisher discounts on multiple-year subscriptions or to provide schools with a 9-month subscription term; (c) provides postcards on which to claim missing issues from the publisher; (d) supplies a list verifying what claims the vendor has forwarded to the publisher; (e) accepts advance payment; (f) notifies publishers of address change if the library moves; (g) requests sample copy from publisher; (h) provides back numbers for new subscriptions; (i) provides online inventory of back issues available; (j) accepts orders for single issues, single volumes, or short runs; (k) accumulates issues of a subscription and sends it to a specified binder so that the library will receive a complete, bound volume. (l) receives and checks in issues, batches them, and supplies them to the library with call numbers, outstanding claim information, and current holdings data; (m) generates union lists of serials; and (n) offers an automated serials control system.

Choosing a Vendor: Establishing Specifications

If the vendor's services and stock match the library's needs, discuss library ordering practices and expectations with the vendor. For firm orders, points to cover include

1. Orders: (a) describe the size and format of the library's order form; (b) give an estimate of the frequency of the orders sent and the average number of titles ordered; (c) state whether one of the library's order copies is to be returned with the book or as a report; and (d) ask whether the vendor will provide mailing labels or self-addressed envelopes for the library's orders.

2. Order processing: (a) determine whether rush orders will be handled more rapidly than other orders and if so, whether discounts apply to rush orders; (b) if an edition is available in both cloth and paper, ask whether the vendor can supply the edition preferred, even if the preference is not stated on the order itself; and (c) specify by what amount above the quoted price for a title the library is willing to pay without having the order returned for clarification.

3. Shipments: determine (a) through what carriers shipments may be made and state the library's preference; (b) whether the cartons will be numbered ("1 of 5," etc.) if there is more than one package in a shipment; (c) whether the invoice is to be included in the carton or mailed separately; (d) where the packing list or invoice will be found in the shipment (i.e., in the first box, in an envelope taped to the box); and (e) whether a copy of the order is to be sent with the book and where it should be placed—in the book, attached to the invoice, or appended in some other way.

4. Invoices: determine (a) how many copies of the invoice are needed; (b) what information should be provided for each title (e.g., author, title, purchase order number, fund); (c) in what order the invoice items should be listed (i.e., alphabetically by title or author, in purchase order number sequence, grouped by fund); and (d) describe any special invoicing needs (e.g., billing items for only one fund per invoice, having a separate invoice for each title, double spacing between invoice items, requiring a definite dollar limit per invoice.)

5. Billing: (a) determine what discount the vendor offers for trade books, scientific and technical books, reprints, juveniles, and no-discount items; (b) ask whether there are any service charges; (c) find out whether the vendor pays for shipping and if not, whether shipping will be charged separately or included in the cost of the book; (d) inform the vendor not to charge tax, if the library has tax-exempt status; and (e) ask whether the vendor has a method for handling vouchers efficiently, if the library requires a voucher for each order.

6. Returns and problems: determine (a) under what circumstances a title may be returned for credit; (b) whether separate permission is required for each case; (c) whether the vendor provides credit memos that the library can prepare; and (d) whether the vendor has a toll-free number for customers to call in order to ask questions and solve problems.

7. Reports and cancellations: determine (a) under what circumstances the vendor sends reports and in what format; (b) whether he or she will regularly produce a list stating the status of all outstanding orders, which will reduce the need for claims, and if so, how the list should be arranged (e.g., by title, by fund); and (c) whether the

vendor should cancel an order automatically if it has not been filled and if so, when.

If the vendor can meet the library's specific requirements, ask that he or she confirm them in a letter or put them in writing and send him a copy. Establish a trial period and begin sending orders.

Continued communication is essential. Throughout a trial period, tell the dealer what the problems are as soon as they arise and seek solutions that are acceptable to both parties. Allow enough time for a proposed solution to take effect. Consider using the vendor on a more permanent basis if he or she performs well during the trial period.

If problems with a proven vendor appear, let the vendor know immediately. Perhaps procedures have been altered, new staff hired, or there is a local strike. He or she may never know there is a problem unless informed of it.

Vendor Performance Standards

During the past 25 years, several committees of the American Library Association (1957, 1977, 1983) have issued documents outlining what librarians and bookdealers may expect from each other. They include guidelines for fair practice; for ordering monographs, serials, and audiovisual materials; and for prepaying orders. These are included in the references. A subcommittee of the ALA Resources and Technical Services Division, the resources section's collection management and development committee is currently drafting a set of guidelines for measuring vendor performance.

Bids

Some institutions require that their libraries get bids for library materials to ensure that the library will get the most for its money. In his 1974 study, Boyer found that the state-wide contracts for library materials frequently require that the staff expend far more time than the resulting discounts can justify. A librarian selects a vendor for the service provided as well as for the discount offered. Melcher (1971) and Osborn (1980) agree that discount alone is emphasized and service suffers in a bid situation. If a bid situation is required, the acquisition librarian should request that the institution arrive at a list of approved vendors, rather than having an entire contract awarded to a single vendor. This provides the institution a method of doing business with reliable vendors, yet it allows the acquisitions librarian to use different vendors according to the services, as well as the discounts, they offer.

RECORDS AND FILES

When deciding which acquisitions records and files to maintain, the basic premise is to use the least number possible. That premise should be followed with the caveat that one must have enough information to accurately acquire what is needed as efficiently and as rapidly as possible. If a file is rarely accessed or if its information is available in another source, do away with it. Remember that each file adds to acquisitions costs in terms of the staff time taken to add, consult, and remove its records.

The Purchase Order

The key acquisitions record is the purchase order, the official library message transmitted to the vendor that requests a certain number of copies of a specific title. Over the years the format of the order has varied from handwritten lists, to typed slips, then magnetic tape, and finally to library-terminal to vendor-computer transmission. Customarily, the library assigns a number to each order issued so that both the vendor and the library can easily identify that order in future communications. Sometimes this purchase order number identifies a list of many titles being ordered, but usually it identifies one title only. The latter method should be preferred because the multiple titles on a list will rarely be shipped, reported on, claimed, or cancelled as a group.

Information on the Purchase Order

The purchase order should include enough information so that the vendor can supply the title wanted. Ideally, the international standard book number (ISBN), the title, the number of copies wanted, and the shipping address should be sufficient. However, if a certain edition is wanted, imprint and edition information should be included as well. Frequently, the author information supplied by a library, especially if it is a corporate author, is superfluous and therefore confusing for the vendor (Scilken, 1972). This confusion may be unavoidable if the order format is used for other purposes.

Libraries holding membership in bibliographic utilities such as the Online Computer Library Center (OCLC), the Research Libraries Information Network (RLIN), the University of Toronto Library Automation Systems (UTLAS), or the Washington Library Network (WLN) may wish to use a printout of the bibliographic record as their order, by adding a purchase order number and highlighting the information that the vendor needs. Schreiner (1978) advocates this practice. Some vendors will accept such printouts and from them generate multiple 3 × 5 in. (7.6 × 12.7 cm) forms, which are sent to the ordering library to use in its manual file system. Other libraries may wish to generate a multiple form from the bibliographic record. This process is described by Brown and DeGraff (1979).

Standard Order Form

The American National Standards Committee Z39 for Library and Information Sciences and Related Publishing Practices has developed a standard order form for single title orders. A copy of this form is shown in Figure 4.1. For more information, consult ANSI Standard Z39.30.

Typical Access Points for Acquisitions Data

An automated acquisitions system should allow entry to the bibliographic records of items on order and in process by title, purchase order number, fund, and any other access points the library deems necessary (e.g., author).

The pages of a typical five-part order form may be used as follows in order to access appropriate data: (1) Copy 1 is sent to the vendor, who is to return it either with the book or as a report. (2) Copy 2 is filed in the on-order–in-process file until the book is received. It goes to cataloging with the book. The cataloger returns this slip to acquisitions after the book has been cataloged so that the on-order–in-process file can be cleared. (3) Copy 3 is the financial record to be filed by fund. (4) Copy 4 is filed in the on-order–in-process file and remains there until copy 2 is returned by the cataloging department. To prevent duplication of orders, this copy should not be removed at all until final removal. (5) Copy 5 is filed by purchase order number. On it, all reports, claiming information, and nonroutine events (e.g., "defective book returned for replacement") may be recorded.

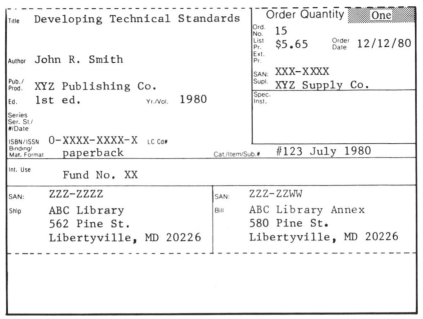

Title Developing Technical Standards	Order Quantity ▓▓ One ▓
	Ord. No. 15
	List Pr. $5.65 Order Date 12/12/80
	Ext. Pr.
Author John R. Smith	SAN: XXX-XXXX
Pub./ Prod. XYZ Publishing Co.	Supl. XYZ Supply Co.
Ed. 1st ed. Yr./Vol. 1980	Spec. Inst.
Series Ser. St./ #/Date	
ISBN/ISSN 0-XXXX-XXXX-X LC Cd#	
Binding/ Mat. Format paperback	Cat./Item/Sub.# #123 July 1980
Int. Use Fund No. XX	

SAN: ZZZ-ZZZZ		SAN: ZZZ-ZZWW	
Ship ABC Library 562 Pine St. Libertyville, MD 20226		Bill ABC Library Annex 580 Pine St. Libertyville, MD 20226	

Figure 4.1   ANSI standard order for single titles. This sample filled-in single-title order form is reproduced with permission from *American National Standard for Order Form for Single Titles of Library Materials in 3-Inch by 5-Inch Format* (ANSI Z39.30-1982), © 1982 by the American National Standards Institute (ANSI). Copies may be purchased from ANSI at 1430 Broadway, New York, NY 10018.

Files

On-Order–In-Process File

The central acquisitions file is the one that indicates what titles are on order and what titles have been received but are not yet cataloged. Occasionally in a manual system, two different files are created for these purposes; one file houses the outstanding orders and the other reflects items received but not yet cataloged. However, having both categories in one filing sequence eliminates the need to remove a slip from the on-order file when its title is received and then file it into the in-process file. Usually, a distinction can be made between the two categories, even though they are interfiled; this is because there is more than one slip for a title on order, yet there is only one slip for a title that has been received. In an automated system a status designation on the bibliographic record indicates whether the title is on order or has been received.

The on-order-in-process file is usually arranged alphabetically by either title or main entry. Title arrangement is preferred because titles change less frequently than do various individuals' interpretations of what constitutes a main entry.

Fund Files

Encumbered and expended files. Commonsense accounting dictates the practice of keeping track of each annual cycle. This includes not only the materials budget allocations and expenditures, but also the encumbrances—the amount of money committed to be spent, but not yet spent. By having such data, the accounting staff can provide up-to-date budget information for the acquisitions and collection management staff; this makes it easier for them to regulate the flow of order requests. Frequently, libraries with manual systems maintain an encumbered file and an expended file; each file is composed of copies of the purchase order that is arranged by fund, and within each fund, by purchase order number. When an order is placed, this financial copy of the purchase order is entered in the ledger in order to keep a running total of commitments; it is then filed into the encumbered file. When the item is received, the amount of the original encumbrance is subtracted from the encumbered column; and the actual amount spent on the title is added to the expenditure column. The financial slip is removed from the encumbered file and inserted into the expended file. Since this one-slip-per-title fund record is very cumbersome, some libraries may find that they can function well without retaining these slips. However, such a file *does* allow a library to determine which titles it has purchased on each fund.

In an automated system, all of these data can be tagged so that current encumbrances and expenditures are known as soon as they are entered. The side benefit is the capability to produce lists of titles received in whatever arrangement is desired (alphabetically by title or main entry, by call number, or by fund). Detailed how-to information with examples of forms is available in Alley and Cargill (1982).

Invoice files. In order to determine that an invoice has been paid, the library retains a copy of the invoice and files it alphabetically by vendor name into an invoice file that contains all other paid invoices for the current fiscal year. All of the invoices of a given vendor are arranged either by invoice number or by date paid. Occasionally, in large institutions, the invoice files are divided by sections that correspond to the organizational units that process the invoices (e.g., monograph orders, serials, binding). A single alphabetical arrangement is simpler because some vendors bill titles for several departments on one invoice; staff members, consulting one section of the file, may overlook the copy of a pertinent invoice filed in another section.

Files for Serials and Standing Orders

Titles that have parts published at different times require a unique set of records for adequate control. Data that should be captured in these files include

1. Basic information: bibliographic description, vendor, description of initial order (when placed, purchase order number), fund, location, and routing information
2. Check-in information: numbers or, if unnumbered, abbreviated titles of parts received
3. Financial information: what was paid for, when it was paid, and on what invoice it was paid (identified by invoice number and/or date)
4. Claiming information: what part was claimed, when it was claimed, and the vendor's report
5. Binding information: what parts were sent to the bindery, when they were sent, the fact that a volume has been bound, type of binding used, which parts are bound together in a single volume, and whether the title page, index, and/or contents are included.

A file that presents all of the above data that a library elects to record is the ideal. Brown and Smith (1980) and Osborn (1980) offer examples of forms to use for a manual system. Boss (1982) candidly describes what an automated system can and cannot do for serials control.

Correspondence Files

It often proves valuable to store some correspondence for a short period of time. However, it is reasonable to keep correspondence that establishes working agreements for the life of those agreements. To economically file correspondence, an acquisitions department can do three things: (1) It can *not* create copies of standard form letters always filled out in the same manner. For example, it can simply make a record at some access point (e.g., on the financial copy of a multiple order form) that its title was claimed on a certain date and not keep a file copy of that letter. (2) It can use authority files that are arranged logically according to their purpose in order to store correspondence that establishes policy. Then the staff can retain copies of the correspondence outlining specifications for establishing business with a particular vendor in a permanent vendor file or retain the initial order request, letter order, original blurb, and any correspondence related to a basic format change in a serial authority file, arranged alphabetically by title. The acquisitions department can also house the correspondence used to establish an exchange partnership in an exchange file arranged alphabetically by country; within each country, alphabetically by city; and within each city, alphabetically by institution. (3) The department can store correspondence of a more ephemeral nature (e.g., the file of letters necessary to solve specific receipt problems) for a short period. Some libraries find it not cost-effective to retain this information after the problem is resolved. Others find it useful to retain such information for several years, especially in evaluating a vendor's effectiveness in problem solving. A general correspondence file in alphabetical sequence by vendor name, including correspondence received and/or resolved during 1 fiscal year and retained for 1 to 3 years thereafter is an effective method of storing such information.

ORDERING PROCEDURES

Basic ordering procedures occur in all libraries, but the degree of detail involved with each depends upon the specific needs of that library.

Receive the Order Request

Order requests may come verbally, in the form of titles checked off in a catalog or selection tool, or on library order request forms. Simplicity suggests that the acquisitions staff work with the catalogs themselves, annotating them as needed, and keyboard the order directly from the printed description. However, searching and verification routines cause titles to be sorted and re-sorted in varying arrangements, and having a separate physical piece for each title requested makes this easier. Thus, many libraries require that order requests be submitted to acquisitions on a particular form. The layout of such a form should closely resemble the format of the purchase order itself, so that transferring data from one to the other will be as easy as possible.

Instead of requiring a request form, acquisitions staff in libraries belonging to a bibliographic utility might generate a printout of the database's bibliographic record for a title when the request for it is received, and use the printout as the basic document from which to work when searching and verifying. This approach is viable only if a very high percentage of the library's order requests are for items already having records in the database.

The person submitting the request form should also be encouraged to submit the advertisement through which he or she discovered the title—or to at least cite the source of the information on the order form. Acquisitions staff will frequently find that such documentation provides important ordering information or additional bibliographic detail that was not included on the request form itself. The person submitting the request form should also be encouraged to indicate any library files that have already been checked, especially if this person is a member of the library staff. Such notation will keep acquisitions staff from repeating that work.

It may be important to know when an order was submitted to the acquisitions area. This is especially true when an irate patron wants to know why a book has not arrived. If this *is* important, each order should be stamped with the date received.

Search and Verify

Acquisitions staff must search the library's holdings records to be sure that the title requested is not already in the collection, on order, or received but not cataloged (the process known as *searching*); and they must prove that the title is indeed available and that its bibliographic description is correct (the process called *verification*).

Searching the Library's Records

Check each title against the catalog, the on-order–in-process file, and pertinent ancillary listings, such as the serial or standing order record if the item is an ongoing one.

Acquisitions staff in a library holding membership in a bibliographic utility can review the database bibliographic record for an order request to determine whether or not the library has already used that record to catalog the book. Thus, acquisitions staff in such a library need check the catalog only for orders with imprint dates earlier than the point at which the library began cataloging through the bibliographic utility and for reprint titles, whose original editions may be in the collection.

The act of adding a new title to the on-order–in-process file may serve as the check to determine if that title is already there. However, if the order production for the number of duplicates found outweighs the amount of effort required to check every title against the on-order–in-process file, each title requested should be checked there before its order is produced. If the serials record indicates that the series for a title requested is on order, the order request should generate a review of this series to see if it should be claimed.

Occasionally, information found when searching the catalog requires further decisions in the selection process. If the library has a different edition of a work, should an order be placed for another? If the order duplicates a title in the collection, should a second copy be ordered for another location? If the order is for volume 3 of a set and the library does not have *any* of the set, should volumes 1 and 2 be ordered as well? If acquisitions staff do not have the authority to make such decisions, the order involved should be referred to those who do.

Care must be taken to check *all* of a library's holdings. If the order request is for a document, and if documents are not included in the catalog, the order should be referred to the documents area. Such distinctions become blurred occasionally. For example, who handles commercially marketed microreproductions of documents when the collection has a unique bibliographic identity? Or, if the library has acquired materials not yet under bibliographic control, is the acquisitions staff committed to review those materials before ordering a title that might already be owned? Procedures should be established and recorded whenever such questions arise.

Verifying Bibliographic Information

If a title is new, has it really been published? If a title is older, is it still in print? Many tools are available to determine this information, and some acquisitions staff consult them to the "bitter end," as described by Fristoe (1966). Some libraries look thoroughly for price information, even though the title to be ordered is a current imprint that is known to be in print. Their encumbrances would probably be just as accurate if they were to use average price estimates by subject, which can be compiled annually from one of the spring issues of *Publishers Weekly,* which gives title output and average price figures for U.S. book production of the previous year; from the periodicals price study published annually in *Serials Librarian;* and from other price information offered occasionally by the Library Materials Price Index Committee in the *RTSD Newsletter,* a publication of the ALA Resources and Technical Services Division.

The acquisitions librarian must determine how much verification is enough, but not too much, for the needs of the library. Some acquisitions staff whose libraries hold membership in a bibliographic utility have not revamped their search and verification sequence to take full advantage of the database. Neikirk (1981) illustrates how dramatic such alterations can be. Reports other than Fristoe's (1966) and Neikirk's (1981) that might be of help in analyzing search and verification processes are those of Groot (1981), Lazorick and Minder (1964), and Reid (1977). Woods' analysis (1978) of the "bare bones" acquisitions tools needed should be particularly useful to those in small libraries. Kilton's 1979 offering will assist serials librarians.

Verification Tools

Verification tools are used to answer four primary questions: (1) Does the title exist? (2) How much does it cost? (3) Is it still in print? (4) Does the vendor have it?

Does the title exist? If a library holds membership in a bibliographic utility, the first step its acquisitions staff should take to answer this question is to see if the title is included in the utility's database. Finding a current imprint in the database does not always mean that the title has indeed been published. Through the Library of Congress Cataloging in Publication program (CIP), titles are cataloged prior to publication from galley proofs or from front matter, such as the title page and table of contents. The CIP record may be prepared as long as 24 months ahead of the title's actual publication, although 3–6 months is a more usual time frame. A CIP record can be recognized by the fact that its bibliographic description lacks collation information, by its encoding level in the database, and by the expected date of publication in the MARC (Machine-Readable Cataloging) 263 field. By checking the number of libraries that have used the database record for cataloging, it is possible to make an educated guess as to whether the CIP title is indeed published. If the Library of

Congress (LC) is reflected as the only location, the title is most likely still in press. Even though there are one or two location other than LC, the book may not be published; some libraries, especially public libraries, strive to have the cataloging done in advance of receiving a title in order to make it available almost as soon as it is received.

The time-honored tool used to verify a title's existence is the national bibliography. The national bibliograhy that U.S. librarians consult first is the National Union Catalog (NUC) and related services that offer Library of Congress contributed cataloging information and cataloging copy contributed by research libraries.

The National Union Catalog, Pre-1956 Imprints is, as its subtitle states, "a cumulative author list representing Library of Congress printed cards and titles reported by other American libraries" (1968). This pre-1956 or "Mansell" (for the publisher) is updated by Library of Congress national union catalogs, published monthly and cumulated quarterly the first 3 quarters of every year, annually, and every 5 years. Arrangement is alphabetical by main entry with some cross-references. Cataloging records created at LC are identified by the LC card number in the lower right corner. Union catalog records are identified by the symbol of the contributing library. Cataloging in publication records are included, and the existence of a CIP record does not always mean that the title described has been published.

The NUC cumulative author list is one of several NUC titles that LC has produced. In their Chapter 10, Bonk and Magrill (1979) describe the history and various parts of the LC catalogs in detail. Beginning with 1983 output, National Union Catalog (NUC) publications are available in four titles produced in microfiche format:

1. *National Union Catalog: Books* (*NUC Books*) incorporates records that previously appeared in the *National Union Catalog*, the *Subject Catalog*, *Chinese Cooperative Catalog*, and *Monographic Series*.
2. *National Union Catalog: U.S. Books* (*NUC US Books*) is a new publication that includes only the U.S. imprints found in *NUC Books*.
3. *National Union Catalog: Audiovisual Materials* (*NUC AV*) contains records that were formerly included in the *Audiovisual Materials* catalog.
4. *National Union Catalog: Cartographic Materials* (*NUC Maps*) is a new publication for maps and atlases.

Each of these NUCs has a register that contains the full bibliographic record for every title included and four indexes (name, title, subject, and series) that access the full records by register number. *NUC Books* and *NUC US Books* appear monthly; *NUC AV* and *NUC Maps* appear quarterly. Each subsequent issue during a year cumulates the information found in all preceding issues of that year.

Since 1968, the Library of Congress has distributed NUC cataloging information on Machine Readable Cataloging (MARC) tapes. Subscribers can select from a number of tape services and use them in connection with their own computerized programs. Several vendors offer MARC records on fiche. Because LC cataloging copy is not copyrighted, it can be reproduced and sold by anyone. However, use of the contributed copy included on the MARC tapes is controlled by the Resources and Technical Services Division (RTSD) of ALA. Names of those vendors who have been awarded a nonexclusive contract to use this contributed copy are available from the executive director of RTSD.

The Library of Congress makes its current cataloging available on a weekly basis through its Catalog Distribution Services (CDS) Alert Service. Through this successor to the Proofsheet Service, the subscriber selects from more than 1800 subject categories those for which he or she wishes to receive 3 × 5 in. (7.6 × 12.7 cm) laser printed notification slips. CIP records are identified by the statement, "Cataloging in Publication."

The NUC and its related services provided by the Library of Congress is only one example of a national bibliography. Ford (1978) describes others in detail.

How much does it cost? The price information supplied to the acquisitions staff along with the bibliographic information for a title to be ordered should generally be accepted if the title's imprint date is for the current year or immediate past 2 years. If the price is not supplied with the order, consult the appropriate books in print for the country of the title's imprint. Sources for the United States follow.

The R. R. Bowker Company in New York publishes a spectrum of works that list in-print and forthcoming trade titles published in or exclusively distributed in the United States. The annual *Books in Print* (BIP) provides access by author and by title, and a list of publishers and distributors. *Forthcoming Books* is a bimonthly cumulation of forthcoming titles and titles published since the previous July. The semi-annual *Paperbound Books in Print* has, since 1978, listed in-print and forthcoming paper trade and paper text editions. The *Publishers Trade List Annual* (PTLA) is a massive collection of catalogs and other data on publisher output issued annually. For a list and description of many of the books in print titles that Bowker publishes, consult the explanatory material at the beginning of volume 1 of the most recent BIP. Consult Ford (1978) for books in print information for other countries.

Is it still in print? If the imprint date for a title is more than 3 years old, acquisitions staff should check the current books in print for the country in which the title was published, even if the price is already included in the order information. The purpose of such a check is two-fold: It verifies that the title is still available, and it establishes the current price.

Does the vendor have it? To find the answer to this question, most libraries simply send the order to the vendor and wait for the book or a report explaining why the book is not being supplied. However, some vendors make their stock information available to libraries in printed, fiche, or electronic format. Titles appearing on such a record should be immediately available from the vendor who produces it. Terminals accessing vendor inventory information give up-to-the-minute information on titles and numbers of copies available.

It is most important to use only the tools that answer the questions that the library needs to have answered. Indeed, some libraries do not need to perform formal steps to answer any of these questions. For example, many elementary school librarians select from current reviews half again as many titles as their budgets will allow and send the list to a vendor, asking that the order be filled up to a specified dollar limit. Reviews evaluate titles which *do* exist, and they give price information, so the first and second primary questions are answered. If the librarian uses current reviews, there is usually no need to consider question 3. Question 4 is asked through the act of sending the order. Because the titles listed have been selected from current reviews, the chances are excellent that the vendor has in stock or can quickly obtain two-thirds of them.

*On Preventing Duplication of Procedures
and Materials*

The flow chart in Figure 4.2 shows how searching questions and verification questions can mesh for a sophisticated searching and

Figure 4.2 Questions to be answered during the searching and verification process. This flow chart indicates how searching questions and verification questions may be meshed into a sophisticated searching and verification routine. To prevent duplication of effort, each step should be recorded on the order request form as it is completed.

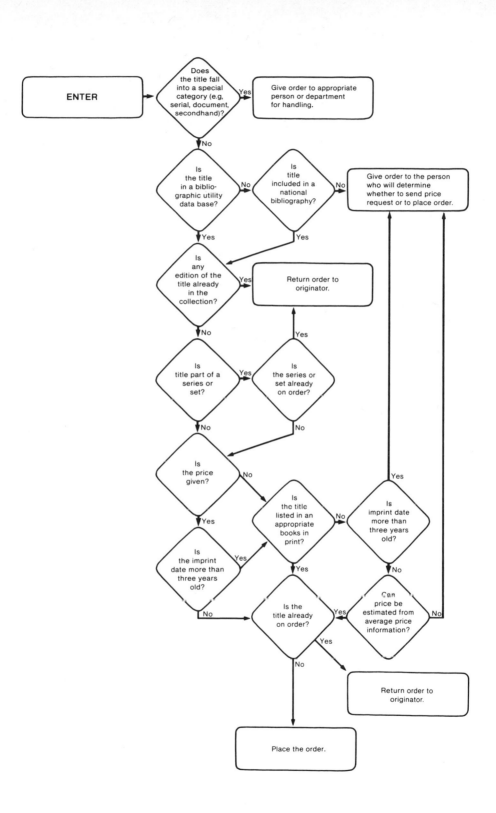

ENTER

Does the title fall into a special category (e.g, serial, document, secondhand)?

Yes → Give order to appropriate person or department for handling.

No

Is the title in a bibliographic utility data base?

No → Is title included in a national bibliography?

No → Give order to the person who will determine whether to send price request or to place order.

Yes

Yes

Is any edition of the title already in the collection?

Yes → Return order to originator.

No

Is title part of a series or set?

Yes → Is the series or set already on order?

Yes → Return order to originator.

No

No

Is the price given?

No → Is the title listed in an appropriate books in print?

No → Is imprint date more than three years old?

Yes

Is the imprint date more than three years old?

Yes → Is the title listed in an appropriate books in print?

No → Is the title already on order?

Yes → Can price be estimated from average price information?

Yes

No → Is the title already on order?

Yes

No

Yes → Return order to originator.

No → Place the order.

verification routine. Several tenets should be followed during this process:

1. Information unearthed by the searcher should be recorded to prevent search duplication. For example, if an order request is held in acquisitions because it is not yet published, all searching and verification steps performed on it the first time around should be noted so that the same steps will not be repeated the next time it is handled.

2. Also, this information should be recorded for the cataloger who will handle the title farther along—again, to prevent duplicate steps. The order request form which reflects all of the searching and verification steps and any printout of the bibliographic record should be forwarded to cataloging with the book when it is received.

3. If, during the verification procedure, the author or title of a requested work is found to be incorrect, re-search the library holdings record under the correct information. Serials or standing order records should be checked for each item discovered to be an ongoing title or part of a series.

4. The routines that acquisitions staff perform *solely* as a service to cataloging staff (e.g., sorting book trucks into certain categories prior to delivery, producing printouts for items after they are received) should be reviewed to determine whether such tasks might be more economically handled by cataloging staff.

Placing the Order and Receiving the Book

A library should use the most convenient ordering method in relation to its acquisitions system. Possible methods include generation via terminal, phone call, typed 3 × 5 in. (7.6 × 12.7 cm) slip, or checked list. When the order is received,

1. Unpack the carton. Keep together a shipment that arrives in more than one carton. Match the books with the invoice or, in the absence of an invoice, with the packing list. If there is no invoice, save the package label; it might later provide clues as to who placed the order.
2. Retrieve the order record. Call it up on the terminal, look it up in the computer printout, or pull it from the on-order–in-process file.
3. Check the book against the invoice and the order. Make sure that the title ordered is the title received and verify that the cost billed is correct.
4. Resolve any problem. Communicate with the vendor concern-

ing an incomplete shipment, incorrect book received, or erroneous billing. Recheck library holdings records if author and/or title information used in ordering was incorrect or if the item is now found to be part of a series or a set.

5. Approve the invoice for payment. Any invoice adjustments must be explained to the vendor so that credit may be issued and reflected on the vendor's statement of the library's account.

6. Process the book. Add theft detection devices, if necessary. Insert special processing flags (such as a rush streamer) for the catalogers or the bindery staff. Forward it with the appropriate records to the cataloging area.

Claim Titles Not Received

If the title ordered has not arrived after an established length of time (e.g., 3 months for domestic titles; 4 months for foreign titles), and if the vendor has not sent a report to explain why, send a claim notice asking for the status of this order. The claim notice may be a form letter generated by computer or it may be a copy of the order slip, with a special note attached. If it is the latter, it should say "CLAIM" in bold letters to keep the dealer from thinking that an additional copy is wanted. Before sending the claim notice, check every holding area in the mail room, in acquisitions, and any possible point in between to make sure that the book is indeed not in the library.

As reports are received from the dealer, they should be recorded in a location that is automatically checked at the beginning of the claiming process. Reports that indicate that the vendor cannot supply a title but that it is available elsewhere should cause the order to be rerouted to the suggested source. Reports that indicate that a title is no longer in print should be reviewed to see if they should be put through the out-of-print procedures.

The ALA Bookdealer Library Relations Committee guidelines for ordering monographs suggest claiming time frames (1974, 1977, 1983). Schenck (1981 b) offers further detail about claiming procedures.

Cancel Orders for Titles Not Received

Orders that have been outstanding for more than a year should be cancelled in order to keep the financial encumbrance records viable. When cancelling, remove the title's entry from the on-order–in-process file and the financial posting from the fund records. Keep a cancellation record that explains when and why the item was cancelled. Return the original order request, along with the reason for the cancellation, to the person who submitted the order.

Throughout the entire ordering procedure it is important to establish routines that are economical, yet detailed enough to assure that the library materials ordered are indeed the library materials received.

OTHER MEANS OF PROCUREMENT

This section describes methods by which a library can obtain materials other than by sending firm orders to a vendor.

Subscriptions and Standing Orders

Orders can be placed for the first part and all future parts of a title on a "til forbid" basis—that is, until the library notifies the vendor that it no longer wishes to receive future parts. Orders can be placed for both serials (ongoing titles with no end in sight) and standing orders (sets with an end in sight), although not necessarily with the same vendor. Standing orders, sometimes called continuations, are generally handled by monograph vendors as a sideline to their firm order services, while serials are handled by a special type of vendor known as a subscription agent. The ALA directory entitled *International Subscription Agents* (Buckeye, 1978) is an alphabetical list of agents that gives address, areas served, and types of materials supplied by each.

The special nature of serials calls for special handling. The unique set of services that subscription agents offer is listed at the end of all vendor services outlined in the section "Choosing a Vendor: Examining Services Offered."

There are general facts to remember in dealing with serials and, to some extent, with standing orders.

They are difficult to start and stop. Contrary to one-shot-purchase monographs, the acquisitions librarian ordering serials must specify exactly with which issue the serials subscription is to begin. The subscription agent must be notified far enough in advance, so that the agent has enough time to contact the publisher, who in turn can actually start the process of sending issues to the library. Subscription agents request orders 10–16 weeks in advance of the time the subscription is expected to begin. There must also be time for the library order to reach the agent and enough lead time for the acquisitions bibliographic searching and verification processes. It is reasonable to require that subscription requests come into acquisitions 5½–6 months ahead of the time the subscription is expected to begin.

Renewals must be done well in advance. Likewise, decisions on renewals must be made far enough in advance to relay the library's cancel and add requests to the subscription agent, for the message to be transferred to the publisher, and for the publisher to act on these requests.

Renewals represent an ongoing financial obligation. Placing a subscription is an act that commits a portion of the library materials budget on an ongoing basis. This commitment is sure to increase as time passes and inflation escalates. Because a subscription represents a lien against future budgets, special care should be taken in the selection process, and each year existing subscription costs plus an inflation factor must be estimated as part of the ongoing commitments for the library materials budget.

Claims require good timing. Do not claim so early that the claim will generate a duplicate, yet do claim soon enough to actually get the missing number. Subscription agents suggest the following timetable for claiming serials with regular publishing frequencies: Claim monthlies/quarterlies 3 weeks after their normal receipt date; claim weeklies 2 weeks after normal receipt date; and claim dailies 1 week after normal receipt date.

Few serial publishers print many copies more than those sent out on subscripton and for sale at newsstands. Thus, many claims for missing issues cannot be filled by the publisher. This means that the library must then decide whether it wishes to search elsewhere.

Replacements are often difficult to obtain. Many issues received do not survive in the library long enough to be found when binding staff gather for binding. If the piece already came, it cannot be claimed. Then another copy must be ordered if the library wants a complete volume. Also, orders must be placed for issues claimed and still not received. To order a replacement, check the publishing information in an issue of the title to see if it states how to order single issues. If it does not, order the missing issue from the publisher. If he cannot supply it, try to obtain it through the Universal Serials and Book Exchange (USBE) or the Duplicates Exchange Union, which are described in the section "Redistribution of Unwanted Materials"; order it from a vendor specializing in back issues; or hope for the miracle that it will come in as a gift.

Consider serials in microform. A library may wish to order some serials titles in microform as an alternative to binding or to searching for needed backfiles. *Serials in Microform* lists nearly 13,000 journals, magazines, and documents available in microform.

The many ramifications of dealing with the ongoing nature of serials are explored in Katz (1971), Katz and Gellatly (1975), and Osborn (1980).

Approval Plans

An approval plan is a plan whereby the vendor supplies the library with books according to a predetermined profile, defining such parameters as subject, country, and language of publication; level of complexity; and publishers. Library staff, after reviewing incoming approval shipments, may return any titles they do not want. Libraries may elect to receive notification slips instead of books for the hazy areas in which they do not want comprehensive coverage but do not want to miss something. One copy of the notification slip for titles desired is returned as an order, with a duplicate retained for the on-order–in-process file.

There are pointers to remember in handling an approval plan:

1. The mechanics of handling approval plans are different from those for firm orders: (a) display space must be set aside so incoming shipments can be reviewed, (b) searching of library holdings files must be done *after* the books arrive, (c) libraries accustomed to fund allotment by subject must evolve a method for allocating approval funds if the approval plan includes titles from many subject areas, and (d) accounting methods will not parallel those for firm orders because titles are not encumbered individually.
2. A positive decision should be made for each title retained. This policy assures that every approval book added to the collection has indeed been examined by a reviewer.

3. The approval plan should provide a mechanism that tells the acquisitions librarian what titles will be coming as part of the plan. Otherwise, knowing when to place a firm order for a title that might come on approval is a problem.
4. Ongoing communication is vital. If not enough titles are being received, or if there are too many returns, the acquisitions librarian and the vendor must revise the profile so it more sharply reflects the library's needs.

Practical Approval Plan Management by Cargill and Alley (1979) provides detailed information on setting up and evaluating a plan. McCullough, Posey, and Pickett (1977) offer acquisitions, subject specialist, and vendor viewpoints concerning an approval plan study. McDonald, Maxfield, and Friesner (1979) describe one method to monitor approval plans. The "International Seminars on Approval and Gathering plans in Large and Medium-sized Academic Libraries," of which there have been four to date, provide an ongoing forum for discussion of approval plan topics (1969, 1970, 1972, 1980).

Other Plans Involving Direct Cost

Several other purchasing methods are worthy of note.

1. Lease plans: some vendors offer lease services, whereby a library can acquire multiple copies of popular titles for recreational reading and, when demand for them has waned, return them. Although Cushman (1976) supports this arrangement as one of worth even for an academic setting, Steinbrenner (1979) offers an analysis that indicates that such a plan does not appear to provide enough savings to allow for purchase of more books.

2. Blanket order: through a blanket order arrangement with a publisher, a library arranges to purchase one copy of each title published.

3. Greenaway Plan: with a Greenaway plan, a library places a standing order for one copy of each trade book to be delivered prior to publication so that each title can be reviewed and multiple copies can be ordered in advance of publication. Such a plan is popular with public libraries needing multiple copies quickly in order to meet patron demand. It is named for the former Free Library of Philadelphia director Emerson Greenaway, who initiated the first such arrangement with Lippincott (G. E. Evans, 1979, p. 71; "Get-em-all theory of book buying," 1969, p. 3387).

Gifts

Libraries receive solicited and unsolicited gifts—both the gift materials themselves and money. If the money is to be used to purchase library materials, acquisitions staff must clarify any stipulations that affect the acquisitions process. Considerations include: Is the money to be spent for a specific type of material? Are bookplates to be used? If so, how should they be worded? Where are these books to be housed? Is the library committed to keeping a list of titles purchased on this fund?

The library should have a written policy establishing methods for handling gifts of library materials. The library may wish to restrict the types of gifts accepted and might want to review the gifts before actually accepting them. It must be tactfully explained that the gift will not be retained if it does not fit in with the library's selection policy, perhaps outlining the means by which the library disposes of unwanted materials. The gifts should be acknowledged in writing if the donor so desires and the quantity of items given should be listed, with a brief description of their nature. The library should select gifts to be added to the collection with the same guidelines used for selection of other materials because gift volumes cost just as much to process and to bind as do purchased ones. Library holdings files should be searched *after* the unwanted gifts have been removed from items to be processed in order to prevent unnecessary searching. Whenever possible, the library should strive to accept gifts with no strings attached. If strings (e.g., bookplates, special location, special room) are necessary in order to make a worthwhile acquisition, they should be outlined for every area involved in processing so unusual stipulations will be honored.

The Association of College and Research Libraries "Statement on Appraisal of Gifts" (1973) strongly suggests that the library should have little involvement with gift appraisals beyond recommending "appropriate professional appraisers" to a donor. Articles by Leonhardt (1979) and Osier (1979a) offer more pragmatic suggestions for assisting donors with appraisal information.

Unwanted gifts may be disposed of in several ways:

1. Offering them to other libraries in the area: relevant items may be offered to a library with a special interest; or, a storage area may be designated for these materials, and staff from other libraries may be invited to review them prior to a prearranged deadline.
2. Offering them to other institutions by issuing a list: requests

should be honored as the lists are returned; the recipient library may be asked to pay the postage.

3. Sending them to USBE, whose stock is accessed by other libraries worldwide (see also the section "Universal Serials and Book Exchange").

4. Selling them to library patrons, to dealers, or by auction, depending on their nature and value: institution restrictions may prevent a library from selling materials.

5. Throwing them away: such outright discard must be done with care, so it will not offend patrons or staff.

The amount of staff a library invests in a gift operation should be governed by both the net gain of gift materials added to the collection and the public relations value received. Much more detail is available in Lane (1980).

Exchanges

Many libraries establish exchange arrangements with other libraries, in which each sends the other library materials without charge. Such an arrangement supports the International Federation of Library Association commitment to the Universal Availability of Publications (UAP) and occasionally is the only method through which some serials titles are available.

Some libraries exchange monographs, but more and more are exchanging serials only. This concentration on serials exchanges is probably due to two reasons: (1) as Kovacic (1980) notes, such an exchange, once established, is easy to maintain, and (2) an exchange of monographs requires tedious attention to titles to be sent and received and is more difficult to evaluate monetarily. Usually the exchange titles that a library supplies to others are items published in association with its institution. However, some exchange titles might be purchased by a library to send or have sent to an exchange partner. Such a buying arrangement may be worthwhile, especially if the titles bought are serials, requiring little maintenance. Buying monographic titles requested by an exchange partner is rarely a reasonable investment of time and money.

Exchange arrangements should be reviewed periodically to determine their true value to the library. Questions to ask include: Does the library really want the titles it receives on this exchange? Is the exchange balanced monetarily? Is it more economical to disband this exchange agreement and purchase the titles received instead? Refer to Lane (1980) for more detail.

Shared Resources Programs

Although many libraries have talked about cooperative acquisitions for years, few viable enduring programs have evolved.

Farmington Plan

One of the most effective, the Farmington Plan, was formulated in 1942 so that participating research libraries agreed to acquire foreign publications in special subject areas in order to "assure that there should be in some collection in the country at least one copy of every current foreign publication of research value" (Goldhor, 1963, p. 97). Selected vendors in foreign countries supplied these materials until the end of 1972, when the plan was terminated because of reduced book budgets, increased use of blanket order arrangements, and the effectiveness of the Library of Congress commitment to comprehensively acquire foreign scholarly imprints (Bruer, 1974, pp. 177–178).

Public Law 480

Under the Food for Peace Program enacted in 1954, U.S. surplus agricultural products are given to a foreign country that, in exchange, sends some of its publications to U.S. libraries (Goldhor, 1963, p. 2). This program, termed by many libraries as "PL-480," is now officially called the Special Foreign Currency Program. At the height of this program, offices in Egypt, India, Indonesia, Israel, Nepal, Pakistan, and Poland supplied publications from those countries as well as from others nearby. Today, through the PL-480 program, American libraries receive publications through offices in India, Nairobi, and Pakistan; and Library of Congress staff are investigating the possibility of broadening the program once more.

Redistribution of Unwanted Materials

Materials not wanted by one library are frequently used to advantage in another. Several mechanisms exist for unwanted material to find a home.

Universal Serials and Book Exchange (USBE). The Universal Serials and Book Exchange in Washington, D.C. was established in 1948 as a "clearinghouse for the receipt, organization and redistribution of surplus and duplicate publications" (Rovelstad, 1979, p. 98). USBE staff have identified a core list of 10,000 periodical titles that are always stocked. This list is available on microfiche, as a Bibliographic Retrieval Services (BRS) database, and through the OCLC Interlibrary Loan (ILL) Subsystem. Libraries can place orders for issues of these titles on forms that USBE provides this service, through the BRS message switching service or the OCLC ILL Subsystem. A standard fee is charged for each issue. The USBE member cost-per-issue is significantly lower than the nonmember cost. USBE members may also order from USBE mailing lists additional items available or send in bibliographic descriptions of what is needed and ask USBE to search for a specified number of months.

Duplicate exchange unions. The ALA Resources and Technical Services Division sponsors a Duplicates Exchange Union in which more than 500 member libraries irregularly send lists of their own duplicates to all other members. A library wanting a title notes the fact on the other library's exchange list and returns the list, along with a self-addressed mailing label. Requests are processed in the order received. Postage costs exceeding 50 cents are repaid by the receiving library in the form of stamps.

Similar programs are offered by the Medical Library Association and the American Theological Library Association. Osier (1979b) describes a serials exchange program in Minnesota.

Other Examples

In the fact of reduced buying power, more libraries are developing effective cooperative acquisitions programs. Kronick (1979, p. 297) reports on the plan developed by the 12 libraries in Region IX of the Regional Medical Library Network, in which each library agrees "to purchase all books of an assigned publisher which fall within a prescribed subject-format profile."

The Research Libraries Group, an information consortium for North American universities with strong research libraries, includes as one of its principal programs collection management and development, through which its members strive to curtail duplication of expensive items while ensuring that research materials in specified areas *will* be collected by at least one institution. Each member records in the RLIN cooperative purchase file all selection decisions for serials and expensive items so that other members may access this data before making their own major acquisition decisions.

SPECIAL MATERIALS AND SPECIAL PROBLEMS

Some library materials require ordering procedures that vary from firm order practices. One such category is serials, which are addressed in the section "Subscriptions and Standing Orders." Others are paperbacks, remainders, government documents, alternative materials, audiovisual materials, and out-of-print items. This section offers suggestions in treating each type.

Paperbacks

Paperbacks are difficult for acquisitions librarians to acquire by title because most are available through magazine distribution channels, rather than through vendors who handle hardback trade and scholarly items. Few of the paperback vendors who *do* distribute nationally accept orders for less than 20 copies of a title. If they *do* accept a single copy order, they will usually fill it only if it is in stock. Abel (1976), Kline (1977), and Melcher (1971) each expound on the difficulties of obtaining paperbacks.

The various methods libraries can use to acquire paperbacks are to encourage the selectors to tell acquisitions staff immediately if a local store or newsstand has a title they request; try local used paperback exchanges; buy titles by category (e.g., Gothic novels) from the local distributor if selection policy allows.

Remainders

When a publisher no longer finds it valuable to stock large numbers of a title, he will sell it in quantity and at low cost to a wholesaler who specializes in such remainder items. This wholesaler, in turn, can offer the title at a price substantially below its list price. To obtain remainders, write to the remainder dealers listed in *Literary Market Place* as Wandres (1979) suggests, asking for lists of in-stock titles from which to select; or choose from the items listed by title, author, and series or set in *Best Buys in Print*. Editor Wall also provides more information (1978, 1979).

Government Documents

Documents—publications produced by local, state, and national governmental agencies—are another category of materials not usually handled by a book vendor. A library that does not receive government publications automatically by virtue of being a depository must acquire them on a title-by-title basis. The basic tools used for verifying American documents are the *Monthly Catalog of United States Government Publications,* which lists publications issued during the preceding month, and the *Monthly Checklist of State Publications,* which lists all of the state documents that the Library of Congress received during the previous month. Sources beyond these and the few vendors specializing in government publications (see *Literary Market Place*), must be cultivated individually. Addresses for federal agencies are available in *The United States Government Manual.* Writings by Blasdell (1977), Erlandson (1980), Nakata and Kopec (1980), Shannon (1981), Shaw (1975), and Wittig (1979) all offer suggestions on obtaining documents.

Alternative Materials

Danky (1980, p. 13) defines alternative materials as those "produced by non-standard, non-establishment groups or individuals." As the definition implies, these materials and their publishers are not usually cited in the conventional selection and bibliographic verification tools, nor are they generally available through vendors. Tools developed specifically for these materials include: *Alternatives in Print: Catalog of Social Change Publications, Alternative Press Index,* the *International Directory of Little Magazines and Small Presses,* and *Small Press Record of Books in Print.* Excellent background information on alternative materials can be found in Glessing (1970). Two articles especially helpful for acquiring these often-elusive materials are those by Danky (1980) and Shore (1979).

Audiovisual Materials

Microforms tend to be handled in the same tools and by the same dealers as printed library materials are. Sullivan (1977) sets forth an excellent discourse on their acquisition.

Guides for other audiovisual (AV) vendor selection are current editions of: *Audiovisual Market Place, Educational Film Locator, Educators Guide to Free Films, Feature Films on 8mm, 16mm, and Videotape, Film Programmer's Guide to 16mm Rentals, Index to 16mm Educational Films,* and *Index to Educational Video Tapes.*

Once an AV item is received, it should be reviewed, not only to make sure that it *is* the title ordered, but also to confirm that its physical condition is good. Thus, library routines should allow records and tapes to be heard and visual media to be viewed immediately after receipt and prior to payment. The need for AV equipment to do this may dictate that the review be done in a location remote from the acquisitions department and by nonacquisitions staff. The acquisitions librarian is responsible for seeing that, even in such a situation, payment for the material goes forward rapidly. Further information on acquiring audiovisual materials may be found in Bloomberg and Evans (1981), G. E. Evans (1979), and J. Evans (1979).

Out-of-Print Items

There is no miraculous formula for finding a specific title that is no longer available in print. Schenck (1981a, p. 4015) describes the second-hand book world as "one of the last bastions of individuality ...a composite of many interesting and fascinating people who operate in their own ways."

Preliminary Steps

There are, however, some steps one can take before turning to the out-of-print market, once the decision is made that a library really wants a title that has been declared out of print (OP).

Is the item indeed out of print? If the item has a recent imprint, did the publisher provide the OP report? Even if a publisher does not list a title in *Books in Print*, he may have several copies left. Requesting recent OP's directly from the publisher often yields some titles. (And it does not mean that the OP report previously received from a vendor was unreliable, for the publisher may have had no copies earlier, and since then received returns from dealers.)

Is an alternate edition still in print? If the title wanted is a U.S. imprint, search *British Books in Print;* if the title is British, search *Books in Print.*

Is a reprint edition available? In 1929 when New York bookman Peter Smith realized that making reprints of some OP titles would be simpler than searching for them repeatedly, the twentieth century reprint world was born (Dempsey, 1969, p. 381). Some of the OP titles a library wants may be available as reprints. Check *Guide to Reprints*, which lists titles available from more than 400 publishers throughout the world. For more background on reprint publishing, refer to Nemeyer (1972).

Is this item available from the Universal Book and Serials Exchange? The nature of a library's OP wants might be such that acquisitions staff will reap success by using the Universal Book and Serials Exchange (USBE) (see also the secton "Universal Serials and Book Exchange [USBE]). Fill out a USBE form for each title to be searched and indicate how long it should be searched, if the title is not already in their warehouse.

Is reproduction available through the University Microfilms books on demand program? University Microfilms (Ann Arbor, Michigan) holds agreements to reproduce on request in film or hard copy the recent out-of-print titles of 350 major trade and university press publishers. More than 100,000 titles are presently available through this program; 3,000 are added each year. Contact University Microfilms in order to obtain the subject, author, and title listings of the items available.

Would it be worthwhile to make a photocopy of the book and bind it for the collection? Even if a good copy can be obtained to reproduce, the prime question here is whether or not such reproduction infringes on copyright law. The complete text of the U.S. copyright law, Public Law 94-553, which underwent major revision in 1976, may be found as the Appendix to Title 17 of the 1976 edition of the *United States Code.* Section 108 sets forth the law in regard to reproduction by libraries and archives.

Out-of-Print Procedures

After eliminating the OP want items that can still be obtained through routine sources, decide whether to rely primarily on the expertise of the OP market or to rely on the expertise of library staff. Both options are discussed in the rest of this section.

Send want lists to out-of-print dealers. Compile a list of desiderata titles and send it to a dealer, asking for a search of these titles for a specified length of time (e.g., 6, 12, or 18 months). The items listed should correspond to the types of materials (subject and/or country of imprint) in which he specializes. The latest editions of the directories such as *European Bookdealers* and *Book Dealers in North*

America and of Patterson's *American Book Specialists* are helpful in determining what dealers to use. Halwas (1977) and Lynden and Meyerfeld (1973) suggest others as well. As Mitchell (1971) suggests, keep records of the dealers that are used and of the success experienced with each. If possible, set up files by subject specialty and by vendor in order to access this information easily.

Develop a lasting relationship with a dealer. During the initial contact, describe expectations in writing. Many dealers prefer to have exclusive listings for a limited period of time, so be aware that sending wants to several dealers at once may cause problems. Always notify a dealer if a title for which he or she is searching is acquired by another means.

Advertise in publications. Advertise desiderata in publications faithfully scrutinized by OP dealers, such as *The Library Bookseller* (formerly called "TAAB"—*The American Antiquarian Booksellers Weekly*) and *AB Bookman's Weekly.* As Smith (1968) points out, such advertising is good for small want lists, for urgently needed materials, or for items that dealers have not been able to supply.

Use out-of-print dealers' catalogs. Select titles needed from dealers' catalogs. This may be a worthwhile procedure if the library's wants are stored in the memory of the person scanning the catalogs, if the catalogs are sent by the fastest means possible so that review of the catalog occurs before many of the items listed have been sold (the library may need to pay the dealer a fee to cover airmail costs), and if titles are selected and ordered immediately. Call or cable to see if items wanted are still available, both to respond as soon as possible and to eliminate acquisitions time spent on verifying orders for titles that are already sold. Of course, the dealer must be contacted immediately if, during subsequent verification, a reserved title is discovered to be already in the collection and, therefore, no longer wanted. The experiences of Kim (1973) and Smith (1968) suggest that relying on the dealers' expertise is more economical than this method.

Go on buying trips. Have a knowledgable member of the library staff or of the institution select material from dealers' stock. Imperatives here are that the dealer reserve the chosen items pending notification as to which titles are indeed wanted and that, prior to notifying the dealer which titles are indeed ordered, a list of the selected items be checked against the library's holdings files to prevent duplication.

Buy at auction. Buying at auction is an acquisitions method usually enjoyed only by the well-endowed research library. The items bid on must be known in advance so that library holdings files are checked to prevent duplication. An upper limit of what the library can afford to pay for each item should be established prior to the auction.

Hire a specialist to handle out-of-print ordering. Lynden and Meyerfeld (1973) describe Stanford University's success in adopting this approach.

The method or combination of methods used depends on the library's quantity of wants and the amount of resources available to obtain them. Articles by Perez (1973), Reichmann (1970), and Schenck (1981a) provide more information for developing acquisitions procedures for OP material.

KEEPING UP WITH TRENDS

In order to keep up with the changing world of acquisitions, read pertinent library literature regularly, communicate with others in the field, and attend meetings when possible.

Read the Literature

Relevant periodicals focusing on acquisitions are *The Acquisitive Librarian,* an R. R. Bowker newsletter available since 1979, and *Library Acquisitions: Practice and Theory,* since 1977. More general publications that include acquisitions as one of their specialties are *Technicalities,* a technical services newsletter produced since 1980, and *Library Resources & Technical Services* (LRTS), published since 1957. LRTS has offered reviews of various technical services areas since volume 3. Refer to those with "acquisitions" or "resources" in the title.

Exchange Information

If other acquisitions librarians live nearby, talk with them regularly to compare notes on special problems. Ask vendor sales representatives about the latest acquisitions news whenever they visit. When possible, visit another acquisitions operation to acquire additional perspective.

Attend Meetings When Possible

Comb the exhibits area to find out what is new. If there is not enough time to visit with every vendor who offers an acquisitions service, collect their brochures and read them later. If the meeting offers a multitude of programs as American Library Association conferences do, formulate a schedule at the beginning of the first day. If one session does not prove interesting, head immediately for an alternative choice during the same time slot. Develop contacts with other acquisitions people. The most valuable part of a meeting is often the information gained informally from those with similar interests.

REFERENCES

AB Bookman's Weekly (Vols. 1–). Newark: Antiquarian Bookman, 1948–.
Abel, M. Paperback practicalities. *School Library Journal*, 1976, *22*, 31–33.
The Acquisitive Librarian (Vols. 1–). New York: R. R. Bowker, 1979–.
Alley, B., & Cargill, J. *Keeping track of what you spend*. Phoenix: Oryx Press, 1982.
Alternative Press Index (Vols. 1–). Baltimore: Alternative Press Centre, 1969–.
Alternatives in Print (Vols. 1–). San Francisco: New Glide Publications, 1971–.
American Library Association. Acquisitions Section. Code of fair practices for dealers and librarians. *ALA Bulletin*, 1957, *51*, 777–779.
American Library Association. Bookdealer Library Relations Committee. *Guidelines for handling library orders for serials and periodicals*. Chicago: American Library Association, 1974. (Monograph)
American Library Association. Bookdealer Library Relations Committee. *Guidelines for handling library orders for microforms*. Chicago: American Library Association, 1977. (Monograph)
American Library Association. Bookdealer Library Relations Committee. *Guidelines for handling library orders for in-print monographic publications* (2nd ed.). Chicago: American Library Association, 1983. (Monograph)
American Library Association. Bookdealer Library Relations Committee. Prepayment dilemma; A consumer's guide. *American Libraries*, 1977, *8*, 571–72.
American National Standards Institute. *ANSI Standard Z39.30.* New York: American National Standards Institute, 1982.
Association of College and Research Libraries. Statement on appraisal of gifts. *College and Research Libraries News*, 1973, *34*, 49.
Audio Visual Market Place (Vols. 1–). New York: Bowker, 1969–.
Best Buys in Print (Vols. 1–). Ann Arbor, Mich.: Pierian Press, 1978–.
Blasdell, L. M. Government publications and the small public library. *Texas Libraries*, 1977, *39*, 172–179.
Bloomberg, M., & Evans, G. E. *Introduction to technical services for library technicians* (4th ed.). Littleton, Col.: Libraries Unlimited, 1981.
Bonk, W. J., & Magrill, R. M. *Building library collections* (5th ed.). Metuchen, N.J.: Scarecrow Press, 1979.

Book Dealers in North America. London: Sheppard Press, 1955–

Books in Print (Vols. 1–). New York: Bowker, 1948–.

Boss, R. W. *Automating Library acquisitions: Issues and Outlook.* White Plains, N.Y.: Knowledge Industry Publications, 1982.

Boyer, C. J. State-wide contracts for library materials: An analysis of the attendant dysfunctional consequences. *College & Research Libraries,* 1974, *35,* 86–94.

British Books in Print (Vols. 1–). London: J. Whitaker, 1874–.

Brown, C. D., & Smith, L. S. *Serials: Past, present, and future.* Birmingham, Ala.: EBSCO, 1980.

Brown, D. R., & DeGraff, K. Practical librarian: From purchase order to processing slip on OCLC. *Library Journal,* 1979, *104,* 2173–2174.

Bruer, J. M. Acquisitions in 1972. *Library Resources & Technical Services,* 1974, *18,* 171–181.

Buckeye, N. *International Subscription Agents* (4th ed.). Chicago: American Library Association, 1978.

Cargill, J. S., & Alley, B. *Practical approval plan management.* Phoenix: Oryx Press, 1979.

Cushman, R. C. Lease plans: A new lease on life for libraries? *Journal of Academic Librarianship,* 1976, *2,* 15–19.

Danky, J. P. Acquisition of alternative materials. *Collection Building.* 1980, *2,* 12–27.

Dempsey, D. OP publishing: The new look in reprints. In J. S. Kujoth (Ed.), *Libraries, readers and book selection.* Metuchen, N.J.: Scarecrow Press, 1969.

Educational Film Locator (2nd ed.). New York: Bowker, 1980.

Educators Guide to Free Films (Vols. 1–). Randolph, Wisc.: 1941–.

Erlandson, J. A., & Boyer, Y. Acquisition of state documents. *Library Acquisitions,* 1980, *4,* 117–127.

European Bookdealers: Libraries d'Occasion Européennes. Europäische Antiquariate. London: Sheppard, 1967–.

Evans, G. E. *Developing library collections.* Littleton, Col.: Libraries Unlimited, 1979.

Evans, J. Evidence for the audiovisual verdict. *Australian Library Journal,* 1979, *28,* 266–268.

Feature Films on 8mm, 16mm, and Videotape (6th ed.). New York: Bowker, 1979.

Ford, S. *Acquisition of library materials* (Rev. ed). Chicago: American Library Association, 1978.

Forthcoming Books (Vols. 1–). New York: Bowker, 1966–.

Fristoe, A. J. Bitter end: The searching process. *Library Resources & Technical Services,* 1966, *10,* 91–95.

Get-em-all theory of book buying (replies by librarians). *Library Journal,* 1969, *85,* 3387–3393.

Glessing, R. J. *The Underground press in America.* Bloomington, Ind.: Indiana University Press, 1970.

Goldhor, H. (Ed.). *Selection and acquisition procedures in medium-sized and large libraries.* Urbana, Ill.: Illini, 1963.

Gregory, R. S. Afternoon of an acquisitions librarian; or, how to hurry up and rush. *Publishers Weekly,* 1972, *201,* 45.

Groot, E. H. Comparison of library tools for monograph verification. *Library Resources & Technical Services,* 1981, *25,* 149–161.

Guide to Reprints (Vols. 1–). Kent. Conn., 1967–.

Halwas, R. G. Buying books from dealers. In *Book collecting, a modern guide.* New York: Bowker, 1977.

Index to Educational Video Tapes. Los Angeles: National Information Center for Educational Media, 1971–.

Index to 16mm Educational Films. Los Angeles: National Information Center for Educational Media, 1967–.

International Directory of Little Magazines and Small Presses (9th ed.). Paradise, Calif.: Dustbooks, 1973.

International seminars on approval and gathering plans in large and medium-sized academic libraries. 1st–, Western Michigan University, 1968. Littleton, Col.: Libraries Unlimited for Western Michigan University Libraries, 1969. 2nd–, Western Michigan University, 1969. Kalamazoo, Mich.: Western Michigan University, 1970. 3rd–, West Palm Beach, Fla., 1971. Westport, Conn.: Greenwood Press, 1972. 4th–: *Shaping library collections for the 1980's.* Phoenix: Oryx Press, 1980.

Katz, W. A. *Magazine selection: How to build a community-oriented collection.* New York: Bowker, 1971.

Katz, W. A., & Gellatly, P. *Guide to magazine and serials agents.* New York: Bowker, 1975–.

Kilton, T. D. OCLC and the pre-order verification of new serials. *Serials Librarian,* 1979, *4,* 61–64.

Kim, U. C. Comparison of two out-of-print book buying methods. *College & Research Libraries,* 1973, *34,* 258–64.

Kline, C. 142,000 paperback titles and how to get them. *Top News,* 1977, *34,* 79–83.

Kovacic, M. Gifts and exchanges in U.S. academic libraries. *Library Resources & Technical Services,* 1980, *24,* 155–63.

Kronick, D. A. Regional cooperative acquisition program for monographs. *Medical Library Association Bulletin,* 1979, *67,* 297–301.

Lane, A. H. *Gifts and exchange manual.* Westport, Conn.: Greenwood Press, 1980.

Lazorick, G. J., & Minder, T. L. A least cost searching sequence. *College & Research Libraries,* 1964, *25,* 126–128.

Leonhardt, T. W. Gift appraisals: A practical approach. *Library Acquisitions; Practice & Theory,* 1979, *3,* 77–79.

Library Bookseller (Vols. 1–). West Orange, N.J.: Albert Saifer, 1949–.

Library Acquisitions: Practice & Theory (Vols. 1–). New York: Pergamon, Jan. 1977–.

Library Resources & Technical Services (Vols. 1–). Chicago: American Library Association. Library Resources and Technical Services Division, Winter 1957–.

Library Resources Market Place (Vols. 1–). New York: Bowker, 1980–.

Library survey on direct ordering. *AB Bookmans Weekly,* 1978, *61,* 3876.

Lynden, F. C., & Meyerfeld, A. Library out-of-print publications. *Library Resources & Technical Services,* 1973, *17,* 216–24.

McCullough, K., Posey, E. D., & Pickett, D. C. *Approval plans and academic libraries.* Phoenix: Oryx Press, 1977.

McDonald, D. R., Maxfield, M. W., & Friesner, V. G. F. Sequential analysis: A methodology for monitoring approval plans. *College & Research Libraries,* 1979, *40,* 329–34.

Melcher, D. *Melcher on acquisition.* Chicago: American Library Association, 1971.

Mitchell, B. J. A systematic approach to performance evaluation of out-of-print book dealers: The San Fernando Valley State College experience. *Library Resources & Technical Services,* 1971, *15,* 215–22.

Monthly Catalog of United States Government Publications (Vols. 1–). Washington, D.C.: Superintendent of Documents, U.S. Government Printing Office, 1940–.

Monthly Checklist of State Publications (Vols. 1–). Washington, D.C.: Library of Congress, Processing Services, Exchange and Gift Division, 1947–.

Nakata, Y., & Kopec, K. State and local government publications. *Drexel Library Quarterly*, 1980, *16*, 40–59.

National union catalog: Audiovisual materials. Washington, D.C.: Library of Congress, 1983–. (Microfiche)

National union catalog: Books. Washington, D.C.: Library of Congress, 1983–. (Microfiche)

National union catalog: Cartographic materials. Washington, D.C.: Library of Congress, 1983–. (Microfiche)

National union catalog: Pre-1956 imprints. London: Mansell, 1968–1980. (685 volumes)

National union catalog: U.S. books. Washington, D.C.: Library of Congress, 1983–. (Microfiche)

Neikirk, Harold D. Less does more; adapting pre-order searching to on-line cataloging. *Library Acquisitions: Practice & Theory*, 1981, *5*, 89–94.

Nemeyer, C. A. *Scholarly reprint publishing.* New York: Bowker, 1972–.

Osborn, A. D. *Serial publications, their place, and treatment in libraries* (3rd ed.). Chicago: American Library Association, 1980.

Osier, D. V. Appraising library material donations: An explanation of the appraisal process for librarians. *Minnesota Libraries*, 1979, *26*, 477–83. (a)

Osier, D. V. Serials exchange—Minnesota style. *Serials Librarian*, 1979, *3*, 423–427. (b)

Patterson, R. H. (Ed.). *American book specialists* (4th ed.). New York: Continental Publishing Co., 1981.

Perez, E. L. Acquisition of out-of-print materials. *Library Resources & Technical Services*, 1973, *17*, 42–59.

Publishers Trade List Annual (1st ed.–). New York: Bowker, 1873–.

Publishers Weekly (Vols. 1–). New York, 1872–.

RTDS Newsletter (Vols. 1–). Chicago: American Library Association Resources and Technical Services Division, 1976–.

Reichmann, F. Purchase of out-of-print material in American university libraries. *Library Trends*, 1970, *18*, 328–353.

Reid, M. T. Effectiveness of the OCLC data base for acquisitions verification. *Journal of Academic Librarianship*, 1977, *2*, 303, 326.

Rovelstad, H. Economics of the Universal Serials and Book Exchange (USBE). *Interlending Review*, 1979, *7*, 98–101.

Schenck, W. Z. Acquisition of out-of-print books. *AB Bookmans Weekly*, 1981, *68*, 4015 ff. (a)

Schenck, W. Z. Claiming: Luxury or necessity? *Library Acquisitions: Practice & Theory*, 1981, *5*, 3–7. (b)

Schreiner, K. J. New use of the OCLC cataloging subsystem; acquisitions. *Library Acquisitions: Practice & Theory*, 1978, *2*, 151–157.

Scilken, M. H. Ordering books by title. *Unabashed Librarian*, 1972, *2*, 3.

Serials in microform. Ann Arbor, Mich.: University Microfilms International, 1972–.

Serials Librarian (Vols. 1–). New York: Haworth Press, 1976–.

Shannon, M. O. Collection development and local documents. *Government Publications Review*, 1981, *8A*, 49–87.

Shaw, G. A. How to locate out-of-print, hard-to-get documents. *Southeastern Librarian*, 1975, *24*, 28–29.

Shore, E. Collecting the alternative press. In *Collection Management* (LJ special report 11). New York: Library Journal, 1979.

Small press record of books in print (1st ed.–). Paradise, Calif.: Dustbooks, 1966–.

Smith, E. Out-of-print booksearching. *College & Research Libraries*, 1968, *29*, 303–309.

Steinbrenner, J. Cost-effectiveness of book rental plans. *Ohio Library Association Bulletin,* 1979, *49,* 5–6.
Sullivan, R. C. The acquisition of library microforms. *Microform Review,* 1977, *6,* 136–144 (Part 1); 205–211 (Part 2).
United States code (1976 ed.). Washington, D.C.: United States Government Printing Office, 1977.
United States government manual (Vols. 1–). Washington, D.C.: National Archives and Record Service, Office of the Federal Register, 1935–.
Wall, C. E. Budget stretching: Remainder books for libraries. *American Libraries,* 1978, *9,* 367–370.
Wall, C. E. Remainder books: A background paper. *Media Spectrum,* 1979, *6,* 15–17.
Wandres, J. Remainder books: An offer you can no longer refuse. In *Collection Management* (LJ special report 11). New York: Library Journal, 1979.
Weaver, K. (Ed.). *Film programmer's guide to 16mm rentals* (3rd ed.). Albany, Calif.: Reel Research, 1980.
Wittig, A. J. *U.S. government publications for the school media center.* Littleton, Col.: Libraries Unlimited, 1979.
Woods, W. E. Bare-bones acquisition tools. *Unabashed Librarian,* 1978, *28,* 3–4.

BIBLIOGRAPHY

Collection Management

American Library Association. Collection Development Committee. *Guidelines for collection development.* Chicago: American Library Association, 1979.
Association of Research Libraries. Office of University Library Management Studies. *Collection analyses in research libraries: An interim report on a self-study process.* Washington, D.C.: Author, 1978.
Boyer, J. W. Selection tools—What's available? *Catholic Library World,* 1976, *47,* 420–422.
Broadus, R. N. Selecting materials for libraries (2nd ed.). New York: H. W. Wilson, 1981.
Cabeceiras, J. *Multimedia library: Materials selection and use.* New York: Academic Press, 1978.
Collection building. 1978–, *1–.*
Collection management. (LJ special report 11). New York, Library Journal, 1979.
Collection management. New York: Haworth Press, 1976–1977–, *1–.* (Vol. 1, nos. 1–2 published under *The De-acquisitions librarian).*
Gardner, R. K. *Library collections: Their origin, selection, and development.* New York: McGraw-Hill, 1981.
Godden, I. P., Fachan, K. W., & Smith, P. A. (Comps.). *Collection development and acquisitions, 1970–1980: An annotated, critical bibliography.* Metuchen, N.J.: Scarecrow Press, 1982.
Katz, W. A. *Collection development: The selection of materials for libraries.* New York: Holt, Rinehart & Winston, 1980.
Kósa, G. A. Book selection tools for subject specialists in a large research library: An analysis. *Library Resources & Technical Services,* 1975, *19,* 13–18.
Magrill, R. M., and East, M. *Collection development in large university libraries* (Advances in librarianship, vol. 8), New York: Academic Press, 1978.

Osburn, C. B. *Academic research and library resources: Changing patterns in America.* Westport, Conn.: Greenwood Press, 1979.

Perkins, Flossie L. *Book and non-book media: Annotated guide to selection aids for educational materials.* Urbana, Ill.: National Council of Teachers of English, 1972.

Smith, M. Book selection sources. *Library Association Record,* 1979, *81,* 131.

Spiller, D. *Book selection: An introduction to principles and practice* (2nd ed.). Hamden, Conn.: Linnet Books, 1974.

Stueart, R. D., & Miller, G. B. (Eds.). *Collection development in libraries: A treatise* (2 Vols). Greenwich, Conn.: JAI Press, 1980.

Technicalities (Vols. 1–). Phoenix: Oryx Press, December 1980–.

Van Orden, P. J., & Phillips, E. B. *Background readings in building library collections* (2nd ed.). Metuchen, N.J.: The Scarecrow Press, 1979.

Van Orden, P. J. *The collection program in elementary and middle schools: Concepts, practices, and information sources.* Littleton, Col.: Libraries Unlimited, 1982.

General

Allardyce, A. UAP (Universal availability of publications) and the exchange of publications. *IFLA Journal,* 1978, *4,* 122–128.

Bluh, P., & Haines, V. C. Exchange of publications: An alternative to acquisitions. *Serials Review,* 1979, *5,* 103–108.

Boss, R. W., & Marcum, D. H. On-line acquisitions systems for libraries. *Library Technology Reports,* 1981, *17,* 115–194.

Coplen, R. Subscription agents: To use or not to use. *Special Libraries,* 1979, *70,* 519–526.

Fast, B. Publishing and bookselling: A look at some idiosyncrasies. *Library acquisitions: Practice & theory,* 1979, *3,* 15–17.

Galejs, J. E. Economics of serials exchanges. *Library Resources & Technical Services,* 1972, *16,* 511–520.

Grieder, T. *Acquisitions: where, what, and how. A guide to orientation and procedure for students in librarianship, librarians and academic faculty* Westport, Conn.: Greenwood Press, 1978.

Hensel, E., & Veillette, P. D. *Purchasing library materials in public and school libraries.* Chicago: American Library Association, 1969.

Heyman, B., & Abbott, G. L. (Comps.). Automated acquisitions: A bibliography. *Library Technology Reports,* 1981, *17,* 195–202.

Keller, D. How fast the book? *California Librarian,* 1960, *21,* 25–26, 72.

Lowy, G. *A searcher's manual.* Hamden, Conn.: Shoe String Press, 1965.

Model policy concerning college and university photocopying for classroom, research and library reserve use. *College & Research Libraries News,* 1982, *43,* 127–31.

Pickett, A. S. An experiment in book buying. *Library Journal,* 1959, *84,* 371–372.

Schenck, W. Z. Evaluating and valuing gift materials. *Library Acquisitions: Practice & Theory,* 1982, *6,* 33–40.

Snowball, G. J., & Cohen, M. S. Control of book fund expenditures under an accrual accounting system. *Collection Management,* 1979, *3,* 5–20.

Tjarks, A. V. Coping with Latin American serials. *Serials Librarian,* 1979, *3,* 407–415.

Weaver, J. Gift appraisal practices in NAPCU (Northwest Association of Private Colleges and Universities) libraries. *PNLA Quarterly,* 1978, *43,* 3–5.

5 Bibliographic Control

Betty G. Bengtson

CATALOGS

The function of a library's catalog is to provide access to the collection of materials housed in that library. Cutter (1876, p. 10) first stated the objectives of a catalog: to allow a user to find a book when its author, title, or subject is known; to show a library's holdings by an author, on a subject, or in a kind of literature; and to assist in the choice of a book bibliographically or by its character.

Cutter's objectives have remained the basis for cataloging theory and practice. In October 1961 the International Conference on Cataloging Principles was held in Paris. A statement of principles, now known as the "Paris Principles," resulted from this international conference. The principles apply to choice and form of headings only and contain a statement of the function of a catalog that clearly derives from Cutter:

2. Functions of the Catalogue
   The catalogue should be an efficient instrument for ascertaining
   2.1. whether the library contains a particular book specified by
      (a) its author and title, or
      (b) if the author is not named in the book, its title alone, or
      (c) if the author and title are inappropriate or insufficient for identification, a suitable substitute for the title; and

2.2. (a) which works by a particular author and
     (b) which editions of a particular work are in the library. (International
         Conference, 1963, pp. 91–92)

The Paris Principles also reflect the work of Lubetzky (1953, 1960) on cataloging theory. He has particularly emphasized the function of the catalog in collocating, or gathering, the works by a given author and the editions of a given work. Uniform headings for authors and titles accomplish this purpose (McCallum, 1977).

The objectives or functions of the catalog have been accomplished traditionally by some ordered arrangement of standardized bibliographic description to which is attached various kinds of access points and subject headings. The entries may be arranged in a variety of ways and formats as discussed in the next section.

Types of Catalogs

The most commonly found U.S. library catalogs are dictionary and divided. The classified catalog is more commonly found in Europe. Any of the three types may be a union catalog.

Dictionary catalog. The dictionary catalog contains entries for authors, titles, and subjects in one file arranged alphabetically. It is the predominant catalog arrangement in U.S. libraries. Its advantages are that users need to consult only one file and the alphabetical arrangement is familiar to everyone. File structure can be very complex, however.

Divided catalog. The divided catalog also is arranged alphabetically but authors/titles and subjects are in two separate files. Some catalogs are divided three ways: authors, titles, and subjects. Some libraries have solved the problem of the separation of materials by and about the same author by putting only topical subject headings in the subject catalog and including name subject headings in the author catalog. Filing is greatly simplified in a divided catalog, but users can become confused about the correct file to consult.

Classified catalog. Entries in a classified catalog are arranged according to subject and are usually based on a classification scheme such as Dewey Decimal Classification. A title may have more than one entry filed in the catalog if it covers several aspects of a subject. A classified catalog generally requires an alphabetical subject index for use plus an author and title index for "known item" searches.

There are few examples of classified catalogs among U.S. research libraries.

Union catalog. A union catalog contains information on holdings in more than one library collection. It may be a union catalog of holdings in a library system with multiple branches or of holdings of independent libraries. The *National Union Catalog* (1956, 1968) is published by the Library of Congress and contains titles from LC as well as from contributing libraries throughout the country. Another kind of union catalog is union lists of serials holdings compiled by various groups of cooperating institutions.

Automation and type of catalog. Card, book, and COM (computer-output microform) catalogs produced from machine-readable records may be arranged in dictionary, divided, or classified order. They also may be union catalogs. The online catalog shares some of the characteristics of a divided catalog; separate indexes usually are constructed for authors, titles, and subjects, and a user must consciously decide the kind of entry he or she is seeking. For instance, the Mission College (California) online public access catalog requires the user to indicate that a search of the title index is desired by keying in "T=" followed by the title to be searched (Hildreth, 1982, p. 94).

Alternative Catalog Formats

Card catalog. The predominant catalog format in U.S. libraries is the card catalog. Such catalogs generally are based on the "unit card" with a card set for each title consisting of a main entry and added entries for subject headings, personal and corporate names associated with a work, title, and series where appropriate. New entries may be added easily in the card catalog, expansion is convenient to achieve, and large numbers of patrons may use it at any given time. Its disadvantages are that the file can be complex, it is not very amenable to revision, it cannot be distributed, and filing of cards can be slow and tedious.

Book catalog. The book catalog enjoyed popularity in the 1960s, especially in public libraries. For the most part, the descriptive information is the same or similar to that appearing in a card catalog, with a main entry and added entries for each title. In some book catalogs, the main entry contains full information with briefer informa-

tion (such as author, title, publisher, and date only) appearing under
the other access points. Some book catalogs are reproduced from
pasted-up cards arranged under various access points. Use of
machine-readable records has greatly simplified production of such
catalogs. Advantages of book catalogs are that they can be distributed and, in a computer-based catalog, filing is automatic. The disadvantages are that they can be out of date as soon as they are
published, high printing costs make new editions very expensive,
and updating can be slow.

Computer-output microform catalog. In a number of libraries the
book catalog has been replaced by a COM (computer-output microform) catalog produced from machine-readable records in either
micro-fiche or film format. It too can be distributed widely, and filing is automatic. Its disadvantages are that it is quickly out of date
and frequent cumulative editions can be expensive. Some libraries
issue supplements to previous editions, but then patrons are faced
with two or more lookups for a title. COM catalogs may also be the
choice as a backup catalog for an online catalog.

Online catalog. Since the 1970s, online catalogs have been successfully demonstrated in a number of libraries. Hildreth's *Online
Public Access Catalogs: The User Interface* (1982) details 10 of the operating catalogs, most of which are either prototypes or have been in
use for only 2 or 3 years. Hildreth emphasizes that "the telling difference between an online catalog and a card catalog does not lie in the
area of bibliographic description, control, or record storage, but
rather in the way the user interacts with and is assisted by the online
catalog. . . . In terms of process, this new dimension is referred to
as human-computer interaction or man-machine communication"
(p. 33). Estabrook (1983) explores other aspects of the social and psychological effects of the online catalog on users. Providing users
(both the public and the library staff) with the skills needed to effectively interact with the new catalogs presents a challenge to the
library professional.

Major advantages of the new online catalogs are that they may be
accessed from many locations, the records maintenance functions
are not as labor intensive, more powerful search capabilities (e.g.,
Boolean) are available, and they may be designed as part of an integrated library system. Current disadvantages are cost and the experimental nature of some models. However, it is now generally assumed that an online catalog will be technically and economically
feasible for a wide range of libraries. Several commercial vendors

are now marketing online public access catalogs, and we can expect very rapid developments in this area in the next few years.

Automation and format. The same cataloging database can be output in any of the formats. Catalog cards and book and COM catalogs are produced from computer records and, of course, the online catalog is made possible by the wide availability of machine-readable records. The versatility of machine-readable records gives libraries choices to meet ever-changing needs of their patrons.

Shelflists

Shelflists are files of cataloging records arranged in call number order or in the same order as materials on the shelf. The shelflist may or may not be available to the public. In general, it is regarded as a tool for the staff and is usually located in or near the units responsible for cataloging activity. The shelflist is consulted by catalogers in the assignment of call numbers to avoid duplication.

The information recorded on the shelflist varies from institution to institution, but most libraries maintain detailed holdings information here. Each title, volume, or copy added to the collection is recorded in some manner. In general, copy number and/or accession number (if used) as well as location appear.

In addition, some libraries record such acquisitions information as cost, source, and date of purchase on the shelflist. Missing or discarded items are noted also on the shelflist. Figure 5.1 is an example of a shelflist.

```
RS
403            Burger, Alfred, 1905-        ed.
.B8               Burger's Medicinal chemistry. -- 4th
1979           ed. / edited by Manfred E. Wolff. --
               New York : Wiley, c1979-
                  v. : llls. ; 28 cm.
                  "A Wiley-Interscience publication."
                  Includes bibliography.
                  Includes index.
v.1 277062    Ballen 3/20/80
v.2 277063    Ballen 3/20/80  msg. 9/82
v.3 325461    Ballen 6/22/81
v.2,c.2 352666   Ballen 11/15/82
                  1. Chemistry, Pharmaceutical.
                  2. Chemotherapy.  I. Wolff, Manfred E.
                  II. Title  III. Title : Medicinal chemistry.
```

Figure 5.1 Representative shelflist.

As catalogs go online, shelflists will be replaced by online access to records by the call number. A very desirable feature is the ability to browse forward and backward in the call number index.

How Many Catalogs?

Many libraries have more than one public card catalog. In library systems with branches, the main library's catalog might be a union catalog of all library system holdings, or it might contain only titles found in the main library with each branch catalog containing only materials in the branch collection. Individual departments within a library may have catalogs; for example, the nonprint or reference departments may have separate catalogs for their collections. Practice also varies with shelflists. Generally the central shelflist is a union shelflist for all library system materials, regardless of location. In addition, separate shelflists may be maintained for materials in branches, departments, or other special locations. Such shelflists may be located in the central processing area and/or in the location with the materials.

The decision on what catalogs to maintain is a local one. Needs of patrons and staff, relative locations of various service units, physical limitations, budget constraints, and resources available for catalog maintenance must be considered. Union catalogs in each branch is the most desirable alternative, but the expense of creating and maintaining union card catalogs has made this an impossible choice for many libraries. The use of computers and availability of machine-readable cataloging and new catalog formats promises to make this ideal a reality for many libraries. One reason many public libraries went to computer-based book catalogs in the 1960s was the distributability of book catalogs. For the first time, library systems with many branches were able to have union catalogs in each location. The same advantage is seen for online catalogs. A central union database file accessible from terminals located anywhere in the library system, or indeed anywhere, is a union catalog.

The Future of Library Catalogs

In 1975 and again in 1977, the Information Science and Automation Division (now the Library and Information Technology Association) of the American Library Association sponsored institutes on the future of the catalog (*Nature and Future of the Catalog*, 1979). At the 1975 institute Bierman (1979) summarized the reasons for interest in automated catalogs:

1. To provide access to the complete and most up-to-date catalog from multiple locations—remote catalog access.
2. To provide more and improved access points and search capabilities.
3. To expand the availability of increased resources through sharing via union catalogs.
4. To eliminate or at least reduce the inconsistencies and inaccuracies of card catalogs and their inhospitality to change (change in headings, filing rules, etc.).
5. To reduce the increasing problems and costs of maintaining card catalogs as they grow in number, in size, in age, and in complexity.
6. To deal with influences and pressures for change which come from both internal and external sources.

In addition, two reasons not mentioned by a majority of libraries, but vehemently stated when mentioned, are to reduce the floor space occupied by the catalog and to arrest the physical deterioration of old and heavily used card catalogs.

The importance of the reason for interest in automated catalogs, and the corresponding perceived inadequacies of the present card catalogs, vary with the individual library situation. Large central research libraries want improved access or searching capabilities most, while multilocationed libraries (public, academic, or special) want remote catalog access the most. Whatever the reasons, many librarians are very interested in alternatives to their present card catalogs. (p. 115)

As we move toward alternative catalog forms, a need has become evident for more research on how patrons use the library catalog and what their real needs are. Atherton (1980) reviewed past user studies at a conference on closing the catalog but suggested we should not rely on such studies for guidance for the future. This position supports Hildreth's previously cited comments on the man-machine interface in the new online catalogs. Hildreth's study (1982) is part of a project funded by the Council on Library Research to develop methods for collecting data on online catalogs and to analyze user requirements. Two additional sources for summaries of user studies are Lancaster (1977, Chapter 2) and Markey (1980).

Access to online bibliographic databases has led to questioning the future role of the catalog in a library. Williamson, in her article "Is There a Catalog in Your Future? Access to Information in the Year 2006" (1982), projects a lessened role for catalogs and an increased use of online files to provide information access. Free-text and Boolean searching and the ease with which multiple descriptors can be assigned make the use of such files very attractive. Nevertheless, the library catalog in card or an alternative format will remain for some time as the chief access mechanism to the collection of an individual institution.

It seems clear that the trend to online catalogs will grow. Many libraries will freeze and close their card catalogs and go online with split files. At one time it was considered unlikely that libraries with large retrospective files (more than 750,000 titles) would be able to afford conversion to machine-readable form. However, the availability of large resource files such as the OCLC (Online Computer Library Center) and REMARC databases puts conversion within the reach of many more libraries. Microcomputers have added a new dimension to online catalog possibilities for small collections. It may be that in this area we shall see the fastest growth of all.

ORGANIZATION AND MANAGEMENT OF CATALOGING ACTIVITIES

The Cataloging Environment

Only a few years ago, the cataloging environment was characterized by little cooperation, slow availability of Library of Congress cataloging copy which led to a large amount of duplicate original cataloging, and nationally accepted standards for descriptive and subject cataloging heavily based on Library of Congress practice. Some initial attempts at international cooperation were evident but, for the most part, they had little direct impact on cataloging operations in libraries.

At the present time cataloging is done in a fast-changing automated environment characterized by rapid access to LC and other cooperative cataloging copy and by strong adherence locally to national and international standards, such as the MARC (machine-readable cataloging) formats, the second edition of the *Anglo-American Cataloguing Rules* (AACR2), and the International Standard Bibliographic Description (ISBD). Decisions made at the national and international level are of direct and vital concern to local cataloging operations. Original cataloging done in one library now appears in national databases, subject to the perusal and judgment of one's fellow catalogers. Previously nonstandard, expedient solutions to cataloging problems could be made for the local catalog. Now cataloging must adhere to agreed-upon standards if a library wishes to participate in shared cataloging. The cataloger's job is at the same time easier and more difficult.

For the moment, catalogers and cataloging managers are consolidating and integrating the changes brought about by the second edition of the *Anglo-American Cataloguing Rules,* adopted January 1, 1981 by the U.S. library community. But no one can afford to pause too long when the move to online catalogs appears to be a reality for many libraries. The building of machine-readable databases and the implementation of online systems will be the prime jobs for the next few years. Change is occurring very rapidly.

Components of Cataloging

Cataloging activities may be divided into several components for convenient discussion.

Precataloging activity. Most of this activity consists of bibliographic searching and verification in various sources. Preorder searching has been previously described in the section "Ordering Procedures" in Chapter 4. It is very desirable to have forwarded to the cataloging department the results of this searching along with the material when it arrives. Such information can save considerable time in the cataloging process and can eliminate duplicate work. Precataloging searching is performed after the material has been received. Typically it may include the following kinds of activities:

1. Search in an online database or the *National Union Catalog* for cataloging copy.
2. Checking the local catalogs to establish relationships with material already in the library.
3. Verification in authority files of the forms of headings for access points.

Some libraries continue to accession books as a control mechanism, and this may be done as a part of precataloging. An accession number is a unique identifying number assigned to each physical volume received in a library. Currently available online circulation systems such as those marketed by C. L. Systems, Dataphase, and GEAC Computers International require an OCR (optical character recognition) or barcode number for circulation and identification of materials. These numbers often are assigned in the precataloging process in place of accessioning.

Some libraries have separate searching units or departments to do both preorder and precataloging searching and verification. Such units may be headed by a professional librarian–manager, but most of the jobs are carried out by nonprofessional library assistants.

Descriptive cataloging. Descriptive cataloging is concerned with the bibliographic description of the material to be added to the collection. This is done by identifying and recording author, title, edition, imprint (place of publication, publisher's name, and date of publication), collation (number of pages, illustrations, and size), series statement if any, and notes. In the process, the descriptive cataloger determines main entry and secondary entries. For the most part, catalogers in U.S. libraries follow national cataloging rules. The current standard is the second edition of the *Anglo-American Cataloguing Rules* (AACR2).

Subject cataloging. Subject cataloging involves the assignment of subject headings and call numbers. The *Library of Congress Subject Headings* (1980a) and the *Sears List of Subject Headings* (1982) are the sources of subject headings for most general libraries. In classifying materials the majority of U.S. libraries use either the Library of Congress (1917) or the Dewey Decimal Classification scheme (1979). Most academic libraries use LC whereas Dewey is favored by public libraries.

Copy cataloging. Copy cataloging refers to cataloging done using cataloging records from an outside source. Most copy cataloging is based on Library of Congress copy available through the purchase of card sets from the Library of Congress, from bibliographic utilities such as OCLC and the Research Libraries Information Network (RLIN) that provide online access to LC MARC cataloging or from commercial vendors of cataloging copy. Many libraries now use copy for the majority of their cataloging.

Catalog maintenance. Catalog maintenance may encompass such activities as filing, revision of descriptive and subject cataloging and classification, correction of errors, shifting cards, maintenance of the cross-reference structure, and replacement of worn out cards. Catalog maintenance activities were complicated by the adoption of the second edition of the *Anglo-American Cataloguing Rules*. This is a very important activity and one that can be too easily neglected when staff shortages occur.

Postcataloging. Postcataloging activities include preparation of the book for the shelf and/or for the bindery. Tasks may include typing and attaching a spine label, pasting in a pocket and a date due slip, and property stamping. Responsibility for this activity may be

assigned to the cataloging department, to a separate physical preparations unit, or to the binding department.

Although it is convenient to discuss cataloging activity by components, in fact cataloging is a continuous process with the parts closely
interrelated. Some insight into the dependency of each part on the
other is necessary to function effectively. Original catalogers must
be aware of catalog maintenance routines and must communicate
constantly with those responsible for them; descriptive and subject
cataloging decisions affect copy cataloging. Materials constantly
flow back and forth between various functional units.

Interactions with Other Departments

Cataloging is an activity that also depends on interractions with
other departments. The quality of this interaction is crucial to effective and efficient procedures in cataloging and in those other departments.

The ordering of material may be done by one or more departments,
but it is important that information on individual items ordered be
passed along. Equally important is information on changes in ordering patterns. For instance, a reduction in the number of titles ordered because of budget cuts affects staffing needs and work
patterns in cataloging activity. A decision to collect materials exten-
sively in a particular subject or a language means that cataloging
staff with specialized subject or language expertise must be provided. It may be necessary to add staff or to provide learning opportunities for existing staff.

Procedures must be worked out for handling material requiring
binding. Are paperbacks to be bound before or after cataloging?
How something can be bound affects how it might be cataloged. For
example, a paperbound work accompanied by a large number of
maps or illustrations may require binding in two physical volumes,
thus affecting the collation. Advice and information must be ex-
changed between the departments.

Generally when new or recataloged materials are ready for shelving, they are sent to the circulation department. Work flow in circulation depends, in part, on the amount of new material arriving. For
planning purposes, they must be kept informed of significant increases or decreases in the processing of new material. Books that
patrons wish to be notifed about must be flagged. Materials needed
by the cataloging department for recataloging or reclassification

should be charged to the cataloging department through the circulation system. And the cataloging staff may make use of the circulation system's hold or recall mechanism to obtain materials needed for reprocessing.

The more the reference and other public service departments know about cataloging policies, the better able they will be to interpret the catalog to the public. Consultation and information exchange between cataloging and public service units should be a continuing process. The move to integrated library systems will increasingly blur the distinctions between public and technical services, making such continuing communications essential.

Organizational Patterns

Organizational patterns for cataloging activities vary from library to library. A single department responsible for all cataloging has been, perhaps, the traditional pattern. The placing of responsibility for serials cataloging in a separate serials department that might or might not also be responsible for the acquisition of serials is a frequent variation. With the growth of bibliographic utilities and the increased use of cataloging copy from outside sources, it has not been uncommon to find separate copy cataloging or automated cataloging departments.

Some libraries have organized their cataloging staffs into teams responsible for original and copy cataloging of materials in subject specialities. Responsibility also may be assigned to individual catalogers, based on type of material (nonbook, audiovisual (AV) material, maps, etc.) or on language. In general a cataloger will do both the descriptive and subject cataloging and classification of the material for which he or she is responsible.

Catalog maintenance is sometimes a separate department but most often is found as a unit or section of the cataloging department. Filing and typing may also be the responsibility of a separate unit. Postcataloging activity, especially that involving shelf preparation, may be the responsibility of the cataloging department.

No particular pattern is best. Local factors such as size of the library and its staff, number of volumes added each year, personalities and abilities of current staff, special collecting or development areas, and curriculum requirements often determine specific patterns and responsibilities. Most important are communication, cooperation, and the willingness to respond to changing needs and circumstances.

DESCRIPTIVE CATALOGING

Purpose of Descriptive Cataloging

The descriptive cataloging function includes describing the physical item, deciding on a main entry, and assigning additional entries or access points. As stated in the 1949 edition of the Library of Congress's *Rules for Descriptive Cataloging in the Library of Congress:*

> The objectives of descriptive cataloging are: (1) to state the significant features of an item with the purpose of distinguishing it from other items and describing its scope, contents, and bibliographic relation to other items; (2) to present these data in an entry which can be integrated with the entries for other items in the catalog and which will respond best to the interests of most users of the catalog. (p. 7)

The currently accepted international standard for descriptive cataloging is the second edition of the *Anglo-American Cataloguing Rules* published in 1978.

Brief History of Cataloging Codes

The earliest modern codes appeared in the nineteenth century and included those of Jewett (1852) and Cutter (1876).

The Library of Congress began distributing printed cards in 1901. As libraries began to use the LC cards, they were interested in learning of LC's rules and practice for cataloging that were based on Cutter's rules, with some revisions. To answer this need, LC issued supplementary rules printed on cards from 1903 until the 1930s. In 1908 the *Catalog Rules: Author and Title Entries* were published by the American Library Association. It was a joint Anglo-American effort with input from the Library of Congress. Like the later first edition of the *Anglo-American Cataloging Rules* (1967), it was published in an American and a British edition. As continued standardization of practice and moves towards cooperative cataloging occurred, pressure increased for a new edition of the rules. A preliminary edition was published by ALA in 1941, but was criticized as too "legalistic." Further work on the code was delayed by World War II.

In 1946 the Library of Congress undertook a study of its descriptive cataloging practice. Dr. Luther Evans, who was the librarian at that time, directed that a code of descriptive cataloging practice be drawn up and submitted to the library profession for comment. The preliminary edition appeared in 1947 with a final edition appearing in 1949. The rules covered description only and not choice of entry and form of headings (LC, 1949).

The American Library Association revised the rules for entry and form of headings of its 1941 preliminary edition and issued a final edition in 1949. Until 1967 the *Rules for Descriptive Cataloging in the Library of Congress* (LC, 1949) and the ALA's 1949 *Cataloging Rules for Author and Title Entries* (known by the color of their binding as "the green book" and "the red book" to a generation of catalogers) were the accepted national cataloging code.

Lubetzky (1953) prepared a critique of the rules for entry for ALA's Board on Cataloging Policy and Research in which he criticized them for being too prescriptive and inconsistent. Proposals were made for a new revision. In the United States code revision began in the mid-1950s with the appointment of an ALA Code Revision Committee. First Seymour Lubetzky and then C. Sumner Spalding served as editor. The move toward a set of rules to include both description and entry and to be based on the 1961 Paris Principles culminated in the *Anglo-American Cataloging Rules* of 1967 (AACR1). Because of the expense of changing old headings to the new AACR1 forms, the Library of Congress adopted a policy of *superimposition* when it implemented the new rules. This meant that only headings newly established in its cataloging would be done according to AACR1. Previously established headings would retain their old forms.

The ISBDs, developed in the early 1970s, were incorporated into the first edition of the *Anglo-American Cataloging Rules* (1967) through revision of selected chapters. Chapter 6 ("Separately Published Monographs") was revised and issued as a separately published chapter in 1974. Chapter 12 ("Audiovisual Media and Special Instructional Materials") and Chapter 14 ("Sound Recordings") were issued in 1975 and 1976, respectively.

Anglo-American Cataloguing Rules, Second Edition

Concurrently with the ISBD revisions, a new edition of AACR was being prepared. It was an international project guided by the Joint Steering Committee for Revision of AACR (JSCAACR) composed of two representatives each (one voting, one nonvoting) from the American Library Association, the British Library, the Canadian Committee on Cataloging, the Library Association, and the Library of Congress. Joint editors were appointed: Michael Gorman, then of the British Library, and Paul W. Winkler of the Library of Congress.

The stated objectives of the sponsoring bodies were to reconcile the American and British texts, to incorporate changes made since the 1967 edition, to consider for inclusion other suggested changes, and to contribute to the development of an international cataloging code (AACR2, 1978, pp. vi-vii). Additionally, the new edition was to adhere to the Paris Principles of 1961 and the ISBD formats and was to consider the needs of machine processing of cataloging records.

Mechanisms were set up in each of the three participating countries to coordinate revision efforts. The Catalog Code Revision Committee (CCRC) of ALA's Resources and Technical Service Division was responsible for the revision proposal and review activities in the United States. Arrangements were made to provide for input from more than 30 organizations within and outside ALA. Groups such as the American Association of Law Librarians, the Educational Media Council, and the Society of American Archivists were asked to participate in CCRC or to review the proposed revisions.

Major Provisions and Changes

AACR2 is divided into two parts: Part I, "Description" and Part II, "Headings, Uniform Titles, and References." The arrangement reverses that of AACR1 in which rules for headings came before description. This arrangement presumably follows "the sequence of cataloguer's operations in most present-day libraries and bibliographic agencies" (AACR2, 1978, p. 1); that is, a cataloger first describes the item and then determines access points.

In each part the first chapter is devoted to rules of general applicability followed by chapters of rules applying to specific situations. Chapter 1 of Part I contains general rules for description, followed by Chapters 2–12 dealing with specific materials or types of publications (books, maps, serials, sound recordings, etc.). In using Part I, the description of a particular item is based on "the physical form of the item in hand, not on the original or any previous form in which the work has been published" (AACR2, 1978, p. 8). Therefore, a map published in microform should be described as a microform following rules in Chapter 11. Chapter 3, "Cartographic Material," will also have to be consulted. In addition, there are many references back to general rules in Chapter 1 for Chapters 2–12.

The rules for description are based on the General International Standard Bibliographic Description (ISBD(G)). (See the section "National and International Formats and Standards" in Chapter 3 of this text for a history of the development of ISBDs and a discussion of their use in the cataloging record). The ISBD influence is seen in the division of the description into eight possible areas: (1) title and statement of responsibility; (2) edition; (3) material (or type of publication) specific details; (4) publication, distribution, etc.; (5) physical description; (6) series; (7) note; and (8) standard number and terms of availability.

Chapter 21 (the first chapter in Part II) deals with the general question of choice of access points (i.e., main and added entries). Subsequent Chapters 22–25 deal with the form of heading for specific kinds of access points: persons, geographic names, corporate bodies, and uniform titles (AACR2, 1978).

During the revision process, the retention of the concept of main entry had been debated. In the end it remained in the new rules. "In Part II, the rules are based on the proposition that one *main entry* is made for each item described, and that this is supplemented by *added entries.* The question of the use of *alternative heading* entries (i.e., sets of equal entries for each item described) was discussed but has not been embodied in the rules, largely because of the lack of time to explore the considerable implications of such a change" (AACR2, 1978, p. 2). The utility of the main entry for single entry listings, single citations for a work, assignment of uniform titles, and standardization of bibliographic citation is acknowledged (p. 2).

With the introduction of AACR2, catalogers became accustomed to some new vocabulary: "access points" instead of "entries," "prescribed source of information" as an extended concept of "the title page," and "prominently" defined as "a formal statement found in one of the prescribed sources of information . . . for areas 1 and 2 for the class of material to which the item being cataloged belongs" (AACR2, 1978, p. 3).

Throughout the new rules, options or alternative rules are presented in the solution of particular problems. "These provisions arise from the recognition that different solutions to a problem and differing levels of detail and specificity are appropriate in different contexts" (AACR2, 1978, p. 2). Most libraries have chosen to follow the options selected by the Library of Congress. This was a very practical decision based on libraries' dependence on Library of Congress cataloging copy.

AACR2 prescribes minimum elements for three levels of description for additional flexibility in applying the rules. This responded to criticisms that previous cataloging codes ignored the needs of nonresearch libraries. Again, as a practical matter, libraries utilizing LC cataloging records will choose to catalog at the second level as LC does. Serials are done at an "augmented" level one. The second level of description prescribed by AACR2 (p. 15) calls for the following elements:

Title proper (general material designation) = parallel title : other title information / first statement of responsibility ; each subsequent statement of responsibility. — Edition statement / first statement of responsibility relating to the edition. — Material or type of publication specific details. — First place of publication, etc. : first publisher, etc., date of publication, etc.

Extent of item : other physical details ; dimensions. — (Title proper of series / statement of responsibility relating to series, ISSN of series ; numbering within series. Title of subseries ; numbering within subseries)

Notes.

Standard number.

Libraries are finding it very useful to have a minimal level record (level one) defined as part of the national standards. Several academic libraries are using the minimal level record for selected materials from backlogs or for lower priority material.

A feature new to U.S. cataloging codes is the mnemonic numbering of the rules. A rule number is composed of the chapter number, followed by a period, then a numeric, an alphabetic, and a numeric character appropriate to various levels. The first numeric after the period corresponds to an area of the description and is associated with that area throughout Chapters 1–12. For instance, in Chapter 1 the rule for the edition area is 1.2; in Chapter 2 the rule for the edition area for books is 2.2. The publication, distribution, etc. area is .4; the physical description area is .5; etc. Other features of the second edition include appendixes with rules for capitalization and abbreviations, a glossary, and a detailed index.

The cumulative effects of the new rules have been many changed forms of headings, fewer main entries under corporate bodies, more title main entries, and more access points per title. The rules call for using personal and corporate names in the forms by which they are commonly or predominantly known. An author who writes under more than one name will have items cataloged under each name. Especially conspicuous is the standardized use of parentheses throughout for the addition of qualifiers; for example, "Chicago (Ill.)" and "Eliot, T. S. (Thomas Sterns), 1888–1965." For serials a major change is the use of the first issue as the chief source of information for cataloging rather than the last issue.

The rules for formulating uniform titles are not significantly changed from AACR1 (1967). The major impact here has been LC's changed policy in applying the rules. Under AACR1, LC used uniform titles in a restricted number of cases. With the adoption of AACR2 (1978), LC announced it would formulate and store all uniform titles prescribed by the rules. The rules also call for the use of uniform titles in place of some form subheadings (e.g., "Law, statutes, etc.") prescribed in earlier rules. Therefore, many more uniform titles appear in cataloging records.

There are several reviews of AACR2 that may be consulted for additional discussion of major rule changes (Richmond, 1980; Simonton, 1979, 1980; Tucker, 1978). Maxwell's *Handbook for AACR2* (1980) illustrates individual rules and is recommended for catalogers using AACR2.

The Library of Congress's Implementation of Anglo-American Cataloguing Rules, *Second Edition*

Before the new edition was published, LC announced that it would adopt the new rules in January 1980. At the same time it announced that it would close its card catalogs. Originally LC had planned to have a public online catalog containing records from the MARC database as a replacement for the closed card catalog. When this proved impossible, plans were made to open a new Add-On card catalog that was to be regarded as temporary and to be discarded when the online catalog became a reality. All entries in the new catalog would be AACR2 cataloging. The new Add-On catalog would be filed by a new edition of filing rules being developed at LC (See the Section "Filing and Catalog Maintenance" of this chapter).

A second decision made possible by the closing of LC's card catalog was to "desuperimpose" forms of headings. This meant that LC would newly establish all headings used for cataloging, except for selected "compatible headings". Initially LC estimated that 49% of the existing MARC records would have headings affected by the new rules. This caused great consternation to librarians in the field. The heavy use of LC cataloging by most libraies meant that the impact would be felt very strongly by library catalogs throughout the country. After selecting options and making further policy decisions, LC estimated that 11% of the headings and 15% of the records in the MARC database would be affected by desuperimposition. Because of the anticipated impact, LC agreed to delay adoption of the new rules for 1 year until January 1, 1981.

Implementation Plans and Impact Studies

The two-year gap between the publication of AACR2 in late 1978 and its formal adoption by the Library of Congress on January 1, 1981 was filled with much discussion and planning activity. ALA's Library and Information Technology Association (LITA) sponsored an institute on closing the catalog in November 1978 (*Closing the Catalog*, 1980). The Association of Research Libraries (ARL) sponsored the Library Catalog Cost Model Project developed by King Research, Inc. as a model to assist libraries in comparing costs of alternative catalog forms. Seventy-two ARL libraries participated in the study (Wiederkehr, 1980).

Numerous local studies of the impact of the new rules and plans for the future of the catalog were conducted. Dowell's study of the impact of AACR2 on library catalogs contains a useful summary and bibliography of impact studies done by libraries (Dowell, 1982, pp. 22–35). Many of the studies and other internal planning documents were reproduced in a very timely microfiche publication issued by the Johns Hopkins University Library, the *Alternative Catalog Newsletter*.

The Library of Congress and ALA sponsored a series of training institutes ("road shows") in 1980 and 1981 to familiarize librarians with the provisions of AACR2 and especially with LC's choice of options. News of LC's choice of options, implementation of AACR2, and rule interpretations began appearing in the *Library of Congress Information Bulletin* and in the *Cataloging Service Bulletin* in 1979.

Closing Catalogs

As the debate continued, several major alternatives for the future of catalogs in light of AACR2 and desuperimposition appeared in favor among libraries: (1) continue the present unified card catalog; (2) close the card catalog and open a new card catalog; (3) close the card catalog and implement a COM catalog; and (4) close the card catalog and implement an online catalog.

Closing or freezing the catalog is not an uncomplicated process (McCallum, 1977). Many questions have to be answered: Should you close by cataloging date or date of publication? What do you do about open entries for serials and continuations in the old catalog? What do you do about material that is recataloged or reclassified? Do you withdraw the old cards? How much maintenance of subject headings do you do in the old catalog? Do you link entries in the old catalog with entries in the new catalog, and if so, how? Research at the Universities of Oregon and Toronto seemed to indicate that users utilized only one part of a split catalog. How could this problem be overcome?

The continuation of a unified card catalog with old and new headings interfiled also presented problems. Strategies that might be adopted to integrate new headings into an old catalog included:

1. Converting all old cataloging (description and form of heading) to AACR2. This clearly was not feasible economically for most libraries.

2. Using AACR2 for all new cataloging and converting all old entries to the new form when they are encountered.

3. Using AACR2 for all new cataloging but superimposing the old form of headings already in the catalog. The heavy reliance on LC copy cataloging from the national database over the years made this impractical.

4. Using the AACR2 for all new cataloging, including form of heading, and adopting a variety of strategies in integrating the new headings with the old. The varying strategies included (a) using split files, that is, leaving the old headings under the old forms and linking the two files with cross-references; (b) changing the old headings to the new form when conflict arises in the catalog; (c) using split files when files are large (e.g., if there are more than 10 cards under a heading) and changing old heading to new if the file is small (e.g., if there are 10 cards or less under a heading); and (d) interfiling old and new headings where possible.

Effect on Work Flow and Operations

The Library of Congress experienced a 30% decrease in cataloging productivity in the year after the adoption of AACR2. Most other libraries experienced similar decreases in productivity.

The cost of training staff to use the new rules was considerable. Catalogers attended formal training programs sponsored by LC, ALA, and state and local associations. Self-training took place, and any library with more than one cataloger generally held group discussions and learning sessions. No estimate of the number of hours involved has been made, but 100 hours per cataloger for initial training, reading, and study as well as ongoing self-training in use of the rules would be minimal.

Another factor contributing to decreased productivity and growing backlogs was the increased amount of authority work to be done. Because of desuperimposition, all previously established names were candidates for being established under AACR2 rules. All existing authority files were in question. The details of authority control procedures are discussed in the section "Authority Control."

Machine-Readable Cataloging (MARC) Formats and International Standard Bibliographic Description

Machine-Readable Cataloging (MARC) Formats

The history of the MARC formats has been discussed earlier (see the section "National and International Formats and Standards" in Chapter 3). Catalogers have become very familiar with the format in the last few years. The majority of non-LC original cataloging done in American libraries now is input on one of the bibliographic utilities such as OCLC, Research Libraries Information Network (RLIN), and Washington Library Network (WLN). In addition, some libraries are developing in-house capabilities to create and manipulate cataloging records in MARC or MARC-compatible formats.

Figure 5.2 illustrates a MARC record for a monograph as it appears on OCLC. Figure 5.3 shows a catalog card produced from the same record. A MARC record consists of record directory information (not displayed on the OCLC record), fixed fields, and variable fields (MARC Formats, 1980). The fixed fields are generally incomprehensible on first glance but contain important coding of characteristics of the bibliographic item. For example, the language of the text (LANG) and country of publication (CTRY) are coded. These fixed fields, though usually not used now, have potential as additional access points or as parameters for Boolean searches in an automated catalog.

The variable fields contain the familiar information that appears on catalog cards, though in a slightly different form. Each field is coded by a three-character numeric with additional indicators and subfield coding. The tagging of each element makes later machine manipulation of that information possible. For a detailed explanation of the MARC tagging, the reader is referred to *MARC Formats for Bibliographic Data* (1980) issued by the Library of Congress in loose-leaf format for updating.

```
OCLC: 8193936          Rec stat: p Entrd: 820204          Used: 830214
Type: a Bib lvl: m Govt pub: s Lang:  eng Source:     Illus: a
Repr:     Enc lvl:    Conf pub: 0 Ctry:  nmu Dat tp: s M/F/B: 10
Indx: 1 Mod rec:     Festschr: 0 Cont: b
Desc a Int lvl:     Dates: 1982,
 1 010        82-2800
 2 040        DLC c DLC
 3 020        0826306020 : c $19.95
 4 020        0826306039 (pbk.) : c $9.95
 5 039 0      2 b 3 c 3 d 3 e 3
 6 043        n-ust-- a n-mx---
 7 050 0      F800 b .W4 1982
 8 082 0      979/.02 2 19
 9 090        b
10 049        TKNN
11 100 10     Weber, David J.
12 245 14     The Mexican frontier, 1821-1846 : b the American Southwest under
Mexico / c David J. Weber.
13 250        1st ed.
14 260 0      Albuquerque : b University of New Mexico Press, c c1982.
15 300        xxiv, 416 p. : b ill. ; c 24 cm.
16 440   0    Histories of the American frontier
17 504        Bibliography: p. 377-407.
18 500        Includes index.
19 651 0      Southwest, New x History y To 1848.
20 651 0      Mexico x History y 1821-1861.
```

Figure 5.2   Machine-readable cataloging record for a monograph as displayed by the Online Computer Library Center.

```
F
800      Weber, David J.
.W4         The Mexican frontier, 1821-1846 :
1982     the American Southwest under Mexico /
         David J. Weber. -- 1st ed. --
         Albuquerque : University of New Mexico
         Press, c1982.
            xxiv, 416 p. : ill. ; 24 cm. --
         (Histories of the American frontier)
            Bibliography: p. 377-407.
            Includes index.
            1464571


            1. Southwest, New--History--To 1848.
         2. Mexico--History--1821-1861.
         I. Title
```

Figure 5.3   Catalog card produced from machine-readable cataloging record in Figure 5.2.

International Standard Bibliographic Descriptions

Another standard with which catalogers have become familiar is the International Standard Bibliographic Description (ISBD) developed in the early 1970s. The generalized format ISBD (G) "lists all the elements which are required to describe and identify all types of materials which are likely to appear in library collections; it assigns an order to those elements; and prescribes punctuation for those elements " (IFLA, 1977, p. 1). Its history and purpose have been discussed earlier (see section "National and International Formats and Standards" in Chapter 3). AACR2 uses the ISBD(G) as the basis for its bibliographic description (AACR2, 1978). Individual ISBDs have been developed for monographic publications, serials, nonbook materials, printed music, cartographic materials, and antiquarian materials.

The prescribed punctuation specifying the use of periods, dashes, colons, slashes, etc., is the most apparent characteristic of an ISBD record. Figures 5.2 and 5.3 illustrate such cataloging records. Detailed explanations of the use of the specialized punctuation may be found in the ISBD(G) document (IFLA, 1977) and in the *Anglo-American Cataloguing Rules* (1978).

SUBJECT CATALOGING AND CLASSIFICATION

Subject Headings

General Principles

The purpose of subject cataloging is to show what a library has on a particular subject, described by Cutter (1876) as one of the functions of a catalog. Subject headings expand the subject approach provided by classification, permitting a cataloger to bring out a secondary subject or opposing concepts. Close coordination of subject headings and classification should be an objective. In U.S. library practice, the catalog generally reflects the subject content of the library material but does not include subject analysis of subunits of these materials, such as book chapters or periodical articles.

There is no code of subject heading practice that corresponds to that for descriptive cataloging. Chan (1978) addresses the problems caused by the lack of such a code. She states that "this lack of consensus and a clear statement of the functions is the cause of many difficulties in defining the basic principles . . . and in both the construction and the application of subject headings" (p. 20). In general, Library of Congress subject headings are used in academic and research libraries and large public libraries, and Sears subject headings are used by small- to medium-size public libraries and by school libraries. The following discussion of subject heading principles reflects LC practice. The same principles also apply to Sears subject headings that are based on LC.

For many years Haykin's *Subject Headings, a Practical Guide* (1951) has been considered the classic statement on subject heading practice for U.S. libraries. Haykin (pp. 7–11) discusses principles for choosing terms to be used as subject headings. The first principle is that the reader should be the focus: "The heading, in wording and structure, should be that which the reader will seek in the catalog, if we know or can presume what the reader will look under." The second principle is that of unity: "A subject cataloger must bring together under one heading all the books which deal principally or exclusively with the subject." The term must be unambiguous, have references from its synonyms, and be qualified if it is a term that can be used in more than one sense. The third principle is that the term must represent common usage. For U.S. libraries this means current American usage. This inevitably means that as currency of terms change then the term chosen for a particular subject may need to change. English terms are to be preferred to foreign terms. The fourth principle is that "the heading should be as specific as the topic is intended to cover. As a corollary, the heading should not be broader than the topic; rather than use a broader heading, the cataloger should use two specific headings which will approximately cover it."

It is impossible to represent all subjects with one-word headings. Haykin (1951, pp. 21–25) has categorized the different forms of subject headings as noun (e.g., "Chemistry"), adjectival headings (e.g., "Botanical gardens" or "English language"), inverted adjectival headings (e.g., "Advertising, Political"), phrase headings (e.g., "Photography of children"), inverted phrase headings (e.g., "Animals, Training of"), compound headings (e.g., "Christianity and economics"), and composite forms (e.g., "Open and closed shop"). Chan (1978, pp. 46–61) discusses forms of headings under the terms single nouns, adjectival phrases, prepositional phrases, headings with qualifiers, headings with subdivisions, and inverted headings.

Cross-referencing is a major component of the subject heading structure of a catalog. References are used to refer from synonyms and unused forms of headings ("see" references):

Tyrants   Architecture, Library
see   see
Dictators   Library architecture

Cross-references also may be made to related headings or subjects ("see also" references):

Ornithology
see also
Birds

See also references may be made from general to more specific subjects but not from the specific to the general:

Literature
see also
Poetry

But one would not make the reference:

Fiction
see also
Literature

General references may be used to refer to an entire category of headings:

Comparison (Grammar)
 see also subdivision COMPARISON under individual
 languages and groups of languages, e. g.
 ENGLISH LANGUAGE — COMPARISON

Library of Congress Subject Headings

The first edition of the *Library of Congress Subject Headings* (LCSH) was published in parts from 1909 to 1914. It was based on the American Library Association's ALA *List of Subject Headings for Use in Dictionary Catalogs* (1911). Eight editions followed in 1919, 1928, 1943, 1948, 1957, 1966, 1975, and 1980. Supplements have been published between each edition. The supplements now are published on a regular quarterly schedule with annual and sometimes biennial cumulations. Beginning with the eighth edition, LCSH also is issued in microfiche format. The quarterly microfiche are cumulative so that each issue is virtually a complete new edition.

An editorial group meets weekly at the Library of Congress to consider additions and changes to the subject headings list. New headings, new references, new subdivisions to be used with a particular

subject, and changes in old headings must be "established editori-
ally" before they can be used. Suggested additions and changes come
from LC staff and from individuals and groups outside LC.

There have been many critics of the LC subject headings over the
years. Cochrane and Kirtland (1981) have identified a "selective catalog of 20 LCSH weaknesses" in their compilation of post-World War
II critical evaluations of LCSH. Among the weaknesses identified are
the lack of a code governing their application, inconsistencies in the
form of headings, lack of currency and specificity, prejudicial
headings, too few headings assigned to individual cataloging records, litle coordination between LCSH and the LC classifications,
and their unavailability in machine-readable form.

The Library of Congress is well aware of these criticisms and has
taken some steps to respond to them. The closing of LC's catalog in
1981 was the occasion for updating some terminology. Geographic
subdivision is now "direct" (with a few exceptions) and LC has plans
to make subject headings available in machine-readable form. This
last step will be sometime in the future.

Changes in a subject heading or the addition of a new one potentially can affect many other headings through the cross-reference
structure. The cumbersomeness of revising subjects in a manual
file has been one factor in LC's conservative approach to making
changes. Some have speculated that the new machine-readable catalogs will alleviate this awkwardness and inevitably will lead to more
rapid and more frequent changes in individual subject headings.

Sears Subject Headings

First published in 1923 as the *List of Subject Headings for Small Libraries,* the Sears subject headings are patterned closely on the Library of Congress form of subject headings. In the Sears list some
LC forms are simplified; others may be broadened to combine two
LC headings into one Sears heading.

The list is now in its twelfth edition published in 1982 under the title *Sears List of Subject Headings.* There is a prefatory guide to the
application of the subject headings. The list also contains the corresponding Dewey Decimal Classification numbers for the subject
headings.

Subject Cataloging and Automation

Many librarians think that some more radical approach to the revision of subject heading practice is needed. Current attention is fo-

cussed on subject access in the online environment. Mandel (1981) has reviewed some of the problems and prospects for online subject access. Her recommendatons for action include the creation and distribution of the LC subject headings routinely in machine-readable form using the MARC authorities format. Computer-assisted indexing techniques (Mischo, 1980) and keyword searching (Gorman, 1980) are two approaches that have been suggested for improving access.

The PREserved Context Index System (PRECIS), developed for use in indexing the *British National Bibliography*, has received a good deal of attention in the last few years as a possible successor to LCSH in automated catalogs. Several reviews and guides have been published (Austin & Digger, 1977; Weintraub, 1979), and a workshop was held at the University of Maryland in 1976 (Wellisch, 1977). In 1978 the Library of Congress investigated the possibility of adding PRECIS strings to its cataloging but rejected the idea, saying that it would be too costly to convert.

Classification

Purpose and General Principles

Paul Dunkin (1969, p. 96) gives the two purposes of classification as "to help the user find a book whose call number he knows" and "to help the user find all books of a kind together." In providing a call number and shelf location, it is generally desirable that it be a relative (to other materials) one rather than a fixed (to a specific spot on a shelf) one to provide for the intershelving of new materials. A shelf location could be provided by sequential or accession numbering as long as the call number on the cataloging record matched the call number on the item; but users would not find all books of a kind together.

In meeting the second purpose, classification schemes traditionally group materials by subject as the way most users want to approach library materials. Materials could be classified according to characteristics other than subject, such as binding, language, size, or type of user. In practice many libraries do just this. For example, most libraries place oversize material on special shelves designated on the cataloging record by such notations as "oversize" or "folio" placed before the call number. Juvenile literature may be separately classified by a designation such as "Juv" plus a Cutter number. Fiction also is sometimes treated separately, even in college and university collections, and shelving non-Roman language material separate from the rest of the collection is not unusual.

Dewey Decimal Classification (Dewey, 1979) and Library of Congress Classification (LC, 1917) are the most commonly used classification systems in U.S. libraries and share a number of characteristics:

1. Both are based on traditional philosophical ideas of the classification of knowledge.
2. Both are enumerative, that is, they provide detailed class numbers for subjects and their subdivision. The LC system is more enumerative, a fact reflected in the size of the LC classification schedule.
3. Both provide close classification, that is, the item is classified with the most specific subject.

In classifying materials according to Dewey or LC, it is often necessary to chose between two or more possible classifications because a title may be about more than one subject or more than one aspect of a subject. Chan (1981, pp. 212–215) has synthesized from a number of sources general guidelines for classifying:

1. Consider where a title should be located to be of greatest use to library users.
2. Consider form after subject, except in literature.
3. Classify in the most specific number.
4. Consult the complete schedule not just its index when classifying a work.
5. Classify with the dominant subject.
6. Classify with the thing being influenced not with the subject doing the influencing.
7. Classify with the subject not with the group of readers for whom it is intended.
8. Classify with the subject not with the tool being used.
9. Classify with the first subject if the dominant subject cannot be determined.
10. Classify with the broader subject a title that covers several facets of that subject.

Both Dunkin (1969, p. 137) and Chan (1981, p. 209) agree that the primary purpose served by classification in U.S. libraries is that of shelf location (often referred to as "mark it and park it"). In most cataloging operations practicality prevails. A cataloger does not have time to ponder for long over choices between two or more possible classification numbers. A general guideline followed in many libraries is to have the call number determined by the first listed subject heading (see item 9 just mentioned).

Library of Congress Classification

History. When the Library of Congress acquired Thomas Jefferson's library in 1815, it decided to use Jefferson's classification system as well. That scheme was used with modification until the late nineteenth century. At that time its inadequacies in the face of an expanding collection of materials forced the Library to examine alternatives. Dewey's Decimal Classification and Cutter's Expansive Classification were considered in the period 1897–1898 but were rejected in favor of developing a system at the Library of Congress.

Unlike other systems, the LC classification is designed to classify a specific collection of materials and is the work of many people. The outline was developed by James C. M. Hanson, the head of the Catalogue Division. Charles Martel, the chief classifier, directed much of the early development effort and the reclassification from Jefferson's system to the new system (LC, 1917). The development of the individual schedules was carried out by subject specialists under the direction of an editor.

Class E-F (History: America) was the first published in 1904. Only the K class (Law) is now incomplete. Table 5.1 lists the currently published schedules.

TABLE 5.1

The Library of Congress Classification System Currently Published Schedules

Class	Schedule	Year published
A	General Works. (4th ed.)	1973
B–BJ	Philosophy. Psychology. (3rd ed.)	1979
BL–BX	Religion. (2nd ed.)	1962
C	Auxiliary Sciences of History (3rd ed.)	1975
D	History: General and Old World. (2nd ed., 1959, reprinted with supplementary pages)	1966
E–F	History: America. (3rd ed., 1959, reprinted with supplementary pages)	1965
G	Geography. Maps. Anthropology. Recreation. (4th ed.)	1976
H–HJ	Social Sciences: Economics. (4th ed.)	1981
HM–HX	Social Sciences: Sociology. (4th ed.)	1980
J	Political Science. (2nd ed., 1924, reprinted with supplementary pages)	1966

(cont.)

TABLE 5.1 (Continued)

Class	Schedule	Year published
K	Law. (General)	1977
KD	Law of the United Kingdom and Ireland	1973
KE	Law of Canada	1976
KF	Law of the United States. (Prelim. ed.)	1969
KK	Law of Germany.	1982
L	Education. (3rd ed., 1951, reprinted with supplementary pages)	1966
M	Music and Books on Music. (3rd ed.)	1978
N	Fine Arts. (4th ed.)	1970
P–PZ	Language and Literature Tables	1982
P–PM	Index to Languages and Dialects. (3rd ed.)	1983
P–PA	Philology. Linguistics. Classical Philology. Classical Literature. (1928, reprinted with supplementary pages)	1968
PA	Supplement: Byzantine and Modern Greek Literature. Medieval and Modern Latin Literature. (Reprinted with supplementary pages)	1968
PB–PH	Modern European Languages. (1933, reprinted with supplementary pages)	1966
PG	Russian Literature. (1948, reprinted with supplementary pages)	1965
PJ–PM	Languages and Literatures of Asia, Africa, Oceania. America. Mixed Languages. Artificial Languages. (1935, reprinted with supplementary pages)	1965
PN, PR, PS, PZ	General Literature. English and American Literature. Fiction in English. Juvenile Belles Lettres. (2nd ed.)	1978
PQ	Part 1: French Literature. (1936, reprinted with supplementary pages)	1966
PQ	Part 2: Italian, Spanish, and Portuguese Literatures. (1937, reprinted with supplementary pages)	1965
PT	Part 1: German Literature. (1938, reprinted with supplementary pages)	1966
PT	Part 2: Dutch and Scandinavian Literatures. (1942, reprinted with supplementary pages)	1965
Q	Science. (6th ed.)	1973
R	Medicine. (4th ed.)	1980
S	Agriculture. (4th ed.)	1982
T	Technology. (5th ed.)	1971
U	Military Science. (4th ed.)	1974
V	Naval Science. (3rd ed.)	1974
Z	Bibliography and Library Science. (5th ed.)	1980

Features. As stated earlier, the LC Classification System is the most enumerative of the systems in use. Synthesis of classifications numbers is not a prominent feature of the scheme. Consequently, it requires more volumes to detail all the classes.

The notation is a mixture of alphabetic and numeric characters. The first element is a single, double, or triple letter combination (e.g., E, PA, KFC). The second element indicates subdivision of each class or subclass and consists of the numerals 1–9999, which may be expanded by the use of decimal extension (e.g., 1949.25). The third element of the notation usually consists of a letter–number combination known as a Cutter number in which the number portion is treated decimally. The classification number often has only the above three elements. However, in a significant number of cases fourth and/or fifth elements consisting of a second Cutter number or date (i.e., year) may be added. A classification number may be further extended by the addition of volume designations as well. Typical LC classification numbers have the appearance:

HG	N	PT	RC	TS
2461	6809	9876.18	280	155
.H4	.C3	.E514	.E9	.H377
1980	H44	V5	H46	
			1980	

LC users may elect to write call numbers on spine labels and to display them in catalogs several ways. Some of the more common choices are:

HG	PT	N6809	N6809	N	N
2461	9876	.C3H44	.C3	6809	6809
.H4	.28		H44	C3H44	.C3
1980	.E514			1982	H44
	V5				

Although each schedule was developed independently, there are some features common to all classes. Within a class or subclass there often are provisions for some common divisions: (1) general form subdivisions, such as periodicals and dictionaries, (2) theory and philosophy of the discipline, (3) history of the subject, (4) general works, and (5) study and teaching.

Several types of tables for recurring patterns of subarrangement may be found throughout the schedules. Immroth (1980, pp. 107–134) has identified six different types: (1) form tables for subarrangement by physical or bibliographic form, (2) geographic tables for subarrangement by place, (3) chronological tables for subarrangement by date, (4) subject tables for arrangement by subtopics, (5) combination tables for subarrangement by two or more characteristics (e.g., by subject and country), and (6) author tables for subarrangement of books by and about an author in classes B (Philosophy, Psychology, Religion) and P (Language and literature). The tables may be of general applicability across several classes or may be applicable only to a specific range of subclass numbers within a single schedule. The application and use of the wide variety of tables in the LC system is one of the more difficult parts of the system. Experience in their use is the only way to learn them adequately.

Notes of various kinds are scattered throughout the schedules. Cross-references and scope notes aid in the use of the LC system. The index to each volume is of great help also in assigning classifications.

Addition and review. The schedules are updated by the quarterly *L. C. Classification—Additions and Changes.* Changes and additions are suggested by subject catalogers at LC and are reviewed by a committee in the Subject Cataloging Division. After approval they are published in *Additions and Changes.* A cumulative of *Additions and Changes* has been issued by the Gale Research Company as *Library of Congress Classification Schedules: a Cumulation of Additions & Changes.* Many libraries have found that the time saved by their catalogers in using the cumulation justifies the purchase price.

The most common ways of expanding the LC classification system are by using previously unassigned numbers or double and triple letters, extending existing numbers decimally, and providing for subdivision by using Cutter numbers. Triple class letters were first used in the KF class (U.S. law) published in 1969. An example of a new double-letter subclass is the creation in 1972 of BQ for the classification of materials on Buddhism. Decimal extension and subdivision by Cutter numbers are the more common ways of expanding the LC system. Each issue of *Additions and Changes* includes many examples.

Cumulative or revised editions of individual schedules are issued at irregular intervals. Cumulative editions represent a cumulation of additions and changes published since the last edition. Revised editions represent a true reworking of the schedule as a whole with many additions and changes not previously published. In addition to new editions, a schedule may be reprinted with supplementary pages cumulating additions and changes but not integrating them into the schedule itself.

Indexes and guides to use of the Library of Congress Classification.
A manual of classification has never been published by the Library of
Congress. Most cataloging departments would find it useful to have
Schimmelpfeng and Cook's *The Use of the Library of Congress Classification* (1968) and *Immroth's Guide to the Library of Congress Classification* (Immroth, 1980) available for reference. Each issue of the
Cataloging Service Bulletin, published by LC, usually contains some
explanations of principles or discusses changes in practice in classification.

The compilation by Olson, *Combined Indexes to the Library of Congress Classification Schedule* (1974), may be of some assistance in assigning LC classification numbers. The microfilmed edition of the
Library of Congress shelflist is also available. The *Library of Congress Subject Headings* (LC, 1980a) serves as a partial index to the
classification scheme because LC classification numbers are given in
parentheses following many of the subject headings.

Dewey Decimal Classification

History. The first edition of Dewey's Decimal Classification System (DDC) appeared anonymously in 1876 under the title *A Classification and Subject Index for Cataloguing and Arranging the Books and
Pamphlets of a Library.* In contrast to the Library of Congress Classification System, it is based on the classification of knowledge rather
than the classification of an individual library's collection. Dewey
himself edited the first three editions and supervised the fourth
through the thirteenth. The nineteenth edition, edited by Custer, was
published in 1980. The present editor Comaromi has written a history of the first eighteen editions that should be consulted for details
(Comaromi, 1976).

Responsibility for day-to-day editing of the DDC now rests in the
Decimal Classification Division at the Library of Congress. The chief
of the division is also the editor of DDC. The Decimal Classification
Editorial Policy Committee, consisting of practicing librarians and
library science educators, acts as an advisory committee. The rights
to the DDC have been vested in the Lake Placid Education Foundation with Forest Press as the publisher. Between editions DDC is
updated by *Dewey Decimal Classification Additions, Notes and Decisions* (LC, 1959). The nineteenth edition is in three volumes: Volume 1, *Tables;* Volume 2, *Schedules;* and Volume 3, *Index* (Dewey,
1979). It was adopted by the Library of Congress at the same time as
AACR2.

In reviewing his years as editor, Custer (1980) highlighted two areas of which he was especially proud. First was the "cosmopolitanization" of DDC or the effort to move away from the Anglo-Saxon Protestant bias. Increased international use of DDC made this especially desirable. Second was the "modernization" of DDC, including "substantive improvements" in classing women, ethnic groups, etc. and "organizational improvements" resulting in a "rational and coherent structure characterized by subject integrity and predictable subject relationships" (p. 102). During Custer's editorship the concepts of citation order and facet analysis also were adopted resulting in more number synthesis, or number-building.

Characteristics of the Dewey Decimal Classification System. The DDC divides knowledge into 10 classes:

000	Generalities
100	Philosophy and related disciplines
200	Religion
300	Social sciences
400	Language
500	Pure sciences
600	Technology (applied sciences)
700	The arts
800	Literature (belles lettres)
900	General geography and history

Each class and subclass, and so on is further subdivided on a base of 10. Thus the 300s, Social sciences, are divided:

310	Statistics
320	Political science
330	Economics
340	Law
350	Public administration
360	Social problems and services
370	Education
380	Commerce (trade)
390	Customs, etiquette, folklore

As illustrated, the classification is hierarchical proceeding from the general (300, Social science) to the more specific (330, Economics).

The notation is pure, being all numeric. The numbers are to be considered decimally with the decimal point appearing after the third digit: 516.37. Some numbers are used mnemonically throughout the scheme. For instance, -73 is used for United States and -03 for encyclopedic or dictionary works.

In using the DDC the classifier synthesizes or builds specific numbers from base numbers in the schedules by adding elements from auxiliary tables or from within the schedules themselves. There are seven auxiliary tables for standard subdivisions: areas; subdivisions of individual literature (used with class 800); subdivisions of individual languages (used with class 400); racial, ethnic, and national groups; languages; and persons.

One practical problem with number building is that it can result in very long numbers of more than 10 digits. Classifiers may choose to truncate or segment classification numbers that are too long. There are libraries (usually the smaller ones) with a policy of not assigning a number with more than a specified number of digits (e.g., 3 or 4) beyond the decimal. Segmentation is possible because of the hierarchical nature of the Dewey numbers. The Library of Congress indicates by using "prime marks" the natural breaks in the Dewey numbers it assigns for the convenience of its users:

346.82'022
362.7'96'09931
743'.6

A 1975 survey (Comaroni, Michael, & Bloom, pp. 100–113) indicated that 70% of DDC libraries use segmentation to some extent.

DDC may be revised by expansion (i.e., using numbers not previously used or extending a number decimally), reduction (i.e., shifting a topic to another number at a different level in the hierarchy), and relocation (i.e., shifting a topic to another number at the same level in the hierarchy) (J. Osborn, 1982). Numbers used in previous editions are indicated by brackets and are to remain unused for a period of time. Another more radical method of revision is the use of "phoenix schedules" to completely revise numbers without regard to how they were used in the past. The term was first used in the eighteenth edition, though the technique was employed in the sixteenth The nineteenth edition included two phoenix schedules: 324 (The political process) and 301-7 (Sociology).

The method of revision of the DDC is at the heart of an old debate between "stability of numbers" and "keeping pace with knowledge." The early editions under Dewey's editorship followed a policy of stability of numbers. Beginning with the fifteenth edition, keeping pace with knowledge, especially in science and technology, became a goal. There is now an attempt to balance the two policies. (Chan, 1981, pp. 219–220; J. Obsorn, 1982, p. 24). In the 1975 survey (Comaromi, Michael, & Bloom, pp. 78–79), 63.6% of the respondents preferred "stability of numbers" to "keeping pace with knowledge" as the guiding editoral policy. If "keeping pace with knowledge" is understood to result in greater movement and revision of numbers, then this can be viewed as a very practical choice. Each change in a number in a new edition means a library may be faced with reclassifying hundreds or thousands of titles. In practice, few libraries can afford to do this, resulting in collections with materials on the same topic scattered in several location and materials on different topics being given the same classification number (Comaromi, Michael, and Bloom, 1975, pp. 47–60).

Library of Congress and Dewey Decimal Classification Systems. In the mid-1960s and early 1970s there was a move to reclassify library collections from Dewey to LC. This was especially popular among college and university libraries. Reasons given for adopting the LC system included: the availability of complete LC numbers on LC cataloging and the expansiveness of LC in accommodating new subjects. Reclassification projects were common. In many libraries reclassification has never been finished and collections in both LC and Dewey systems exist side-by-side. Most reclassification taking place today is done as part of retrospective conversion projects.

Book Numbers

A library may use the Dewey Decimal or the Library of Congress Classification system to provide a classification number for a work. To provide a unique call number for that title a book number must be added. Book numbers are also called "author numbers" and "Cutter numbers." Lehnus (1980, p. 6) prefers book numbers as the more precise term, pointing out that not all book numbers are derived from the author's name and that Cutter numbers refer specifically to book numbers derived from a Cutter table. The activity of assigning book numbers is often referred to as "Cuttering" or "shelflisting."

A book number is a letter and number combination usually representing the main entry in the cataloging record for a work. It always is considered to be a decimal. The majority of libraries using Dewey derive book numbers from the Cutter two-figure and three-figure tables and the Cutter-Sanborn three-figure author table (Cutter, 1969a,b,c). Book numbers are not assigned to the Dewey Decimal Classification numbers appearing on LC cataloging. Libraries using LC Classification apply the Library of Congress book number tables that appeared most recently in the Winter 1979 issue of *Cataloging Service Bulletin.*

A work mark may be added to a book number to distinguish two works by the same author under the same classification. Work marks are not generally used with LC Classification. Instead, the book numbers are varied decimally. Other situations may call for the addition of dates, a second Cutter number, and volume and copy numbers to form a complete call number. Lehnus (1980) should be consulted for more detailed guidance in the use of book numbers with Dewey. Sources of assistance with book numbers for LC Classification include Immroth (1980).

ORIGINAL AND COPY CATALOGING

Original Cataloging

Distinction should be made between original, copy and near copy cataloging. *Original cataloging* refers to cataloging done for a unique item for which there is no cataloging record available. The cataloger must determine description according to the rules and must assign subject headings and classification. *Copy cataloging* refers to cataloging done using a cataloging record from an outside source such as LC or a network member library. It is assumed that a professional cataloger at another institution has done the cataloging. *Near copy cataloging* refers to cataloging done with copy that describes another edition or another manifestation of the work. The copy may be for another edition, for the title translated, or for the title issued in another format.

The responsibility of professional catalogers for original cataloging generally is well-defined in libraries. In the majority of OCLC libraries surveyed by Braden, Hall, and Britton (1980), original cataloging was performed exclusively by professional catalogers or by professionals with support staff used for verification. Their responsibility for copy and near copy cataloging is less clearly defined. The pattern that emerged from this survey was the involvement of both professional and support staff in the cataloging of these materials. There was a tendency to allow support staff to catalog with LC copy and to have greater professional involvement with member-contributed copy. As a rule, those activities in copy cataloging regarded as professional include assignment of subject headings and classification, establishment of new headings and the authority work associated with them, and the decisions on series treatment.

Original cataloging is now input on a bibliographic utility in many libraries. Often the professional cataloger is responsible for the MARC tagging of the cataloging record. Typically, cataloging work-forms, such as that illustrated by Figure 5.4, have been designed for the convenience of catalogers and support staff. Work flows from the cataloger to a staff member who keys in the record and places it in a temporary file; another staff member then revises for inputting errors and permanently adds the record to the cooperative database.

Copy Cataloging

One of the goals of bibliographic utilities has been to share the burden of original cataloging by making available cataloging done not only at the Library of Congress but also at member libraries. With the quick distribution of LC and member-contributed cataloging copy available through the bibliographic utilities, such as RLIN and OCLC, the proportion of copy cataloging to original cataloging done in most libraries has increased dramatically.

In the discussion that follows, the focus is on using LC as the standard and generally assumes that cataloging is done via one of the online utilities.

Availability of Copy

When LC began making its cataloging available through the printed card program, libraries were immediately aware of the advantage of using it. It was economical and authoritative. Until the middle 1970s most libraries depended on ordering LC cards for copy. There were some experiments with "catalogers cameras" in photographing and enlarging entries from the *National Union Catalog* and using those as a master for photocopying a card set in house. Commercial firms also offered photocopying of card sets for libraries. When the card set was received, the local call number had to be added. Photocopying from a master did offer the advantage of being able to type a call number on it and having it appear on each card. However, in both cases the added entries had to be overtyped.

In 1968 LC began doing its English language cataloging in machine-readable form. Shortly afterwards, magnetic tapes of these records were made available for sale. At the present time, LC distributes its cataloging records as machine-readable records, on printed cards, and in the series of *National Union Catalogs*.

Another source of LC cataloging copy is Cataloging in Publication (CIP). Under this program publishers submit prepublication infor-

INPUT CATALOGING WORKFORM
(MONOGRAPHS)

Type___ Bib lvl___ Govt pub___ Lang___ Source___ Illus___

Cat &   OP &

Repr___ Enc lvl___ Conf pub___ Ctry___ Dat tp___ M/F/B___

Date_____Date_____

Indx___ Mod rec___ Festschr___ Cont___

Save No. /_____ _____XC

Desc___ Int lvl___ Dates: _____, _____

010

040   015

020   025

041 _   0 _ 0 _

086 _   0_ 2

099

1_ _ _

240 _ _

245 _ _

250

260 _

300

4 _ _ _ _

5_ _ _

6_ _ _ _

7_ _ _ _

8_ _ _ _

Figure 5.4 Sample cataloging workform for machine-readable cataloging tagging.

mation on a book in the form of galley proofs. From this information LC staff provide partial cataloging information including main entry, partial title, series statement, subject headings, and added entries that are sent to the publisher to be printed in the book, usually on the verso of the title page. Figure 5.5 is an example of a CIP record. CIP cataloging records are also distributed as part of the MARC Distribution Service. They are later replaced by the full cataloging record in the MARC file and are redistributed to subscribers.

Most libraries have access to LC MARC records through a bibliographic utility. Cooperative networks, such as OCLC and RLIN, provide online access to a database containing LC MARC records and cataloging in the MARC formats from member libraries. Each member may call up individual records, make changes online to edit records according to local guidelines, and produce card sets. The cards arrive several days later already printed with call numbers and added entries and arranged for filing in the catalog. In addition, the library now has the cataloging record in machine-readable form.

Problems in Copy Cataloging

Any library using cataloging copy must make some very basic decisions about how much will be accepted without checking, which may involve a range of reviewing or editing activities. The more checking that is done, the less economical copy cataloging becomes. Almost all libraries accept the form of the description (pre-1949, pre-ISBD, etc.), but practices vary widely regarding access points, subject cataloging, and classification. Checking access points may involve verifying headings and series tracings in authority files maintained by a li-

```
Library of Congress Cataloging in Publication Data

Rosenthal, Gerald A.
     Plant Nonprotein Amino and Imino Acids: Biological, Biochemical, and
Toxicological Properties.

     (American Society of Plant Physiologists monograph
series)
     Bibliography: p.
     Includes index.
     1. Amino acids.  2. Amino acids--Toxicology.
3. Imino acids.  4. Botanical chemistry.  5. Plants
--Metabolism.  I. Title.  II. Series.
QK898.A5R67        582'.019245        82-1651
ISBN  0-12-597780-8                    AACR2
```

Figure 5.5 Cataloging in publication record.

brary and establishing any new headings. Subject headings may be verified in the latest edition of the *Library of Congress Subject Headings* or in a subject authority file, and the classification numbers may be verified in LC or Dewey classification schedules and/or in the local shelflist. The spectrum ranges from libraries that check every heading, call number, and subject heading to those libraries that accept all copy without checking anything. Most libraries fall somewhere in the middle of the two extremes. It is not uncommon to find libraries accepting LC copy but checking member-contributed copy. Other libraries accept copy from all but a few libraries, or they accept copy from LC as well as a few other libraries but check other copy.

Dowell's *Cataloging with Copy* (1976) is a comprehensive guide to the use of cataloging copy in a library and should be consulted for additional guidance and advice. In the final chapter, she discusses the integration of cataloging copy into the local catalog, that is, how much checking of copy against the local catalog must be done. She sees the potential consequences of not checking as "varying forms of entry; lack of some locally needed entry points; subject separation of editions and other related materials; errors or discrepancies that cause mis-filing or that convey misinformation; widely variant classification for the same subject, editions, or translations; and insufficiently complete call numbers" (p. 231). The three methods she discusses for integrating the copy are to change the new cataloging copy to agree with the old, change the old cataloging already in the catalog to agree with the new, or to split the files and connect the old and new cataloging with cross-references. There are pros and cons to each alternative. The general practice in U.S. libraries is to change the old to match the new, but in individual cases the new may be changed to agree with the old. For example, some libraries choose always to classify new editions with old, even if new developments in the classification scheme place the new edition elsewhere. The use of cross-references to connect split files is much more widespread since the introduction of AACR2 and the greatly increased number of changed forms of headings.

Cataloging copy represents cataloging done under several cataloging codes. Even if the cataloging was complete and accurate when it was done, established forms of headings, series treatment, and subject headings may have been revised in the meantime. To work effectively with copy cataloging, one must be familiar with the provision of earlier cataloging codes in order to know if something is an error or if it is a difference in cataloging rules.

*Copy Cataloging Workflow
in an Automated Environment*

Procedures and workflow will vary from library to library, depending on the interaction between the automated cataloging system's capabilities and unique local conditions. To realize fully the benefits from the system, a library should constantly scrutinize its procedures for ways to improve.

Copy cataloging operations in a typical medium- to large-size library might be sequenced something like the following. All new titles are searched on the database for copy. Information passed on from the ordering–receiving unit, such as a LC card number, may make this a very quick process. If a record is found, it is printed, then checked, and edited offline. The record is called up again and edited; then cards are produced. The item is forwarded for shelf preparation. Cards arrive several days later arranged in order for filing and are filed in the public catalog.

The nonhits are usually recycled for searching again after a period of time. RLIN offers an automated researching service by creating a search file from the nonhits and automatically researching the database at specified intervals. OCLC users must manually research each title. The number of researches and the length of time between them vary depending on staffing levels. Older imprints are often searched in the *National Union Catalog* before recycling. Any cataloging copy found is coded and input in the MARC format. Each network has standards for upgrading such records to current cataloging standards—usually by inputting headings established according to AACR2 but leaving undisturbed the descriptive cataloging. After the required recycling any remaining nonhits are sent for original cataloging.

Terminal availability and response time are familiar problems in the automated environment, and work scheduling and procedures are often dependent on them. Many cataloging departments schedule work in the evening to take advantage of evening system hours and to gain maximum benefit from hardware. This has introduced supervisory problems previously unknown in technical services.

Staffing Levels and Training

The Braden, Hall, and Britton (1980) study cited earlier showed a trend toward using more support staff for copy cataloging activities. The study results are supported by the experience in individual libraries (Gapen, 1979; Scott, 1979) in the reduction of professional staff involved in cataloging. An Association of Research Libraries survey (*Automated Cataloging*, 1978) showed that staff reductions averaged two FTE (full-time equivalent) professionals and six FTE support staff among libraries switching to automated cataloging. A number of libraries have been able to upgrade staff as a result of increased responsibilities in copy cataloging. Therefore, fewer staff are involved in cataloging, reductions have been experienced in the top and bottom grades, and some of the remaining staff positions have been upgraded.

Dowell (1976, pp. 23–29) summarizes "knowledge required in order to perform various cataloging functions." Libraries responsible for determining staffing levels and training needs may find this useful. Most training is done on the job. Adaptive, or copy, catalogers must be familiar with MARC, AACR2 and previous cataloging codes, ISBD, subject headings, and subject classification. In addition, changes in various standards—national, international and network—are constant and provision must be made for continued updating of skills.

SERIALS

Definition

A serial is defined in AACR2 as "a publication in any medium issued in successive parts bearing numerical or chronological designations and intended to be continued indefinitely. Serials include periodicals; newspapers; annuals...; the journals, memoirs, proceedings, transactions, etc., of societies; and numbered monographic series" (AACR2, 1978, p. 570). It is the publication over time, with its accompanying bibliographic changes, that makes the cataloging of serials particularly difficult. A serial may change title, publisher, or issuing body; cease publication; resume publication, split into two or more new serials; merge with one or more other serials; and be published in a different physical format. In a sense, the cataloging of serials is predictive, and each new issue of a serial that is received could potentially have changes that should be reflected in the cataloging record.

Descriptive Cataloging

Unlike earlier cataloging codes, the second edition of the *Anglo-American Cataloguing Rules* (1978) does not contain separate rules for the choice of entry for serials. Chapter 21, "Choice of Access Points," is applied to both monographs and serials. The most significant change under AACR2 for the description of serials is the designation of the title page of the first issue of a serial as the chief source of information. Pre-AACR2 rules called for the use of the latest issue for cataloging. The Library of Congress has chosen to catalog serials at an "augmented" level one. The major elements excluded from the description are other title information and the secondary statement of responsibility.

The first edition of the *Anglo-American Cataloging Rules* (1967) called for the successive entry of serials under each title or changed main entry, resulting in multiple records for the same serial. Earlier cataloging rules had used entry under the latest title or form of main entry, with earlier titles noted on the cataloging record and with access to them through appropriate added entries. The Library of Congress implemented this provision in 1971. All new titles are cataloged under the successive entry rules. Libraries using retrospective cataloging copy done under latest entry will need to decide if they are going to use the cataloging done under the old rules or if they will break out the cataloging record into multiple successive entries.

Subject Cataloging and Classification

Both the *Library of Congress Subject Headings* (LCSH) (1980a) and Sears (1982) provide subdivisions for use with subject headings assigned to serials. LCSH uses Periodicals; Collected Works; Congresses; Directories; Indexes; Societies, etc.; Societies, Periodicals, etc.; and Yearbooks.

There are provisions throughout the LC Classification System for classifying periodicals and yearbooks in special numbers at the beginning of a class number. When a class number is further expanded by the use of Cutter numbers, the .A1 Cutter is often reserved for classifying serial publications. Most newspapers are classified in the As.

The Dewey Decimal Classification provides for general serial publications in 050 and for newspapers in 071–079. The standard subdivision -05 for serial publications may be added to classification numbers throughout the schedules where applicable.

Conversion of Serials Project

The CONSER (Conversion of Serials) Project has as its objective the cooperative conversion to machine-readable format of serials cataloging records. Current national and international standards are observed. The CONSER database is mounted on the OCLC computers. Cooperating libraries upgrade existing cataloging records and input new titles. The Library of Congress, the National Series Data Program, and the Government Printing Office authenticate various elements of the record. To date over 200,000 CONSER records have been authenticated.

Treatment of Serials in Libraries

Some libraries treat serials, and more specifically periodicals and newspapers, differently than monographs and do not fully catalog them. The reasoning is that such materials are accessed through periodical and newspaper indexes and representation in the library's catalog is not necessary. Variations in treatment include

1. Full descriptive and subject cataloging and classification
2. Full descriptive and subject cataloging but no classification
3. No descriptive or subject cataloging and classification.

The shelving of periodicals in a library's collection also shows a great deal of variation. Classified titles may be intershelved with other materials or shelved in a separate location. Unclassified titles may be arranged by main entry or by title. Current issues may be shelved with completed volumes or located separately in a current periodicals room.

Serials holdings information (i.e., the specific volumes and issues held by a library) presents problems in recording and in making the information available to the public. In card catalogs, the holdings information may be recorded only on the main entry, or it may appear only in the shelflist that is accessible to the public. Some libraries maintain separate computer-based serials holdings lists. In many libraries information on receipt of current issues is available in a central serials check-in record maintained by serials department personnel. Such records generally must be interpreted for the public by the library staff. The automation of serials control holds great promise for improved access to such holdings information. Already some libraries, such as those at the University of California at Los Angeles and Northwestern University, have online serials check in with information immediately accessible to the public. At least two serials agents, F. W. Faxon Co. and Ebsco Subscription Services, are offering online check-in systems, as well.

Further guidance on the treatment of serials in libraries may be found in A. D. Osborn's *Serials Publications, Their Place and Treat-ment in Libraries* (1973) and Smith's *A Practical Approach to Serials Cataloging* (1978).

AUTHORITY CONTROL

Definition and Interrelationship with Catalog Maintenance

A library's authority file is a record of the authorized or estab-lished forms of headings or access points used in the catalog. Author-ity records may exist for names, series, and subjects. In general, an authority record contains the established form of the heading, cross-references made in relation to the heading, sources searched for verification of the heading, and information about the work for which the heading was established.

Auld's survey (1982) of the literature on authority control is recom-mended as a starting point for a more in-depth study of the subject. Especially helpful is an article by Schmierer (cited by Auld, 1980) that serves as an introduction to the concept of authority control in the library catalog and traces the need for it to the gathering or col-location function of the catalog.

Responsibility for authority control has traditionally been some-what diffused throughout the cataloging department. In general, the cataloger is responsible for establishing new headings as they are en-countered. Copy catalogers check authority files for proper forms of headings to be used on cataloging copy. If they encounter a heading not yet established locally they may or may not establish such head-ings in local files. This is considered to be a professional task in some libraries. Another variation is for copy catalogers to establish locally the headings for which LC established headings can be found and for professional catalogers to establish other headings according to cur-rently accepted national standards.

Resolution of heading conflicts in the existing catalog often are the responsibility of special catalog maintenance staff. Conflicts may ap-pear in filing or information may be passed on from catalogers about headings in the card catalog that need revision.

With the increased need for authority control with the adoption of AACR2, some libraries have expanded the authority and responsibil-ity of catalog maintenance units vis-à-vis authority files. Catalog edi-tors have been appointed to assume responsibility for authority work. Procedures have been examined and revised. For the first time, many libraries have written authority procedures. An excellent example of an authority manual created in response to AACR2 is that of the University of Texas at Austin (Miller, 1981).

Library of Congress Name Authority Files and the Machine-Readable Cataloging (MARC) Authorities Format

The Library of Congress's first attempt at distributing authority information was its *LC Name Headings with Reference* that was published 1974–1980 and included name headings newly established in LC's cataloging along with cross-references made for those headings. Names that did not require cross-references were not included. In 1980, it was replaced by *Name Authorities* (LC, 1979) in a cumulative microform edition. All personal, corporate, conference, and uniform title headings and geographical names of political and civil jurisdictions that are newly established by the Library of Congress are included, whether or not they require references.

These same name authority records also are distributed in machine-readable form in the LC MARC authorities format (LC, 1981). A preliminary edition of the authorities format was issued in 1976. The first edition was published in 1981. The structure of the MARC authority format is similar to that of the MARC bibliographic formats with leader, record directory, and fixed and variable fields. The tags, indicators, and subfield codes used for content designation also are similar but may have a different definition; for example, in the bibliographic formats 4xx fields contain series information whereas in the authorities format they contain "see" reference information.

Figure 5.6 contains an example of an LC MARC authority record. Figure 5.7 shows the same record as it appears in the *Name Authority* microfiche edition. In summary the MARC authorities format tags designate the following:

> 1xx fields: established headings
> 4xx fields: "see from" reference headings
> 5xx fields: "see also from" reference headings
> 64x fields: series treatment information
> 66x fields: notes

Beginning in late 1982 the Library of Congress began adding records for series to its online authority files.

```
Rec stat:  n Entrd:  801127 Used:  801127
Type: z Bib lvl: x Govt Agn:  Lang:  Source:
Site: 004 InLC: a Enc lvl: n Head ref:  a Head: cc
Head status: a Name: a Mod rec:  Auth status: a
Ref status:

1 010     n 79083921
2 100 10  Jackson, William Keith, $d 1928-  $w n001800128aadann ----nnnn
3 400 10  Jackson, W. K. $w n004800128aanaan ----nnnd
4 500 10  Jackson, Keith $w n003800128aanaan ----nnnd
5 670     His New Zealand, 1969.  $w n002800128aanann ----nnnn
```

Figure 5.6 Machine-readable cataloging authority record from online file.

```
Jackson, William Keith, 1928 -
  Found:
    His New Zealand, 1969.
  x Jackson, W. K. (004)
  xx Jackson, Keith (003)
  AACR 2-d RETRO        UNEVAL
  DLC              n  79-83921
```

Figure 5.7 Authority record from *Name Authorities,* microfiche edition.

FILING AND CATALOG MAINTENANCE

Filing Rules

Major Rules

Rules for arranging entries in a catalog are not as well standardized as rules for descriptive and subject cataloging. Both the American Library Association and the Library of Congress have published several editions of filing rules since 1942. In many instances libraries have developed their own rules or have adapted filing rules from other sources. The American Library Association subcommittee working on the second edition of the ALA filing rules assembled 59 such rules during its work on the new edition (*ALA Rules,* 1968, pp. 246–247). It is not uncommon to find that a library's only filing rules are a few typewritten sheets or even entirely oral tradition.

The *A.L.A. Rules for Filing Catalog Cards* was first published in 1942. The rules are complex and offer many options for treatment of filing problems. Consequently, two libraries filing their catalogs by the first edition of the ALA rules may have catalogs filed in significantly different ways. The second edition of the *A.L.A. Rules for Filing Catalog Cards* was published in 1968 in correlation with the *Anglo American Cataloging Rules*, first edition (1967). The subcommittee working on the filing rules had as an objective the simplification of the rules, and the basic order of the rules is straight alphabetical, ignoring punctuation. The preface to the second edition states specifically that these rules are intended for a manual file. It suggests that filing rules might have to be revised again in the not-too-distant future to take into account the question of machine filing.

This proved to be an accurate prediction. Both the American Library Association and the Library of Congress published newly revised filing rules in 1980 that attempted to provide rules for filing in a machine environment (*ALA Filing Rules*, 1980; *LC Filing Rules*, 1980b).

Filing rules at the Library of Congress had previously been based on the classed order proposed by Charles Cutter in his 1904 *Rules for a Printed Dictionary Catalogue* (cited in *Filing Rules*, 1956). In 1945 a filing manual was issued for internal use at LC. A revised version of this manual, *Filing Rules for the Dictionary Catalogs of the Library of Congress*, was published in 1956 for general distribution.

The new editions of both the ALA and LC filing rules (*ALA Filing Rules*, 1980; *LC Filing Rules*, 1980b) were written for the new types of materials and new types of entries. The ALA rules represent the most radical departure from past rules. They are based squarely on the "file-as-is" principle and are intended for use with headings formulated under a variety of cataloging rules and for arrangement of displays in all kinds of catalogs, card and otherwise (*ALA Filing Rules*, 1980, p. 1). Entries are filed as they appear. Personal names are interfiled with other entries beginning with the same word, without regard for the comma separating the surname and forename. Exceptions and optional rules have been kept to a minimum. The committee's success in simplifying the rules is illustrated by its length of 50 pages versus the 260 pages of the 1968 edition.

The 1980 LC rules preserve a more traditional structured order in the catalog. They too are based on the "file-as-is" principle but also on the principle that "related entries should be kept together if they would be difficult to find when a user did not know their precise form" (*LC Filing Rules*, 1980b, p. 4). Headings beginning with the same elements are arranged in the order: person, place, thing, and title. LC began applying these new rules in its new Add-On Catalog in 1981.

Special Filing Problems

There are filing problems with which all filing rules must deal. The most common are discussed here.

1. Numbers: Traditionally numerals have been filed as though spelled out, even when they appear as digits, for example, "20" filed as "twenty." The new editions of both the ALA and LC rules file numerals before all letters so that entries beginning with numerals appear in the catalog before "A." The same numbers spelled out are filed as words. Thus "100" and "one hundred" are filed in different places in the catalog.

2. Abbreviations: Abbreviations may be filed as is or as if spelled out, for example, "Mr." filed as "Mr" or as "Mister." Again the new rules file as is, the old rules file as if spelled out.

3. Initial article: In all published filing rules, articles appearing as the first word of an entry are ignored. The problem here is to distinguish in some languages an initial article in the nominative case from the same word used for the cardinal numeral "one", for example, the German "Eine," or the Portuguese "Um." Articles appearing as an integral part of place names and personal names may or may not be ignored, depending on the rules being followed.

4. Initials, initialisms, and acronyms: These might be filed as single-letter words or as a single word, thus "I.B.M." and "I B M" are filed as "I B M" (three single-letter words), but "IBM" is filed as "Ibm" (one word). Generally, if they are separated by spaces or punctuation they are filed as words; if not separated, they are filed as one word.

5. Names with prefixes: Should "De la Torre" be filed as "De la torre" (three separate words) or as "Delatorre" (one word)? How should "Mac," "Mc" and "M" names be filed? Both the LC and the ALA rules file prefixes in names as separate words unless joined to the rest of the name directly or with an apostrophe with no space.

6. Headings beginning with the same elements: Traditionally it is in this area that library catalogs have been structured in some kind of hierarchy with similar headings grouped in the order: person, place, thing, and title. The 1980 edition of the *LC Filing Rules* preserves this structured approach that considers some punctuation significant for filing purposes. Thus, headings beginning with "Stone" would be arranged:

> Stone, Alan, 1904–
> Stone, Andrew

Stone, John
Stone, William Eric
STONE
STONE, CRUSHED
STONE AGE—AFRICA
STONE AGE—ASIA
STONE QUARRIES
Stone and rock
Stone age archeology
Stone Mountain (Ga.)

The ALA rules, however, disregard punctuation and interfile headings beginning with the same element:

STONE
STONE AGE—AFRICA
Stone age archaeology
STONE AGE—ASIA
Stone, Alan, 1904–
Stone and rock
Stone, Andrew
STONE, CRUSHED
Stone, John
Stone Mountain (Ga.)
STONE QUARRIES
Stone, William Eric

Filing Procedures

When new national filing codes are introduced, it usually is not economically feasible for libraries to refile their catalogs. Typically a library will continue to file by old rules. When new types or forms of entries are introduced because of changes in cataloging codes, as happened with AACR2, local decisions are made on where to file such new entries. If the staff is fortunate, a local filing manual is maintained that can be updated with these new instructions. Both the new editions of the LC and ALA rules recognized this problem and attempted to include forms of heads formulated under older cataloging rules (*ALA Filing Rules*, 1980; *LC Filing Rules*, 1980b).

Typically in large research libraries with card catalogs, cards arrive from the bibliographic utility prearranged for filing in the catalog. In some instances, several card shipments will be interfiled for efficiency of work at the card catalog.

The level of staff doing the actual filing varies. Student assistants are used in many cases. In other libraries, filing is done by full-time filers or by regular staff who routinely file as part of their assigned duties. Filing may or may not be revised. When it is, some method of flagging the newly filed cards is needed. Specially colored filing flags may be placed in front of the newly filed cards. The revisor then checks the filing and removes the flags. In other libraries, the cards are filed "on the rod" and are dropped by the revisor. Training aids include sample packs to be arranged and programmed texts. Filing rule summaries to be used at the catalog also are helpful.

Further complicating the filing procedures in most libraries is integration of headings formulated under a variety of cataloging codes. The desuperimposition of forms of names and the decision in many libraries to retain the integrated dictionary catalog after the adoption of AACR2 has created greatly complicated situations for the filing staff. Splitting of files, the existence of two forms of the same heading, and the creation of complex cross-references has made the job of filing more difficult.

It is at the point of filing that many conflicts in the catalog may be discovered. For example, a filer may discover already in the catalog a "see" reference from the form of heading used on a new card being filed, indicating that another form of the heading has been used in the local catalog. Provision must be made for handling such discrepancies. The filer may refer the problem to a supervisor or may be trained to investigate further. Often questions of authority control or establishment of headings are involved and high-level staff may be required to solve the problem.

Some libraries follow a practice of making no subject cross-references until a unique subject heading is filed in the catalog. The filer or revisor then is expected to pull out that card and refer it to a staff member charged with creating subject cross-references.

The published general filing rules, such as ALA and LC, offer guidance for making cross-references. The 1968 ALA rules are especially helpful in this respect (*ALA Rules*, 1968; *ALA Filing Rules*, 1980; *LC Filing Rules*, 1980b).

Filers also need to be alert to the need for raised guide cards and for additional cross-references. Explanatory cards for outlining special subarrangements under voluminous authors or complex subfiles should also be added as necessary.

Filing is not a function that can be left to poorly trained staff. It requires constant supervision. It is a highly complex, extremely meticulous procedure. Although it may seem tedious, it is essential that it be done carefully. A misfiled entry is one that is lost to a user. In a catalog of 1 million cards, an error rate of 2% (unrealistically low for most libraries) means 20,000 cards misfiled.

Catalog Maintenance

The need for catalog maintenance activities has been mentioned through the previous sections. Most libraries have a unit or at least a member of the staff charged with the responsibility for coordination and implementation of catalog maintenance. Traditional catalog maintenance has been concerned with the card catalog. The newer automated forms present their own problems.

Card catalog. Filing of cards, addition of cross-references and guide cards, expansion of files, and replacement of worn cards are aspects of card catalog maintenance. The adoption of the AACR2 added duties in splitting files between two forms of a heading, pulling cards and changing headings to the new form, and replacing card sets to reflect updated cataloging practice. Planning for workflow should include careful control over cards that are out of the files and use of a temporary "cards out" notice in selected cases.

Book and computer-produced microform catalogs. Misfiling is possible in these catalogs as well, but they cannot be corrected until the next edition of the catalog. Other error corrections and desired changes also must await until the new edition. Methods must be worked out for recording desired changes. Expansion of files causes no additional catalog maintenance work.

Online catalogs. One of the great advantages of online catalogs is that errors can be corrected immediately. The ability to change a heading once in a file and to have that change appear wherever the heading occurs ("global update") makes catalog maintenance chores much easier. The problem of machine filing is not an easy one to solve. Careful attention and thought must be given to the problem. Filing indicators in the MARC formats are very helpful but cannot solve all the problems. One strategy is to be aware of especially difficult areas (such as "a," which may be an English article or a French preposition) and to routinely check the indexing of entries beginning with those words.

Maintenance of machine-readable archival tapes. Each time an OCLC member library produces or updates on a record, that record as edited is added to an archival tape for the library and cannot be called back for re-editing. Libraries interested in using these machine-readable records in the future for an online catalog are advised to work out a scheme for updating the machine-readable records to match changes made in the card files. This usually means going back to the OCLC terminal and reediting the entire OCLC record to reflect the latest changes and reproducing (if new cards are desired) or updating the record. Some libraries have worked out schemes of coding that allow them to update only the changed fields.

RLIN members do not have the same problem as they have online access to their local records and can simply change the element in the record to be revised.

RETROSPECTIVE CONVERSION

As libraries have implemented online circulation systems and moved toward online catalogs and integrated library systems, the need to begin conversion of retrospective cataloging records has become greater. Since the mid-1970s some libraries have been engaged in retrospective conversion (recon) projects. A number of writers have noted a lack of guidance for recon projects in the professional literature (Johnson, 1982; *Retrospective Conversion*, 1980). An indication of the increased interest in sharing information on problems in retrospective conversion was the recent formation of a LITA (Library and Information Technology Association) Discussion Group on Retrospective Conversion within the ALA.

Uses of Machine-Readable Records

Before undertaking a retrospective project, the library should have a clear idea of what use will be made of the machine-readable records. A library must look at both short-term and long-term uses (Butler, Aveney, & Scholz, 1978). A number of other decisions, such as fullness of record and level of authority control, depend on planned uses. Given the state of development of online catalogs, a library that fails to fully convert existing records and that does not use the MARC formats is being extremely short-sighted. The cost of going back to upgrade or "fill out" records in the future would probably closely equal initial conversion costs. This, of course, does not mean that a library that has elected to use minimal-level cataloging for selected materials should upgrade this cataloging during conversion. It does mean that the converted records should not have any less information than the manual records.

Choice of Approaches

A library may choose one of two basic methods: in-house or contract-out. The choice is generally based on time limit as well as money and staff available locally for conversion activity. Each has its own advantages but involve the same principles of project planning and management.

In-house. An in-house project is generally undertaken by libraries with access to a bibliographic utility such as OCLC. The library retains total control over the process and is responsible for all its aspects. Johnson (1982) has described such a project undertaken by the University of South Carolina's Cooper Library. This project is especially interesting because conversion of three differing collections in the same library system was involved.

Contract-out. A library may elect to contract out the conversion process. The contract may be for total keying of records from some library source (usually the shelflist) or for matching of the library's holdings against a resource database for extraction of the matching records. A common practice is to provide the shelflist in microfilm from which the contractor works. Matching against a resource database is generally done by creating a machine-readable brief record (done by either the library staff or by the contractor). The brief record may contain just the LC card number or an ISBN, but more often it also contains truncated information, such as the first four letters of the author's name, the first four or five letters of the title, and last two digits of the publication date or the pagination, etc.

Resource Databases

Most resource databases have as their basic component the MARC records distributed by the Library of Congress. A library may purchase a subscription directly from LC for mounting on its own computer, or it may access the records through a third party, such as bibliographic utilities and commercial vendors.

A new source for retrospective records is the REMARC database being keyed by the Carrollton Press under contract to the Library of Congress. All non-MARC LC cataloging is involved. Eventually more than 5 million records are to be keyed into the MARC format. The project is scheduled for completion in the second quarter of 1984. Access to the database is being marketed in a number of ways: via contracts with individual libraries and consortia of libraries and via the DIALOG system. As of this writing, none of the three large not-for-profit bibliographic utilities has purchased the REMARC records.

Libraries using utilities for conversion also have access to the non-LC MARC records on those databases. This considerably increases the "hit rate."

Planning a Project

In a presentation to a PALINET workshop, Wetherbee (1980, p. 3) outlined seven steps in planning and implementing a successful retrospective conversion: (1) assess institutional needs, (2) specify the scope of the project, (3) outline resources available, (4) decide on a plan of action in some detail, (5) decide on conversion method, (6) implement the method, and (7) assess the results.

Specific components will include

1. A clear statement of use planned for records
2. Assessment of local catalogs and cataloging practices and standards
3. Assessment of matching possibilities with a particular resource database (usually done by a sample of records scheduled for conversion)
4. Appointment of a project coordinator with commensurate authority and responsibility
5. Careful consideration of impact of conversion project on regular work in the technical services departments.
6. Proper attention to controls by statistics and reports
7. Realistic assessment of the time needed to clear up problems resulting from a conversion project.

Costs and Conversion Rates

Butler *et al.* (1978, p. 130) have given the factors affecting the cost of retrospective conversion (and also conversion rates) as the size, age, language mix, and uniqueness of the collection to be converted;

the fullness of cataloging desired; the degree of standardization in the library's cataloging records; and the library staff available for conversion activities. The cost of individual projects will vary considerably, and it is probably useless to suggest average costs that will be valid for an individual institution. Direct cost elements that should be included are staff, equipment and supplies, and per record charges. Inclusion of indirect costs should be specified. An uncontrollable variable affecting costs and conversion rate is response time for those institutions using an online system.

For additional assistance in planning a retrospective conversion project the reader is referred to the recently published *Data Conversion* by Carter and Bruntjen (1983).

KEEPING UP

Citations in the text provide guidance for a survey of the current situation in cataloging. As with any rapidly changing field the best sources for keeping up-to-date are reading the professional journals and talking with colleagues in the field.

Recommended journals include *Library Resources & Technical Services*, for coverage of all aspects of cataloging and classification, and *Information Technology and Libraries* (formerly the *Journal of Library Automation*), for coverage of automation and cataloging. The *Cataloging & Classification Quarterly, The Serials Librarian* and *Serials Review* are specialized journals that have excellent articles. Also helpful are the *RTSD Newsletter, LITA Newsletter, Cataloging Service Bulletin* and the *Library of Congress Information Bulletin*.

Constant scanning of the literature, continuing education, site visits, conference attending, and communication with professional colleagues is necessary if one is to keep up. The increasing number of discussion groups formed within the American Library Association's Resources and Technical Services Division and Library and Information Technology Association is a reflection of this need to share information.

REFERENCES

Alternative Catalog Newsletter, (Nos. 2–26) Baltimore: Milton S. Eisenhower Library, Johns Hopkins University, June 1978–December 1980.
American Library Association. *Catalog rules: Author and title entries* (American ed.).

Compiled by Committees of the ALA and the British Library Association. Chicago: Author, 1908.

American Library Association. *List of subject headings for use in dictionary catalogs* (3rd ed.). Mary Josephine Briggs (Ed.). Chicago: Author, 1911.

American Library Association. Catalog Code Revision Committee. *A.L.A. catalog rules, author and title entries* (Preliminary American 2nd ed.). Chicago: Author, 1941.

American Library Association. *A.L.A. rules for filing catalog cards*. Chicago: Author, 1942.

American Library Association. Division of Cataloging and Classification. *Cataloging rules for author and title entries* (2nd ed.). Clara Beetle (Ed.). Chicago: Author, 1949.

American Library Association. *A.L.A. rules for filing catalog cards* (2nd ed.). Chicago: Author, 1968.

American Library Association. Filing Committee. *A.L.A. filing rules*. Chicago: Author, 1980.

Anglo-American cataloging rules, North American text. Chicago: American Library Association, 1967.

Anglo-American cataloguing rules (2nd ed.). M. Gorman & P. W. Winkler (Eds.). Chicago: American Library Association, 1978.

Atherton, P. Catalog user's access from the researcher's viewpoint: Past and present research which could affect library catalog design. In D. K. Gapen & B. Juergens (Eds.), *Closing the catalog: Proceedings of the 1978 and 1979 Library and Information Technology Association Institutes*. Phoenix: Oryx Press, 1980.

Auld, L. Authority control: An eighty-year review. *Library Resources & Technical Services*, 1982, *26*, 319–330.

Austin, D., & Digger, J. A. PRECIS: The Preserved Context Index System. *Library Resources & Technical Services*, 1977, *21*, 13–30.

Automated cataloging. Washington, D.C.: Systems and Procedures Exchange Center, Office of Management Studies, Association of Research Libraries, 1978. (SPEC Kit, No. 47)

Bierman, K. The future of catalogs in North American libraries. In M. J. Freedman & S. M. Malinconico (Eds.), *The nature and future of the catalog*. Phoenix: Oryx Press, 1979.

Braden, S., Hall, J. D., & Britton, H. H. Utilization of personnel and bibliographic resources for cataloging by OCLC participating libraries. *Library Resources & Technical Services*, 1980, *24*, 135–154.

The British national bibliography. London: British Library. Bibliographic Services Division, 1950–.

Butler, B., Aveney, B., & Scholz, W. The conversion of manual catalogs to collection data bases. *Library Technology Reports*, 1978, *14*, 109–206.

Carter, R. C., & Bruntjen, S. *Data conversion*. White Plains, N.Y.: Knowledge Industry Publications, 1983.

Cataloging & Classification Quarterly (Vols. 1–) New York: Haworth Press, 1980–.

Cataloging Service Bulletin, Washington, D.C.: Library of Congress, Processing Services, 1978–.

Chan, L. M. *Library of Congress Subject Headings, principles and application*. Littleton, Col.: Libraries Unlimited, 1978.

Chan, L. M. *Cataloging and classification: An introduction*. New York: McGraw-Hill, 1981.

Closing the catalog: Proceedings of the 1978 and 1979 Library and Information Technology Association institutes. D. Gapen & B. Juergens (Eds.). Phoenix: Oryx Press, 1980.

Cochrane, P. A., & Kirtland, M. *Critical views of LCSH—the Library of Congress Subject Headings: A bibliographic and bibliometric essay and an analysis of vocabulary central in the Library of Congress list of subject headings.* Syracuse, N.Y.: 1981. (ERIC Document Reproduction Service No. ED208 900)

Comaromi, J. P. *The eighteen editions of the Dewey Decimal Classification.* Albany, N.Y.: Forest Press, 1976.

Comaromi, J. P., Michael, M. E., & Bloom, J. *A survey of the use of the Dewey Decimal Classification in the United States and Canada.* Albany, N.Y.: Forest Press, 1975.

Custer, B. A. The view from the editor's chair. *Library Resources & Technical Services,* 1980, *24,* 99–105.

Cutter, C. A. *Rules for a printed dictionary catalogue* (Public libraries in the United States of America, their history, conditions and management, Part II). Washington, D.C.: Government Printing Office, 1876.

Cutter, C. A. *C. A. Cutter's three figure author table* (Swanson-Swift revision). Chicopee, Mass.: H. R. Huntting Co., 1969. (a)

Cutter, C. A. *C. A. Cutter's two-figure author table* (Swanson-Swift revision). Chicopee, Mass.: H. R. Huntting Co., 1969. (b)

Cutter, C. A. *Cutter-Sanborn three figure author table.* Chicopee, Mass.: H. R. Huntting Co., 1969. (c)

Dewey, M. *A classification and subject index for cataloguing and arranging the books and pamphlets of a library.* Amherst, Mass.: 1876.

Dewey, M. *Dewey Decimal Classification and relative index* (19th ed.). B. A. Custer (Ed.). Albany, N.Y.: Forest Press, 1979.

Dowell, A. T. *Cataloging with copy: A decision-maker's handbook.* Littleton, Col.: Libraries Unlimited, 1976.

Dowell, A. T. *AACR2 headings: A five-year projection of their impact on catalogs.* Littleton, Col.: Libraries Unlimited, 1982.

Dunkin, P. S. *Cataloging U.S.A.* Chicago: American Library Association, 1969.

Estabrook, L. The Human dimension of the catalog: Concepts and constraints in information seeking. *Library Resources & Technical Services,* 1983, *27,* 68–75.

Filing rules for the dictionary catalogs of the Library of Congress. Washington, D.C.: Processing Department, 1956.

Gapen, D. K. Cataloging: Workflow and productivity. In A. M. Allison and A. Allan (Eds.), *OCLC: A national library network.* Short Hills, N.J.: Enslow, 1979.

Gorman, M. Fate, time, occasion, chance, and change; or, how the machine may yet save LCSH. *American Libraries,* 1980, *11,* 557–558.

Haykin, D. J. *Subject headings: A practical guide.* Washington, D.C.: U. S. Government Printing Office, 1951.

Hildreth, C. R. *Online public access catalogs: The user interface.* Dublin, Ohio: OCLC, 1982.

Immroth, J. P. *Immroth's guide to the Library of Congress Classification* (3rd ed.). Lois May Chan (Ed.). Littleton, Col.: Libraries Unlimited, 1980.

Information Technology and Libraries. (Vols. 1–) Chicago: Library and Information Technology Association, American Library Association, 1982–.

International Conference on Cataloging Principles, Paris, 1961. *Report.* London: International Federation of Library Associations, 1963.

International Federation of Library Associations and Institutions. Working Group on the General International Standard Bibliographic Description. *ISBD(G): General International Standard Bibliographic Description. Annotated text.* London: IFLA International Office for UBC, 1977.

Jewett, C. C. *On the construction of catalogues of libraries ... with rules and examples.* Washington, D.C.: Smithsonian Institution, 1852.

Johnson, C. A. Retrospective conversion of three library collections. *Information Technology and Libraries,* 1982, *1,* 133–139.

Lancaster, F. W. *The measurement and evaluation of library services.* Arlington, Va.: Information Resources Press, 1977.

Lehnus, D. J. *Book numbers: History, principles, and application.* Chicago: American Library Association, 1980.

Library of Congress. Subject Cataloging Division. *Library of Congress Classification: Classes A–Z.* Washington, D.C.: Author, 1917–.

Library of Congress. Subject Cataloging Division. *L.C. Classification—additions and changes.* Washington, D.C.: Author, 1928–.

Library of Congress. *Rules for descriptive cataloging in the Library of Congress adopted by the American Library Association.* Washington, D.C.: Author, 1949.

Library of Congress. Decimal Classification Division. *Dewey Decimal Classification: Additions, notes and decisions.* Washington, D.C.: Author, 1959–.

Library of Congress. *Library of Congress name headings with references.* Washington, D.C.: Author, 1974–1980.

Library of Congress. Catalog Publication Division. *Name authorities* (Cumulative microform ed.). Washington, D.C.: Author, 1979–.

Library of Congress. *Library of Congress Subject Headings* (9th ed.). Washington, D.C.: Author, 1980. (a)

Library of Congress. Processing Services. *Library of Congress filing rules.* Washington, D.C.: Author, 1980. (b)

Library of Congress. Processing Services. *Authorities, a MARC format.* Washington, D.C.: Author, 1981.

Library of Congress Classification schedules: A cumulation of additions & changes. Detroit: Gale Research, 1982–.

Library of Congress Information Bulletin. Washington, D.C.: Author, 1972–.

Library Resources & Technical services (Vols. 1–). Chicago: ALA Resources and Technical Services Division, 1957–.

LITA Newsletter (No. 1–). Chicago: Library and Information Technology Association, American Library Association, 1980–.

Lubetzky, S. *Cataloging rules and principles.* Washington, D.C.: Processing Department, Library of Congress, 1953.

Lubetzky, S. *Code of cataloging rules, author and title entry: An unfinished draft.* Chicago: American Library Association, 1960.

Mandel, C. A. *Subject access in the online catalog: A report prepared for the Council on Library Resources, Bibliographic Service Development Program.* Washington, D.C.: 1981. (ERIC Document Reproduction Service No. ED 212 286)

MARC formats for bibliographic data. Washington, D.C.: Automated Systems Office, Library of Congress, 1980.

Markey, K. *Analytical review of catalog use studies.* Dublin, Ohio: Online Computer Library Center, Inc., 1980. (ERIC Document Reproduction Service No. ED 186 041)

Maxwell, M. F. *Handbook for AACR2 explaining and illustrating Anglo-American Cataloguing Rules, second edition.* Chicago: American Library Association, 1980.

McCallum, S. H. Some implications of desuperimposition. *Library Quarterly*, 1977, *47*, 111–127.

Miller, R. B. *Name authority control for card catalogs in the General Libraries*. Austin: University of Texas at Austin, The General Libraries, 1981.

Mischo, W. H. Expanded subject access to library collections using computer-assisted indexing techniques. In *Communicating information: Proceedings of the 43rd ASIS annual meeting 1980, v. 17*. White Plains, N.Y.: Knowledge Industry Publications, 1980.

The National union catalog. Washington: Library of Congress, 1956–

The National union catalog, pre-1956 imprints. London: Mansell, 1968–

The Nature and future of the catalog: Proceedings of the ALA's Information Science and Automation Divisions 1975 and 1977 institutes on the catalog. M. J. Freedman and S. M. Malinconico (Eds.). Phoenix: Oryx Press, 1979.

Olson, N. B. *Combined indexes to the Library of Congress Classification schedules*. Washington: United States Historical Documents Institute, 1974.

Osborn, A. D. *Serial publications, their place and treatment in libraries* (2nd ed. rev.). Chicago: American Library Association, 1973.

Osborn, J. *Dewey Decimal Classification, 19th Edition: A study manual*. Littleton, Col.: Libraries Unlimited, 1982.

Retrospective conversion. Washington, D.C.: Systems and Procedures Exchange Center, Office of Management Studies, Association of Research Libraries, 1980. (SPEC Kit, No. 65)

Richmond, P. A. AACR2—a review article. *Journal of Academic Librarianship*, 1980, *6*.

RTSD Newsletter (Vols. 1–). Chicago: Resources and Technical Services Division, American Library Association, 1976–.

Schimmelpfeng, R. H., & Cook, C. D. (Eds.). *The use of the Library of Congress Classification*. Chicago: American Library Association, 1968.

Sears, M. E. *List of subject headings for small libraries* (1st ed.). New York: H. W. Wilson, 1923.

Sears, M. E. *Sears list of subject headings* (12th ed.). Barbara M. Westby (Ed.). New York: H. W. Wilson Co., 1982.

The Serials Librarian. New York: Haworth Press, 1976–.

Serials Review. Ann Arbor: Pierian Press, 1976–.

Scott, J. W. OCLC and management in a medium-sized university library. In A. M. Allison and A. Allan (Eds.), *OCLC: A national library network*. Short Hills, N.J.: Enslow, 1979.

Simonton, W. An introduction to AACR2. *Library Resources & Technical Services*, 1979, *23*, 321–339.

Simonton, W. AACR2: antecedents, assumptions, implementation. In M. H. Harris (Ed.), *Advances in librarianship* (Vol. 10). New York: Academic Press, 1980.

Smith, L. S. *A practical approach to serials cataloging*. Greenwich, Conn.: JAI Press, 1979.

Tucker, B. R. Anglo-American Cataloging Rules, second edition. *Library Resources & Technical Services*, 1978, *22*, 209–226.

Weintraub, D. K. An extended review of PRECIS. *Library Resources & Technical Services*, 1979, *23*, 101–115.

Wellisch, H. H., ed. *The PRECIS index system: Principles, application, and prospects*. New York: H. W. Wilson, 1977.

Wetherbee, L. Planning a retrospective conversion project. In *Retrospective conversion*. Washington, D.C.: Systems and Procedures Exchange Center, Office of Management Studies, Association of Research Libraries, 1980. (SPEC kit, No. 65)

Wiederkehr, R. R. V. *Alternatives for future library catalogs: A cost model. Final report of the Library Catalog Cost Model Project.* Rockville, Md.: King Research, 1980.
Williamson, N. J. Is there a catalog in your future? Access to information in the year 2006. *Library Resources & Technical Services,* 1982, *26,* 122–135.

BIBLIOGRAPHY

Application of the Anglo-American cataloging rules, second edition, in the General Libraries. Austin: The University of Texas at Austin, The General Libraries, 1980.
Authority control: The key to tomorrow's catalog: Proceedings of the 1977 Library and Information Technology Association Institutes. M. W. Ghikas (Ed.). Phoenix: Oryx Press, 1982.
Freezing card catalogs. Washington, D.C.: Association of Research Libraries, 1978.
Malinconico, S. M., & Fasana, P. J., *The future of the catalog: The library's choices.* White Plains, N.Y.: Knowledge Industry Publications, 1979.
The management of serials automation: Current technology & strategies for future planning. Edited with an introduction by P. Gellatly. New York: Haworth Press, 1982.
Saffady, W., *Computer-output microfilm: Its library applications.* Chicago: American Library Association, 1978.
Wynar, B. S. *Introduction to cataloging and classification.* (6th ed., with the assistance of A. T. Dowell and J. Osborn) Littleton, Col.: Libraries Unlimited, 1980.

6 Preservation and Materials Processing

A. Dean Larsen

ORGANIZATION OF PRESERVATION DEPARTMENTS

There is no set pattern for the organization of a library preservation department. Although many preservation functions are performed in all libraries, the assignment of various activities to departments often depends upon organizational structure and tradition in a particular library and also upon available personnel with specific interests in a given aspect of preservation or processing. The preservation department as a separate organizational unit is of recent origin in most libraries, and the patterns of organization vary tremendously across the country. All aspects of processing have a potential impact on the life and maintenance of library materials. Proper procedures and handling are, therefore, more important than a specific organizational structure.

In larger libraries a preservation department may include a binding preparations unit for both monographs and serials, a repair or mending unit, a conservation laboratory, and a microfilming unit. In recent years, as preservation problems have received more emphasis, many libraries have organized preservation departments to deal with the numerous facets of conserving and maintaining collections, often including security, handling, microfilming, disaster preparedness planning, the physical environment, etc.

The Association of Research Libraries' Office of Management Studies (Darling, 1982) published a self-study manual for libraries that outlines the procedures to be followed in initiating a self-study. Although the program is designed for the use of large research libraries, it can, with adaptation, become the guide and basis for implementing a library preservation program. Patterson (1979) presents a model for organizing library preservation programs and stresses that there can be success only if each library develops its own program and organization. Patterson also suggests a committee approach and outlines 10 tasks for a library committee setting up an organizational structure and program:

1. Examine the library's physical environment and make recommendations for enhancement of environmental factors, including an effective monitoring system.
2. Prepare a disaster plan for the library.
3. Examine current handling, bindery, and processing practices, and make recommendations to bring these practices into conformity with accepted conservation principles.
4. Explore avenues which will provide the library with access to professional conservation expertise and facilities.
5. Recommend what in-house physical treatment can be undertaken for minor cleaning and/or repair of materials.
6. Develop an integrated systems approach in responding to material identified as unusable, and develop a systematic number of options as to handling, including a photoreproduction program.
7. Identify possible sources of funding for conservation programs, examining local, regional, and national sources.
8. Establish a clearinghouse of conservation information for in-house and external use.
9. Explore the feasibility of joining cooperative conservation efforts at local, regional, and national levels.
10. The committee will equitably divide the responsibilities for all of the charges listed above, and will accept the responsibility for monitoring the program resulting from the discharge of their responsibilities. (pp. 1117–1118)

Preservation and Binding

Preservation

Preservation is a problem that all libraries face. Although not all libraries can or will attempt to preserve all materials, good managers will preserve materials needed to serve patrons for as long as it is practical. The organizational structure of the library and the degree of support from the library administration can make or break a preservation program. Preservation is a function that affects almost all aspects of both library and archival operations. The organizational structure and the individual in charge of preservation programs must be such that they are not submerged in administrative obscurity, in which there is no influence on library practices and programs.

A successful program may require centralization under the direction of an administrator with a knowledge of binding practices, collection maintenance, and restoration. This applies to small as well as large libraries. In large research libraries the preservation problems become much greater, and in most instances the policy must include preservation and conservation programs to ensure the use of library materials indefinitely. Such programs must be carefully initiated to ensure success with the resources available.

A preservation program does not necessarily mean setting up a preservation department, although that may be the best course of action in a larger library. A successful program does, however, require an administrative organization to establish policies and ensure the implementation of programs as they are established. In one way or another all libraries are involved with preservation whether or not they have a formal preservation program. Any handling of library materials has an effect on their lifetime, including all aspects of processing, marking, circulation, and shelving practices, as well as the total physical environment.

The literature about preservation has grown tremendously over the past 10 years, and libraries can now turn to a large body of technical information previously unavailable. Preservation of library materials is not new; it has, in fact, been a problem since the establishment of the first library in antiquity. Deterioration and decay are part of the inherent factors affecting all organic materials. In order to preserve the knowledge of past generations for the use of future students and scholars, steps can be taken to slow down these natural processes. Well-planned and well-executed preservation programs are essential in order to succeed.

Not all library material can or perhaps should be preserved in its original form. Nor is it possible to economically preserve all library collections. However, large research libraries, with unique materials, have an obligation to establish policies and programs to extend the life of such collections insofar as it is possible. Additionally, not every library will be able to establish a conservation laboratory, but those with the necessary resources must take the lead. Through re-

gional or state cooperative centers, smaller libraries with limited resources will be able in the future to contribute to the preservation
and rescue of our national library and cultural heritage.

The need to acquire the services of a well-trained conservator is
another problem facing many libraries that initiate preservation
programs. There is presently a shortage of personnel available, both
as administrators and as practicing conservators. New programs,
such as the one established at Columbia University in 1981, will
begin to have an impact.

The development of conservation laboratories in American libraries has taken a quantum jump in recent years. A major program
was initiated at the Library of Congress only in 1971. This laboratory
was preceded by the W. J. Barrow Research Laboratory in Richmond, Virginia (1960). Individual conservators have operated both in
America and in Europe, but it was not until the 1966 flood in Florence, Italy, however, that the possibility of major losses of materials
essential to our written cultural heritage became alarmingly apparent.

To understand the problems of preservation, the administrator as
well as the conservator must have a knowledge of (1) the history of
the book and paper, including its chemical makeup; (2) binding materials, including leather and adhesives; (3) effects of the environment
on library collections; (4) commercial binding methods and their effects; and (5) what can or cannot be done to specific library materials, based on a knowledge of restoration practices, techniques, and
products.

Preservation is an expensive operation, and costs for binding and
conservation must be emphasized in library budget requests. Great
sums have been expended in the past quarter-century for library materials, but few libraries have expended adequate funds for preservation. Frazer G. Poole (1972), former head of the preservation depar-
tent for the Library of Congress, suggested a binding budget equal to
25% of the book budget and a budget for restoration and preservation equal to 10% of the book budget. Rogers and Weber (1971, pp.
177–178) suggest a somewhat smaller percentage. These figures need
to be adjusted to match the needs of specific libraries, but the point
is well taken that as a whole most libraries have seriously neglected
preservation.

Conservation is more than just preserving rare books and manuscripts. Procedures should be followed to lengthen the life of all materials, dependent upon the many factors relating to individual items
in the collection. Only the large research library or special library

with archival responsibility will usually attempt to permanently preserve all or part of its collection. In such libraries, highly technical laboratories will be established, with equipment and well-trained personnel to restore and preserve cultural and historical treasures. The Library of Congress is a leader in the field both in its laboratories for research and in its rare book and paper conservation programs. Other such laboratories have been and are being established in many major libraries with large rare book and manuscript collections.

Binding

Binding is an important function in providing the protection that will extend the life of library materials. No library can acquire all of its materials in bound form, so it must in some manner make provisions for binding to preserve or extend the life of materials acquired. Problems and methods vary with each category of library material (e.g., monographs, serials, pamphlets). Few libraries operate extensive in-house binderies today. It is essential that staff members responsible for bindery operations become familiar with all binding procedures and standards in order to select and determine the binding practices to be followed.

In smaller libraries, the practice would generally be to assign a single staff member to prepare materials to be sent to local binders. In large libraries, however, a more complex organization is necessary, and binding preparation operations are often separated according to types of materials—serials, monographs, etc. In addition, larger libraries may operate repair units and conservation laboratories as well.

The choice of a binder is very important. Often commercial binders are selected through competitive bidding. Although there are no required national standards for binding or certification of binders, membership in a national trade association such as the Library Binding Institute does give some guarantee that a binder adheres to high standards as set by and required for membership in the association. D. A. Weiss (1969, pp. 510–512) has reviewed the development of standards, noting that in 1935 the American Library Association issued its first *Minimum Specifications for Class A Library Binds*, and then in 1939, *Standards for Reinforced (Pre-Library Bound) New Books*. Revisions that have been adopted by the Library Binding Institute have occurred over the years. Libraries that are required to ask for competitive bids must often select the lowest bid offered, regardless of quality. Those libraries that can make free selection should consider many additional factors, including quality, service, and pricing schedules. It is usually necessary to carefully spell out specific responsibilities of the bindery and the library; for example, collation, specifications for lettering, financial responsibility for lost or damaged materials, etc.

The binder needs to be prepared to service the amount of material to be bound, and approximate volumes should be specified in a contract. The financial solvency of the bindery and its ability to have on hand sufficient types of cloths and supplies to service a contract are also factors. Shipping costs may be another major factor unless competing binders are nearby. Usually a binder will maintain records of binding style and rubbings to insure uniform style of periodicals and other serials. Some automated serials record systems now produce instructions to the binder on each title. Application of automated serials records for producing binding instructions will become more and more important as library records are put into machine-readable formats.

Binding decisions must be made on the basis of the projected usage and life desired for material to be bound, as they relate to the mission and goals of each library. There is, and should be, considerable divergence. Some material that should be preserved for its historical importance or because of its fragility should not be bound but stored in portfolios, archival boxes, etc. Material added for only temporary use should be treated appropriately to meet its projected usage.

Organization of Binding and Conservation

There is no standard functional organization of binding and preservation in libraries. Traditionally a library operates a binding unit in technical services as a facility to mend books and to facilitate sending materials to a commercial bindery. Processing of serials for binding may have been included in the binding unit, although in many libraries serials binding preparation is often part of a serial department or current periodicals room operation. Consolidated operations are not the norm except in larger research libraries. Far too often the approach to preservation has been haphazard and ineffective, in both major and smaller libraries. Proper organization is imperative if preservation practices are to become effective.

In a large research library a preservation department should be organized with a trained administrator and might have subsections, including a conservation laboratory, book repair unit, preservation microfilming unit, serials binding unit, and others as the operation warrants.

Conservation Laboratory

In recent years conservation laboratories have been established in many research libraries. The Library of Congress has been the leader, both with its Restoration Office and its Research and Testing Office. Conservation laboratories are usually responsible for treatment and preservation of rare books and manuscripts rather than items from circulating collections. The conservator should be a highly trained individual. Peter Waters (cited in Shelley, 1976) stated:

> The enormous complexities of modern library preservation problems cannot be solved unless librarians take the responsibility of ensuring that their collections are receiving the best possible attention. One solution to this is to employ a conservator preferably scholarly with a broad knowledge of librarianship, mathematics, chemistry and physics, the history of culture and of book technology, who also has had a solid physical training in restoration! S/He should either be responsible for or be part of a preservation department which would control everything concerned with preservation. (p. 276)

Repair

Many libraries operate repair or mending units. Circulating materials are normally referred to this unit. Criteria for the repair operation should be carefully planned. The need for repair, both minor and major, will always be present. Repair decisions must be based on knowledge of the book, its importance, construction, and value—both in terms of monetary value and value to the collection of which it is a part. Rare and valuable books needing specialized treatment should always be referred to a conservator. Minor repair techniques for circulating materials can be learned by staff members, but as greater repairs become necessary, such items should be handled by those who are specially trained. Many libraries operate repair units with one or more full-time trained repair technicians supplemented by part-time workers.

Evaluation

Proper evaluation is necessary not only to determine rare and expensive items in general collections, but also to make sensible and proper judgments in repair decisions. In a circulating collection for which the main purpose of repair is to extend the use or life of an item, a number of factors should be considered: (1) Is the title in print and what is the cost of replacement? (2) Are other suitable editions of the title in print or already in the collection? (3) Is the material outdated and should the title be referred as a candidate to be withdrawn rather than repaired? (4) Is the paper brittle and is repair feasible? (5) Should the title be a candidate for preservation microfilming? These and other relevant factors should all be considered in the repair decision. If repairs are to be made, then a trained, knowledgeable technician should make the decision on the type of repair. Cunha (1971), in his chapter on repair and restoration, thoroughly reviews factors to be considered.

Serials Binding

Very few libraries now operate in-house binderies. Some states operate state binderies at which state institutional libraries must have library books bound. Generally, a library must choose a commercial bindery. Care should be taken in the selection of a binder, not only to obtain the most favorable pricing structure, but also to select a binder with high standards and one who follows the standards set forth by the Library Binding Institute.

Oversewing is the binding method most often used in periodical binding. This process gives great strength to the bound volume, but it is less flexible and rebinding or repair is difficult.

Serials binding is often the responsibility of the serials department, but is sometimes assigned to other areas or as a separate department in the organizational structure of libraries. When a preservation department is formed, a serials bindery preparations unit could be one unit of the department. As part of a department whose entire goals are based on preservation practices, the quality control of serials binding could be monitored and improved in some libraries when quality is uneven.

Relationship to Other Departments

Preservation is a library-wide function and is not restricted to only one department or area. All library materials may be damaged through use, mishandling, improper storage, etc. It is only when library-wide programs are organized and administered that there can be major successes in library preservation programs.

Collection Development

The selection of materials is the first rung in the ladder of preservation. Whenever possible, materials in good condition that do not need serious preservation attention should be selected. Materials needing binding or other repairs add immediate costs to library operations. Care should particularly be taken in exchange and gift programs to avoid the acquisition of materials needing repair and binding. In all selection decisions the selector needs to be cognizant of the ramifications of the condition of materials selected.

Catalog Department

The catalog department in its processing of all materials acquired by the library is in an excellent position to detect and route for preservation or binding those items that were not previously routed in the acquisition and receiving processes. All personnel responsible for handling library materials should be familiar with the repair, conservation, and binding policies and practices of the library.

The catalog department usually has the responsibility for marking, labeling, or affixing identification stamps on library materials. Therefore, policies should be established and supervision given so that these processes do not damage library materials.

Circulation

Inasmuch as the circulation department is the principal library department in the handling, shelving, and identification of materials that may need preservation attention, there must be careful coordination between the preservation department and circulation. Circulation staff should be carefully instructed in the handling of library materials, particularly in shelving and by demonstrating correct book handling to patrons. It is often the circulation department that is responsible for dusting and cleaning book stacks. Well-planned housekeeping and handling will prolong the life of library materials as much as any other factor. In addition, book drops should be specifically designed to avoid damage to books and other library materials when returned.

Special Collections, Archives, and Manuscripts

The relationship of the preservation department with special collections is one of the most important. If conservators are on the staff, they must coordinate the selection of items for conservation treatment with the special collections staff, setting forth criteria and schedules. The conservator, who will usually be the most highly trained staff member in preservation techniques, should also be a major resources person in recommending preservation treatment for all library materials as warranted. Most archives and manuscript collections will entail paper conservation; thus many conservation laboratories will have paper conservators as well as book conservators on their staffs.

Preservation Policy Statements

Preservation of a library's collection is as important as the acquisition of the collection. A formal, well-prepared policy statement will, therefore, provide the guidelines necessary for the implementation and carrying out of a preservation program. Like book selection policy statements, the preservation statement should be broadly based and developed with the input of the entire library staff. Preservation policy will affect every library department and future service to library patrons. Morrow (1979) defined preservation as

> The action taken to prevent, stop or retard deterioration: "conservation" means maintaining in usable condition, each item in the collection; and "restoration" implies returning the deteriorated item to its original or near-original condition. "Information preservation," as opposed to preservation of the physical object, consists of reformatting materials in order to preserve their intellectual content. (p. 3)

Morrow (1979) provides an excellent outline of what might be included in a policy statement and also guidelines for organizing a preservation department. Although not specifically a formula for developing a policy, Darling (1982) outlines step-by-step the review of preservation needs in a library. A policy statement would be one of the products of this self-study.

Organization and Personnel

The scope of the library's program, its mission and goals, and its financial resources are major determining factors in establishing a preservation department. At the very least, each library should have a preservation officer, full- or part-time as dictated by the size and scope of the library's collections. In research libraries the staff might include a head of preservation and subunits, each with necessary staff. Morrow (1979, p. 18) provides a basic outline of a conservation department organization. Figure 6.1 is a modification of Morrow's organizational structure.

Staffing a preservation department requires careful recruiting. It may be necessary to assign present, interested staff and provide in-house and workshop or intern training at another institution to initially establish a preservation department or program. A fully organized preservation department will need an administrator with experience or training in preservation practices. Other staff will need appropriate education and training in relevant conservation or microfilming laboratories, binderies, etc., to fulfill their job responsibilities.

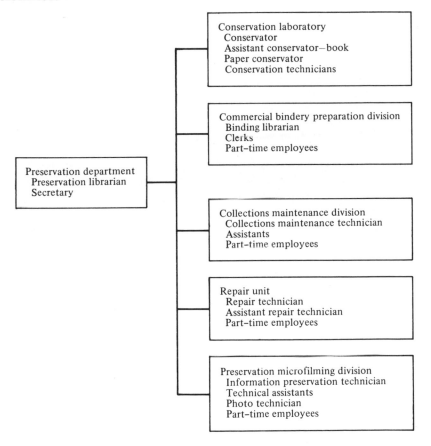

Figure 6.1 Basic organizational model for a preservation department. The preservation department may be a department within technical services or collection development, or report directly to the director of libraries.

PHYSICAL ENVIRONMENT

All library materials will deteriorate and decay with time, but this natural process can be slowed and controlled by taking the necessary steps to regulate the physical environment insofar as possible. Human beings are perhaps the greatest enemy of library collections through abuse and mishandling. However, humans can also produce the means to maximize the major factors affecting the longevity of library collections. Wessel (1970) notes the following environmental factors—many of which can be controlled. Advance planning can minimize the effect of most of those factors over which there is little control. Wessel's list includes

1. The atmosphere (pollution)
2. Light
3. Temperature and its variation
4. Humidity and its variations
5. Insects, rodents, and molds
6. Accidents, vandalism
7. Flood, fire
8. Mechanical failure of control system

Proper environmental care is perhaps one of the most neglected areas of conservation in many libraries. Generally the comfort and convenience of library users are considered without any thought as to their effects on library collections.

Temperature

A review of the literature relating to the temperature indicates that a range of 65 to 75° F (18 to 24° C) is optimum for the storage of most library and museum collections. Wessel (1970, p. 52) notes that with each 10° F (5° C) increase in temperature most chemical reactions approximately double; therefore, the higher the temperature, the faster the deterioration of library collections. Banks (1974) reports that the J. W. Barrow Research Laboratory's long-term data indicate that the colder the temperature, the slower the deterioration of paper. It would, therefore, follow that for storage areas a cooler temperature should be maintained. Public areas need to be kept in a comfort-range of around 72° F (22° C) (Banks, 1974, p. 339). Major deterioration can occur with large, frequent, or quick fluctuations in both temperature and humidity. The range usually recommended is ±5° F (2.5° C). If a larger fluctuation becomes necessary, the changes should be made slowly over a number of days.

Expansion and contraction caused by rapid changes in heat and humidity can cause warping, cracking, drying, and many other reactions. For example, one can note, in just a few hours, changes in vellum bindings as the temperature rises and the humidity lowers.

Generally, other factors combine with heat to cause problems in the library environment. Another example is the lowering of temperatures so rapidly that condensation occurs, with the resultant possibility of moisture damage to library collections. Torrence (1975) states in his article on air conditioning in libraries:

> When one considers the need for reasonable preservation of the collection, that is in the terms of temperature range, relative humidity, degree of filtration of dust and sulphur content—together with the lucky coincidence that people and books require about the same environmental conditions—all lead to the suggestion that the only system that can embrace the above is air-conditioning. (p. 200)

Building planners should become more conversant with preservation factors in order to communicate the special needs, to architects and funding agencies, of new library buildings and in the refurbishing of older structures that lack adequate environmental controls.

Humidity

There is less agreement on the optimal humidity for the storage of library materials. One notes variations in the literature from 30 to 65% RH (relative humidity). Banks (1974) recommends 50% RH but notes that the Library of Congress recommendation is 40–50% and that the British Museum Library's standard is 55–65%. Banks (1974) states:

> Fluctuations in humidity seem to be considerably more serious even than fluctuations in temperature; certainly some of the effects of extreme changes in humidity are quite evident on the visible level, as distinct from variations in temperature whose effects are more on the microscopic or molecular level. Variations should certainly be kept within + or − 6 percent from the level decided upon, and closer control would undoubtedly be desirable if economically and technologically feasible. (p. 340)

Wessel (1970) describes the importance of water in most chemical reactions and the problems that can occur if the air is either too dry or too wet. Both temperature and humidity together largely determine the rate of deterioration. A certain moisture level is necessary to maintain most leather, paper, and other library materials in a pliable state, or drying, cracking, and brittleness will occur. On the other hand, too much moisture can cause damage to adhesives and some paper starches and bring about attacks of mold and fungi.

Air Impurities

Air conditioning is, of course, the principal means of controlling temperature and humidity, and the only material means of controlling and cleaning the air in a building. A number of filtration processes are available, and careful study should be made in planning new buildings or adding atmospheric control systems to older buildings. Wessel (1970, p. 43) lists the following atmospheric substances considered as pollutants:

Particulate Matter (Aerosols)	Gases
Dust, dirt, smoke	Carbon monoxide
Coal and coke dust	Nitric oxide
Fly ash	Nitrous oxide
Salt particles	Sulfur dioxide
Calcium and ammonium sulfates	Ozone
Nitrates	Olefins
Clorides	Aromatic hydrocarbons
Solid oxides	Aldehydes
Soot	Paraffins
Tars	Hydrogen sulfide
Spores	Halogen compounds
Bacteria	Ammonia

Those substances that can cause the greatest damage to library materials are the oxidizing and the acidic agents. Banks (1974) states that "All impurities in the air are harmful to books. The most serious gaseous pollutant is sulfur dioxide, but also important are oxidants such as nitrogen oxides and ozone. These should be removed entirely from the air entering the library" (p. 340)

Cunha (1971) notes that the most practical method to control pollutants, temperature, and humidity is through central air conditioning. Such systems are usually most efficient where they are part of the design of new buildings, but they can also be installed in already existing structures. Filtering will clear the air of most of its contaminants. Passing incoming air through a water spray is also effective, but electrostatic precipitation is not usually recommended for libraries because of the formation of ozone and nitrogen oxides.

Light

According to Dureau (1979):

> Light in all forms promotes the decay of organic materials; ultraviolet light is the most dangerous. Light levels must, therefore, be kept as low as possible, both in storage and in use conditions. Storage conditions should ideally be dark, but if in natural light all windows should be overlaid with UV filters and provision should be made (e.g., with blinds) to reduce any heat gain. It may be necessary to provide UV filters for artificial lighting. In reading rooms the light level falling on library materials should not be more than 100 lux (and preferably UV filtered). In exhibition cases the constant level falling on the surface of library materials should not be more than 50 lux and all lighting must be UV filtered. Lighting level and the UV content of light should be measured (standard photometer and UV monitor) in all areas containing library materials. (p. 5)

Light as a problem in preservation of library materials is often overlooked. Inasmuch as library materials are housed indoors, direct sunlight is not a great problem except from exposure through windows, skylights, etc. Shades, tinted glass, or filters should be used as necessary to protect materials. Incandescent lights do not need filters, but fluorescent lights should be filtered.

Cunha (1971) includes in his appendix a chapter on the physics of light, which is recommended reading. Although damage by light cannot be entirely eliminated, it can be minimized. Banks (1974) summarizes:

> My specific recommendations regarding lighting are: as a guiding principle, lighting levels should be kept as low as is consistent with efficiency of the activity involved wherever library materials are stored, used or displayed (including those hung on walls). In these areas any fluorescent lighting should be protected with UV filtering sleeves. Switches with timed shut-offs might be considered in stack areas. The question of lighting for use should be considered as the purview of a light engineer and not that of the conservator. (p. 341)

Insects, Rodents, and Fungi

Insects

Cunha (1971) notes that there are more than 70 varieties of insects that can be destructive to library materials. The most common are cockroaches, silverfish, termites, book lice, bookworms, mud wasps, and moths. The problem of insects is less of a problem in the continental United States, particularly in the northern states, than in many other parts of the world. Problems with insects are particularly acute in tropical and subtropical climates. All libraries can be vulnerable through the introduction of insects in new acquisitions. Incoming materials should be monitored and fumigated as warranted.

Poor housekeeping, excessive moisture, darkness, etc., may all contribute to insect problems. Insects should generally not be a problem in newer libraries, with modern buildings equipped with air conditioning or ventilation systems, temperature control, and proper lighting. Even with these advances some species may flourish in spite of cleanliness and ideal or nearly ideal moisture and temperature levels and will, therefore, need to be controlled. Weiss (1945) reviews the history of insect enemies of books, noting that Aristotle, writing in his *Historia Animalium,* described insect attacks on books as did Pliny, other classical writers, and Robert Hooke in his *Micrographia* published in 1665. Plumbe (1964) reviews some of the early methods used to control and eradicate insects but notes their ineffectiveness until the development of insecticides in modern times. Gallo (1963) addresses more recent advances in the use of insecticides.

There are hundreds of species of cockroaches, but only a few pose a problem for libraries. They are most commonly found in tropical and subtropical climates and attack paste and glue in book covers. They excrete a dark liquid that discolors pages or other objects over which they crawl. Silverfish, like cockroaches, are attracted to glue and paste and will eat through covers to get at adhesives. They thrive in cool, damp areas and are generally not a problem in dry, well-ventilated places or among books in frequent use. Termites are more common in tropical and subtropical climates but also appear even in far northern climates. They eat cellulose and will attack all papers. Termites can be difficult to detect because they eat into the interior of objects, leaving only an outer shell.

Book lice, also called psocids, occur frequently in old, damp, musty volumes. They thrive best in warm, damp rooms that are not often disturbed. Book lice are generally not a problem in well-ventilated areas. Some authors have not considered them a menace to books, but Cunha (1971) notes that more recent investigation has proven book lice to be destructive to books, papers, and photographs —not just mere nuisances.

Cunha (1971, p. 80) notes that "bookworm" is a generic term for hundreds of beetles found throughout the world. They lay their eggs on the outer edges of books; after hatching, the larvae eat . . . (tunnel) into the pages and covers. Bookworms have been known since ancient times, attacking papyri in Egypt, and in modern times, destroying emulsions on film. They can be a problem in all climates. Mud wasps are not a problem in North America, but in parts of South America, Asia, and Africa their nests on the rear edges of books will seal the pages as well as cement books to the shelves. The brown house moth, common throughout North America and other parts of the world, will attack book cloth and leather.

Insects are not a major problem in most North American libraries. Weiss (1945) notes that cleanliness, awareness, and periodic inspections easily control insects and that they can be eradicated by fumigation or the application of insecticides. Good housekeeping practices are most important, including the removal of food residues that attract insects. The danger of introducing insects through acquisition of old collections must also be monitored.

Rodents

Rodents can potentially be a problem in libraries. Rats and mice can do tremendous damage to stored papers and books. Proper housekeeping practices and eradication programs should eliminate this potential problem altogether.

Fungi

"Mildew or mold are interchangeable terms to describe those fungi which, living in or on organic tissues obtain their food by sending root-like organs (hyphae) into the host's cells" (Cunha, 1971, p. 84). Fungi are a major problem in tropical and subtropical climates with high temperatures and high humidity. The problem will not occur in well-ventilated or air-conditioned libraries. Damage can be extensive, but the spores can be killed through proper conservation treatment. One problem in controlling fungi is their capability of remaining dormant for long periods of time, then becoming active when temperature and humidity become favorable. Cunha (1971) and Plumbe (1964) both provide good reviews of the effects of mold on various types of paper and leather.

In the event of a major or even a minor disaster in which water is introduced into library materials, the growth of mold can be a major problem (see the section "Water Damage").

Disasters

"A disaster . . . is an event whose timing is unexpected and whose consequences are seriously destructive" (Bohem, 1978, p. 1). The consequences may be a result of floods, earthquakes, fire, vandalism, etc. Damage may be large and far reaching, as in the flood in Florence in 1966, or may be limited to a few volumes of soaked books from a leaking water pipe. To salvage and preserve that which should and must be saved will be largely dependent upon disaster preparedness plans that are developed and ready for implementation.

Libraries, regardless of size, should make plans to be followed in case of a disaster in order to save those items or collections predetermined to have regional or national significance as part of our cultural heritage. Large research libraries with rare collections of books and manuscripts are particularly vulnerable. Many factors affect the type of program to follow should a disaster occur, including replacement possibilities and capabilities weighed against the cost of restoration. Unique items that form part of our cultural heritage should have first priority in preservation programs following a disaster.

Bohem (1978, p. 3) recommends a disaster prevention team as the first step in disaster preparedness. Disaster preparedness planning includes meetings with all relevant personnel—police, fire chief, building marshals, relevant members of the library staff, and officers of the parent institution. This team should prepare a written disaster manual, listing names of those to be called and procedures to be followed. The manual records local facilities for restoration, drying, freezing, etc. The team should plan for the acquisition of needed supplies to meet the needs of repair and/or restoration of what might be accomplished in house. Emergency facilities should be listed and contacts should be made with regional and/or national agencies who can assist in the event of a major disaster.

Major disasters such as earthquakes and floods cannot be prevented, but preventive action can be initiated to diminish the effects and/or eliminate many potential disaster occurrences. Shelving can be anchored to prevent a domino effect of shelving falling in a minor earthquake in areas that might be subject to such occurrences. Regular maintenance of facilities in which plumbing leaks might occur should be undertaken. Good maintenance and housekeeping can result in the avoidance of many problems that might lead to major damage of library collections.

Water Damage

Water damage may occur as a result of a leak, flood, wetting caused by fire control, plumbing problems, etc. Water damage can be complicated, depending on where the water came from. In a flood, oil and mud are usually introduced. In the case of a fire, other debris might also be present.

The action to be taken after water damage occurs depends upon the extent of the damage and the volume of material to be treated. Conventional drying methods can be used if staff, facilities, and supplies are immediately available and if the volume is not too great to be accomplished within a few days. The growth of mold will usually begin to occur within a few days; the cooler the wetted items, the slower the growth. One of the best ways to inhibit mold growth is by freezing. Storing books frozen not only will inhibit the growth of mold but will allow staff time to gradually bring out the volumes for drying and restoration in the case of large numbers of wet books.

There are several methods for drying water-soaked books, but all should be administered by a conservator. A manual prepared by the Library of Congress Preservation Office in 1972, *Emergency Procedures for Salvaging Flood or Water Damaged Library Materials*, is an excellent guide on procedures to be followed. Drying methods include conventional air drying, freeze drying, and vacuum drying. Buchanan (1979) reports the success of a large-volume vacuum drying project to dry the books damaged in the Stanford University Library flood of 1979. Vacuum and freeze drying both necessitate the use of elaborate equipment that may not be accessible or practical for the drying of smaller numbers of books. On the other hand, conventional drying requires a sufficiently large area, with good circulation, for the needed staff and supplies. In order to avoid mold growth, books that are not disbound and are placed on drying racks need to be interleaved with thymol-impregnated absorbent paper. Spawn (1973) states that when proper salvage operations are immediately put into effect, it is possible to save almost all items.

Fire

Most librarians are complacent about the possibility of fire, and many misconceptions are prevalent concerning the effect of fire on book collections. Some think that books do not readily burn and that greater damage will occur from water used to extinguish fires. Apart from total consumption, great damage can occur from smoke, heat, and residue from other objects used in building construction. Many plastics used in modern construction burn at very high temperatures; paper will become brittle and residues of plastic may melt over volumes and cement the pages, making them unusable.

The number of major library fires in history is not small, and many treasures of cultural heritage have thus been lost. All know of the loss of the great Alexandrian library, the fires at the Library of Congress in the nineteenth century, and a number of fires in American university libraries in the late 1960s. The Library Technology Project of the American Library Association (1963) reported its study of 359 library fires between 1911 and 1961. The major causes were as follows: electrical failure, 29%; housekeeping and operations, 27%; heating plants, 23%; and other (lightning, arson, etc.), 21%.

Good housekeeping practices, including the proper disposal of waste and the maintenance of electrical systems, as well as not overloading circuits with the many additional electrically operated machines now used in libraries, can reduce potential fire hazards. Arson is a problem that cannot be predicted and for which there are few safeguards.

Fire prevention can be successful if a prevention program is established and carried out on a regular and continuing basis. The first consideration should be for human life. Each library should have a detailed evacuation plan that includes staff training on the procedures to be followed. Detection devices that will respond to heat, smoke, or other products of combustion are important. Such devices should be tied into an alarm system to notify security and fire department personnel, as well as to alert library staff and patrons of a fire danger.

Lowell (1979) notes that detection devices can be installed that recall elevators, shut down building ventilation systems, and initiate protective actions automatically. Suppression systems, including automatic sprinklers, can be automatically activated. Although the installation of sprinkling systems in libraries has been questioned because of potential water damage, current thinking still finds sprinklers the most effective fire suppression system. (General Services Administration, 1977, p. 21.)

Modern salvage technology for water-damaged materials has been developed to a high degree of success. Potential damage of fire and resultant dangers from high temperatures from the burning of modern building materials can be much greater than damage from a sprinkling system. Gaseous suppression systems are also available.

The Halon 1301 system, although expensive, is appropriate for rare book or manuscript vault areas of a library. Hand extinguishers should be readily available for use, and staff should be trained in their operation.

Disaster Planning

A well-organized, written disaster plan should be completed by all libraries and updated on a regular basis. Precautionary and emergency procedures should be outlined to effectively handle any emergencies that may arise to threaten the destruction of library materials. Bohem's (1978) manual is an excellent guide in planning for a disaster. This manual presents a model that could be followed in developing a disaster plan. The Association of Research Libraries (1980) has issued its SPEC Kit *Preparing for Emergencies and Disasters*, which also provides some excellent information and formulas to be followed in disaster planning.

A major factor in the planning and implementation of a disaster plan is the involvement of library staff. The staff should be thoroughly oriented, including educational programs on the procedures to be followed in the event of a disaster. The staff must be well trained and aware of their primary and secondary responsibilities. The written disaster plan or emergency manual should give detailed procedures, including personnel to be contacted. There will be a much greater potential for success in decreasing the damaging effects of a disaster if planning has been thorough.

Lowell (1979) emphasizes that frustration need not occur in the event of a disaster if preparation in advance has occurred.

> When a library collection is damaged by a disaster or when vandals mutilate or steal parts of it, the natural reaction for every librarian is to feel anger, shock and frustration. Such human emotions are justified. The feeling which is not justified is helplessness. Disaster preparedness offers an alternative to helplessness. Disaster preparedness is a carefully considered series of policies, procedures and action steps which are designed to minimize a damage situation and enable a library administrator and staff to cope in time of crisis effectively. (p. 6)

Insurance

Loss from a major or minor disaster can have a tremendous effect on library operations if the losses cannot be recovered. Insurance can be highly complicated in its management, but its necessity cannot be overemphasized. In addition to the building and its contents, the possibility of litigation due to personal claims is ever present. Liability insurance is very important, as Gosnell (1974) suggests, "A slight tripping over a carpet or a fall on a stairway may result in an award that would make a severe dent in the library budget, or even take a sizeable chunk of endowment" (reprinted from Gosnell, 1974, p. 161, by courtesy of Marcel Dekker, Inc.).

Libraries are usually a part of a larger governmental or institutional organization and as a result may often be self-insured. Trelles (1973) cautions:

> This type of decision, of course, can be reached only by those in charge of administering the destinies of any given library. No general statement can be made either in favor of or against such a theory. However, in order to reach that decision, a very careful study of the individual assets of the given institution should be undertaken. Such a study would clearly reveal whether or not that institution could stand a loss of a given substantial amount of money without being insured. (p. 248)

There must be communication and coordination between the librarian, the parent agency, and its business or insurance agent to keep everyone informed about the current and ever-increasing value of library collections, as well as the physical facilities, including furniture and equipment. Self-insurance may not mean insurance in the usual sense. Reserve funds may be set up by the parent institution to cover major risks to property. Unless such reserves are sufficient, a library may not be able to recover losses from a major disaster. When insurance is carried, there will usually be certain deductables to reduce claims for insignificant damage. Rare books and manuscripts over a certain value may need to be scheduled, but for other collections, an average cost per volume can usually be calculated.

The library building and its potential destruction by fire are usually the focus of insurance attention. Thus, bringing a building up to fire codes, including detection devices, sprinkling system, etc., is very important in reducing danger. Good housekeeping practices cannot be overemphasized in avoiding risks not only for minor disasters, but also in the event of injury to individuals. The National Fire Protection Association issued in 1979 a new edition of *Protection of Library Collections* that contains an excellent checklist of principles of fire safety in construction and maintenance of libraries.

Insurance coverage varies greatly from company to company and as a result of various state insurance regulations. The Committee on Insurance of the American Library Association has attempted to compile information and establish standards for library insurance;

their publications should be reviewed when establishing a library insurance program.

Gosnell (1974) concludes his excellent review of library insurance by stating:

> It is well to recognize and remember that all losses, whatever the intermediate arrangement for compensation or spreading the risk, are losses to society as a whole and are eventually paid for by the public at large. Insurance is a fine device for softening the blows of loss, but is not in itself productive. Productivity occurs when the losses are prevented, and society is therefore so much the richer. (reprinted from Gosnell, 1974, pp. 168–169, by courtesy of Marcel Dekker, Inc.).

PROCESSING AND PRESERVATION PROCEDURES

All materials acquired for library use must be prepared for inhouse use or circulation. The type and placement of materials will dictate some of the methods to be used for identification, processing, and circulation procedures.

Marking and Identification

Circulating materials will need an identification stamp or label, as well as spine labels for shelving. Care should be taken to avoid defacing materials, and stamping should be concise and neatly applied. There is a wide variance in the application of identifying marks on library books, but the usual standard is an identification stamp on the verso of the title page and on the inside front cover. Some libraries also stamp the edges of books or a selected page inside. Bookplates may be used to identify gifts and specific collections, but should be applied neatly and generally should not cover presentation inscriptions of previous owners or bookplates of former owners. Call numbers are usually printed on labels that are affixed to the spine of the book, but some libraries use ink or a stylus. These latter methods are more difficult to correct or remove in the case of necessary changes to the call number or if books are withdrawn. Many libraries affix date-due slips and pockets on the inside front or back cover for circulation purposes. The use of paper clips to hold date-due slips or processing slips is discouraged as there is always resultant damage to the page, especially if the clip is left in for a long period of time.

Books for special collections or rare books should always have special handling, and markings should be kept to a minimum. Mate-

rials in a secure area, such as a vault, may need very minimal marking, that is, a slip with call number for shelving purposes and a
tipped-in label or small stamp (not on the title page) for identification.

Some libraries, particularly school and public libraries, cover
books with plastic book jackets to lengthen their service. It is also
possible through jobbers or commercial cataloging service agencies
to acquire processing with completed book cards, spine labels, etc.,
ready to be placed in the book or on other library materials. The use
and manner of application of all marking devices will have an ultimate impact on the preservation of the book or other library items,
and procedures should, therefore, be taken to identify as necessary
but not to damage or deface. Embossing and perforations have historically been used, but this practice has been almost totally discontinued in libraries due to objections because of its defacement of title pages. Circulation records are now often automated, and a bar
code may be necessary for reading with a wand for circulation
records.

Security and Theft Detection

Every library must be conscious of the probability of theft, mutilation, and vandalism. Perhaps realistically there is no way to avoid
some problems, but measures should be taken to bring as much control to protecting library collections from theft and/or multilation,
as with other factors in the preservation of library collections.
Again, only through the planning, cooperation, and training of the
library administration and the education of the entire staff can there
be success. Not many libraries are aware of the extent of loss by both
theft or mutilation. Physical inventories are expensive, and in many
large libraries, extensive inventories may not have been taken in
many years. A continuing inventory program should be established
that identifies missing materials.

Circulation systems are necessary to maintain records of materials not on the shelves and to regulate the loan of items for library collections. Lax surveillance at circulation departments may allow uncharged books to leave the library; this potentially causes patron
inconvenience, as the library would be unable to indicate when an
item might be returned for other partons' use. Most likely, many who
leave the library with uncharged books mean to return them ultimately, but an operation without a viable, well-run circulation system would soon mean chaos. Daugherty, Gapen, Keller, and Miller

(1977) isolated five major factors possibly contributing to a high rate of book theft: the library, academic pressure, individual personality, social and psychological pressures, and the general criminal framework of theft:

> The library factor included such items as insufficient copies of highly desirable books, circulation restrictions, availability of copy machines, fine rates, and book selection policies. The variables within the academic dimension include academic pressure to succeed, class assignment requirements on a limited collection, and the pressure of scholastic achievement in association with freedom of access to persons who are not permitted to borrow. The factor of individual personality is exemplified by the desire to own. Variables within the social and psychological factor include inadequate personal funds to purchase desired books, peer group pressure, revolt against large organizations, or a rebellious act to assert individuality. Finally, the general criminal framework of theft includes such considerations as whether or not the behavior is systematic and habitual, or premeditated rather than spontaneous; is the definition of book theft one in which the behavior is not considered as seriously deviant or illegal, and is it the user's opinion that the librarian does not view book theft within the criminal context of such words as steal, theft, or deviant. (pp. 1–2)

Jenkins (1982) lists five basic types of book thieves:

1. The kleptomaniac, who cannot overcome a compulsion to steal
2. The thief who steals for personal use
3. The thief who steals in anger
4. The casual thief
5. The thief who steals for profit

Preventing book thefts is a very complex problem that cannot be totally overcome. It must be the responsibility of each library to secure its collections insofar as possible. Like a general preservation policy, a security policy should be written. Jenkins (1982) recommends that a security officer be appointed from among senior staff members to carry out the security program and that:

> A policy on the security of the collections should be written by the security officer, in consultation with the administration, staff, legal authorities, and other knowledgeable persons. The policy should include a "standing operating procedure" on dealing with possible theft; deterring suspected thieves reporting thefts to the proper authorities within an organization, and to the local legal authorities. (Sec. II)

As a major deterrent to theft, thousands of theft detection systems have been installed in libraries in recent years. Knight (1979, p. 221) reports an increase from approximately 2100 systems in 1976 to 6600 systems in operation in 1979. The purpose of such systems is to identify books or other library materials that are being removed from the library without authorization. All such systems use a type of sensitive material inserted in the spine or other places which, when not desensitized, will sound an alarm or close a gate when passed through an enclosure set up for detection. Knight reviews the five systems now on the market, including completed questionnaires by the manufacturing companies and a number of library users. Knight (1979) concludes by stating:

> In selecting a theft detection system, a library must identify the special needs of his or her own library, staff, and patrons, and match these needs with the specifications supplied by the manufacturers. There is no one perfect system— all have both advantages and limitations. Nor will any one of the systems totally eliminate all theft. They will certainly serve as successful deterrents to the absentminded patron who has simply forgotten to charge out library materials, but as indicated earlier, the skilled and determined thief can beat any of the systems. (p. 234)

Other factors play a role in stopping theft. Security devices and adequate locks are important. Access points should be as limited as is practical. Windows should also be secure. One library reported that patrons regularly used windows for "long-term circulation." Alarm systems for larger libraries, especially those with rare book and manuscript collections, are also desirable. Doors and accessible windows should be alarmed. Motion detection systems are also recommended. If possible, the alarm system should be tied in with the dispatcher of a local police or security office. The public should not have access to processing areas in which unmarked and unprocessed books and other materials might be easily obtainable. Reading rooms for rare books and manuscripts should have an attendant on duty who can see patrons at all times. Users should be requested to present current photographic identification and should not be allowed to carry personal materials, such as notebooks, briefcases, and coats, in to reading rooms for rare books and manuscripts.

In discussing possible problems of thefts by members of the staff, Jenkins (1982) states:

> An atmosphere of trust and mutual concern for the collections is probably the best insurance against theft by staff, although close and equitable supervision is essential. The staff should be chosen carefully, and background checks should be made at the time of hiring. Bonding of the staff should be considered. A major weak point in any security system is disgruntled staff who may seek revenge through the destruction of collections. Staff should know their responsibility for security and know their legal rights in handling possible problems. Staff should also adhere to the same security procedures as readers, in general, including keeping records of use of materials by staff, checking their belongings when leaving the secure area, and keeping unnecessary personal items out of the secure work areas. The security officer should consider training the staff in security measures a high priority. (sec. V)

Another major problem in libraries is mutilation. More effective theft detection systems may have increased mutilation, but there seems to be no concrete evidence to date. It was also projected that the availability and easy access to copy machines in libraries would reduce mutilation. Weiss (1981) reports little effect of the availability of copy machines on decreasing mutilation. Weiss concludes that some university students who mutilate or remove pages and also steal library books do so because of academic pressures. Whatever the reason, mutilation is a continuing problem and one not easy to solve.

Scott (1980) suggests the following techniques or policies to reduce theft and mutilation:

1. Installing duplicating machines for public use that are as inexpensive as possible for the patron
2. Purchasing multiple copies of popular titles
3. Increasing the number and variety of items that a patron can check out at a time
4. Making it easier for patrons to acquire a library card
5. Circulating older copies of various reference tools like dictionaries, almanacs, atlases, and encyclopedias
6. Making the check-out process as speedy and as pleasant as possible by having enough staff at the circulation desk during busy times
7. Insisting that staff be as friendly and as helpful as possible so that patrons feel comfortable and welcome
8. Making it possible for a patron to check out materials at any library in the system rather than at the library specifically set up in that person's service area
9. Having a reasonable loan period for all items
10. Making it possible for a patron to renew loans over the phone
11. Having convenient points for book-return outlets
12. Increasing the number of hours and days that the library is open
13. Arranging library hours around the convenience of the patron rather than the staff (pp. 29–30)

Many of these factors can reduce security problems, but they also take more staff time and more funds for implementation. They can, however, bring extended service to the library patron—for which reason the library operates.

Photoduplication

Copying of library materials as a service to patrons has tremendously increased in recent years. There are few libraries that do not provide copy service to library users today. Photocopying is a tremendous time saver to patrons, who formerly had to copy by hand material needed for research. It also provides quick and easy dissemination of information for interlibrary loan of periodical articles, etc., without the danger, expense, and inconvenience to other patrons of loaning the bound volumes.

Libraries must be aware of copyright laws and their revisions, but more important from the preservation point of view is the handling of books in making photocopies. Serious damage is possible if books are not carefully handled. When pressure is applied to flatten the pages for copying, the spine can easily be broken. A particular problem exists with bound volumes of periodicals that have been oversewn. Centralized copy centers with trained and supervised personnel would ensure the least amount of damage, but in practice most libraries also have coin-operated copy machines for direct patron use. Patrons should be requested to handle books carefully while making copies through instruction, posters, and signs.

Restoration and Preservation

Survey of Collection

In order to design a viable preservation program, a survey of the collection is necessary to compile information about the preservation needs of the collection as a whole and also to consider individual subcollections. The information obtained can then be used to plan conservation programs in terms of priorities for treatment and estimating costs of personnel, materials, and physical facilities. Surveys may be approached by any number of categories that are determined to have the greatest need of preservation or are the most important to a particular library's collection. The approach might be by classification, date or place of publication, serials, selected subject categories, language, etc.

Ultimately each individual item must be examined to determine preservation needs, but in an initial survey of the collection, a random sample can be used. In a survey, the collection data would be collected on volumes needing rebinding (commercial or inhouse); volumes with brittle or highly acidic paper, mold or mildew, or insect damge; mutilated or incomplete volumes; unbound materials needing binding; minor repairs; and broken bindings, including loose or broken stitching, loose spines or hinges, etc. Care must be used in visual examination programs that do not remove items from the shelves; deteriorating paper and bindings are not always apparent to the eye. Few if any libraries can afford to preserve all items in a collection. So, in addition to identifying materials needing preservation, an evaluation process must also be concurrently planned to determine that which is to be deaccessioned, converted to microform, repaired, or preserved.

Evaluations might also extend to include studies on cleanliness, shelving practices, temperature and humidity fluctuation, lighting, etc., all of which have an influence on potential deterioration. The information to be sought must be carefully planned in order to facilitate a study that is neither too time consuming nor too expensive. Surveys should also be planned to avoid overtaxing the expertise of available survey staff, but with enough detail to establish conditions to enable planning for future preservation programs. Darling (1982, pp. 59–70) in her manual on preservation planning presents a detailed outline for surveying the physical condition of library collections.

Repair Evaluation

The decision to repair a volume must be made for each individual item, taking into account the many factors involved in the relevance of that item to the library and its total collection, as well as the cost of repair. Tauber (1972) states, "Few if any libraries have the funds to provide the optimum care for all the materials in their collections. Decisions must constantly be made as to which materials are to be given priority. Hence, the classification of materials must proceed in accordance with function or end-use of materials" (pp. 20–21). Each item referred for repair must be evaluated as a necessary part of the whole collection. The following factors should be considered:

1. Currency of information
2. Artifactual value or rarity
3. Replacement availability, that is, reprint or another edition
4. Condition of item, including binding, paper, sewing, etc.
5. Possibility of converting to microfilm
6. Cost of repair
7. Withdrawal from collection

When all such factors have been considered, the item should then be referred to the library repair unit, microfilming unit, conservation laboratory, or acquisition department for order replacement, etc., as appropriate. A policy and procedure manual should be prepared that gives specific instructions for the evaluation of items referred from circulation or new acquisitions, including gifts, and so forth. Coordination is necessary with all units or agencies in the preservation processes. Once an item has been determined to be of permanent value in the collection and referred to appropriate units for preservation, additional evaluation will be necessary as to treatment.

General Repair and Rebinding

Many items may only need a minimal amount of repair, such as mending simple tears, tipping in loose pages, recasing (if sewing and covers are sound), cleaning, etc. Care must be taken not to overtreat, as incorrectly applied repairs may cause serious problems in rebinding or preservation at a later date. In-house repair units may also be capable of rebinding, including resewing, making new cases, etc. Smaller libraries may have to send such materials to a commercial binder. Some categories of materials will probably be sent to commercial binders by larger libraries because of volume, lack of equipment, or trained personnel to adequately rebind in house.

Tauber (1972) lists the following as processes that may be carried on in an in-house binding and repair unit of a library:

a. *Mending.* Restoration, not involving replacement with any new material or the separation of book from cover. (For example, the mending of a tear in a page or the tipping in of a loose leaf.)
b. *Repairing.* Partial rehabilitation of a worn volume, the amount of work done being less than the minimum involved in rebinding and more then the maximum involved in mending. (For example, the repairing of the cover cloth or restoring loose leaf corners.)
c. *Reinforcing.* Strengthening the structure of a weakened volume, usually by adding material. (For example, the strengthening of a hinge with cloth or the reinforcing of a page by covering it with tissue.)
d. *Recasing.* Replacing the cover on a volume which has come out of its cover or has loosened in its cover, the sewing and cover being still in good condition.
e. *Rebacking.* Attaching a new shelf back on a volume without any other binding.
f. *Re-covering.* The process of making a new cover and of attaching it to the volume.
g. *Re-sewing.* The process of taking the volume out of its cover, removing the old sewing, sewing anew, and replacing in the same cover. (p. 25)

Paper Impurities and Brittle Paper

Brittle books are a major problem in all libraries, and the literature on this problem has multiplied over the past two decades, particularly since the pioneering research of William James Barrow at his laboratory in Richmond, Virginia. Smith (1969), in his paper entitled "Paper Impermanence as a Consequence of pH and Storage Conditions," presents a thorough discussion of the literature and history of the introduction of impurities (acid content) in paper manufacture in the nineteenth and twentieth centuries. Cunha (1971) states:

> Major sources of acid in paper are sulphur dioxide in polluted air, lignin in wood pulp, alum-rosin sizes, residual bleaching chemicals, iron gall ink, and migration from other materials. Leather is acidified by chemicals added during manufacture, by absorption of sulphur dioxide from polluted air, or by migration of acid from other acidified materials. (p. 89)

The gravity of this problem is illustrated by such reports as the Barrow laboratory study (Church, 1959) that sampled nonfiction books printed and published in the United States from 1900 to 1959. This study indicated that a high percentage had a useful life of 50 years or less. Frazer G. Poole (1976), the chief preservation officer for the Library of Congress, reported that there are 6 million volumes in its collections, "so brittle they cannot be given to a user without significant risk or damage" (p. 444). Such dramatic reports have emerged from a number of other research libraries. Not all such volumes must be physically preserved. The content of many may be preserved through conservation microfilming programs. Physical conservation will vary widely from library to library, depending upon the importance of specific volumes to each library's collection.

Deacidification

Embrittlement of paper resulting from deterioration due to acid content is one of the major problems facing all libraries. Deacidification is the process of reducing the acidity of paper to a neutral or alkaline state. A number of methods are effective, but they can only arrest continued deterioration of acid, not restore paper to its original state. Barrow (1976) developed a method in the 1940s that involved bathing the paper first in a solution of calcium hydroxide to neutralize the acid, followed by bathing it in calcium bicarbonate to add buffering agents. A later method was developed using magnesium bicarbonate which both neutralized the acid and alkalized the paper.

The principal drawback to aqueous methods for deacidification of books is the necessity to disbind, treat one sheet at a time, and follow by drying, resewing, and rebinding. There may also be problems with inks, fragility of paper, etc. These processes should be undertaken only by trained conservators conversant with the chemistry and techniques involved and having a thorough knowledge of the materials to be treated.

A number of nonaqueous processes have been developed, but most have not had widespread adoption because of toxicity or the flammability of the chemicals used. Harris (1979) describes a number of these processes as well as the process developed by Richard D. Smith and marketed by Wei T'O. Associates, Inc. and the morpholine process developed by the Barrow Laboratories. Smith (1979) states:

> Deacidification and mass deacidification method in particular are necessary because:
> 1. Essentially all library records are printed on paper.
> 2. Acid attack causes 80 to 95 percent of this deterioration in libraries. Deacidification is the only known cure.
> 3. Deacidification must be mechanized to reduce unit costs and to provide a substitute for non-available personnel.
> 4. Collections are deteriorating so rapidly that they will be lost if preventive measures are not taken in a few years. (p. 328)

A great deal of research has occurred in recent years on the mass deacidification of books. Mass deacidification is necessary to preserve our deteriorating collections, as the cost of deacidification of single items is prohibitive unless an item is of sufficient rarity to justify such an expenditure. Mass deacidification experiments have been undertaken by both the Library of Congress and the Canadian National Archives. The process that seems to hold the most promise is mass deacidification with diethyl zinc. Williams and Kelly (1974) report their research and state that vapor phase neutralization and buffering must include the following elements:

> 1. The paper must be uniformly neutralized.
> 2. The paper should be buffered as close to pH 7 as possible, on the alkaline side. Higher pH changes the color or tint of inks and art work and yellows paper which contains groundwood.
> 3. The paper should be given an alkaline reserve equivalent to 3 percent calcium carbonate.
> 4. The treatments must penetrate books and masses of books in a reasonable time.
> 5. The treatment, although applied as a gas, must not come back out of the paper. This implies that a reaction with cellulose takes place or that there is a polymerization of gaseous material in the cellulose or that two gases react to make a non-volatile product in situ, etc.
> 6. The treatment should not impart an odor to the paper.
> 7. The treated paper should be nontoxic to humans.
> 8. No new problems should be introduced by the treatment such as darkening of the paper, damage to the leather, etc.
> 9. The treatment should be reasonable in cost. Binding a book costs roughly $5.00. The book paper may degrade so as to be unusable within fifty years.

> Treating the book so that it will last 500 years should be worth at least another $5.00. However, price schedules and what is "reasonable" have not been established. (p. 70)

Kelly and Williams (1978) report their test results on 400 books, indicating the feasibility of this process and noting preliminary cost estimates of about $5 per book on a 5000-book scale. Testing on this process continues at the Library of Congress. Five thousand books were treated in 1982. The process involved using a chemical vapor of diethl zinc vapor in a vacuum chamber to permeate the paper, thus neutralizing the acid and buffering the paper with an alkaline reserve. Testing continued during 1983, and results are expected to be announced in 1984. Kelly (1980) describes the method of treatment and concludes by praising the process:

> The treated books have a pH of about 7.8, making this one of the mildest deacidification treatments available. This is reflected in the stability of colors in the treated materials. Well over 100 maps of various materials, ages, and colors have been treated with no indication of any color changes or other adverse effects. Similarly, treatment of all common binding materials such as leather, vellum, plastics, pyroxylin, cloth, and gilt has shown no adverse effects. The improvement in expected life, as determined by an accelerated aging test, is about five times that of the untreated paper or book. (p. 7)

Preservation Microfilming

Poole (1976) in making recommendation for a national preservation program stated:

> Of the millions of embrittled and deteriorating volumes on the shelves of the nation's libraries, only a relatively small number have such intrinsic value as to justify the cost of repair or restoration. . . . The Library of Congress believes that a National Preservation Program, initially at least, should emphasize microfilming of the brittle materials published during the last century, with storage of the master microfilm negatives under ideal environmental conditions. (pp. 445–446)

The Library of Congress and the New York Public Library have been leaders in microfilming deteriorating library materials and have microfilmed thousands of titles to date. Libraries initiating a microfilming program should avoid filming titles previously filmed by other institutions. Many titles have also been reprinted in recent years and are available in reprint editions on permanent paper. The *National Register of Microfilm Masters,* compiled annually since 1965, lists master negatives used for production of other copies and maintained under archival conditions. This compilation includes negatives owned by libraries and commercial publishers. A number of other guides are also available, including the annual *Guides to Reprints,* published since 1967. Darling (1974) outlines procedures to be followed in establishing a preservation microfilming unit.

Book Handling

Proper handling of books is one of the most important factors in their preservation. Bindings can be readily broken and pages and spines torn, if not carefully handled. Shelving staff should be instructed as to proper handling. Books should not be placed on their fore edges as this will weaken bindings. Book drops for return of circulating books should be designed to avoid damage as books are deposited and should be emptied regularly to prevent overcrowding.

Cleanliness

Cleanliness is important, as dirt on shelves can cause abrasion and staining of covers and pages. Cleaning schedules, including vacuuming and dusting, should be established. If all areas are not regularly cleaned and refuse is not removed, problems with vermin may occur. New acquisitions, if necessary, should be cleaned before being placed on shelves as well as the shelves themselves. Apart from the aesthetic factors, cleanliness is important in maintaining library collections in good condition.

Shelving

Proper placement on shelves will prevent much damage that can occur to books. Darling (1980) notes that

1. Shelves should not be packed. If a book will not slide back on a shelf with a gentle push, the shelf is too full; a too-full shelf can crack spines and cause damage when someone tries to remove a volume.
2. There is a right and a wrong way to remove books from shelves. Tilting and tugging at the headcap can cause the top of the spine to tear and the bottom corners to wear very badly.
3. Spines should be kept vertical. When a book sits on a shelf at a cockeyed angle, stresses are placed on the spine which lead to premature cracking and tearing.
4. Good bookends should be used.
5. Huge books should be kept flat. Gravity wears out the covers and spines of extremely tall or fat volumes if they are stored in the normal vertical position. Such volumes should be shelved flat, preferably one to a shelf to avoid damage to one when another is removed.

6. Air spaces should be left at the back of the shelves. The fore-edges of books pushed up against the back wall of a shelf may be bent and abraided, and insufficient air circulation can encourage mildew in warm, damp weather. (pp. 9–10)

Displays and Exhibits

Improper display techniques can damage library materials in many of the same ways as improper handling. Unsupported books lying open and flat may have bindings broken or damaged due to stress. Display cradles should always be used if possible. Cunha (1971) states, "display cases should have protective glass that absorbs both heat and damaging radiation," and also that illumination should be from the outside or "concealed fluorescent lamps that are screened by plastic ultraviolet filters" (p. 99). For extended exhibits, pages should be turned periodically to avoid fading. Temperature and humidity inside a display case can become a hostile environment and should be controlled to avoid damage. Descriptions on cards or paper should be checked for acidity before being placed on covers or pages.

DEACCESSIONING

Weeding

All libraries, regardless of size or purpose, will deaccession certain titles, if not by design then because of wear, loss, etc. *Weeding* may be defined in terms of removal from the collection (deaccession) through transferring titles to a storage facility, replacement in a microformat, or complete withdrawal. Evans (1977) cites three reasons for weeding a collection: (1) to save space, (2) to improve access, and (3) to save money. A well-planned weeding program is essential to a professionally managed collection. Many factors will determine the program to be developed, including the purpose of the library and clientele served. A small public library whose clientele is interested in the latest information and editions, and with limited space, will develop a much different program than a large research library whose purpose may be to collect in depth a wide variety of research materials in many areas.

Space is most likely to be one major determining factor that will force weeding, as most libraries cannot indefinitely provide new facilities for shelving. Compact storage may be a temporary solution; converting to microforms may also be a solution in some instances to solve shelving needs.

Organizing a weeding program is not an easy task, and unless weeding is given some priority, it is often an area of collection management that is overlooked in many libraries. Some view the removal of any book from the collection as a sacrilegious practice, but practicality dictates the need for management of the collection through a well-developed weeding program. There is a wide divergence of opinion on the type of weeding programs that may be best; a study of the purpose and use of the collection (both current and projected) will help dictate the weeding program to be implemented.

In a public library in which browsing is important, the titles most circulated should be on the shelves. In a research library or a closed stack collection, shelving the most highly circulated materials together may not be an important factor. Access must be considered, however, in order to give an acceptable level of service to patrons.

Standards

A number of associations and organizations have issued standards for weeding, but they are uneven and quickly outdated. Many book selection or collection development statements of individual libraries contain weeding statements that when applied can be useful to other libraries establishing a weeding program.

Slote (1982) recommends the following standards:

a. The objective of weeding would be to maintain a core collection of books that would satisfy 95 percent to 99 percent of the present demands made upon the entire present collection.
b. All books weeded would be considered for secondary or centralized storage.
c. One complete weeding of the library should take place in each year.
d. The weeding criterion to be used should be based solely upon the likelihood of a volume's being used in the future.
e. The shelf-time period established for each library should satisfy the above standards and should result in an objective similar to this: "All volumes should be removed that have not been circulated since (date)." This shelf-time period should take into account the use patterns of no less than one full year.
f. Similar criteria should be established and utilized, in modified form, for the different *types* of material as follows:
   1) For runs of periodicals, remove all before a specific publication date. This date should be established separately for each run.
   2) For reference books, weeding should be performed as for circulating

works, attempting to keep a core representing 99 percent to 99.5 percent of the present usage.
3) For archives and special works (such as works of local authors) no weeding should be done. (p. 33)

These and other recommended standards need to be carefully applied and adapted to each library, taking into consideration the collection development policies for each library and its various collections.

Circulation Records

One of the most often used criteria for weeding is the circulation record of a title. If the library wishes the most used titles readily accessible, circulation is an excellent standard. A method must be developed to determine the amount of time a title remains on the shelf uncirculated and projection of any future circulation. If the title is to be stored rather than deaccessioned, the problem is not as great because an item in storage could be brought back into the core circulating system. An informative study by Slote (1971) suggests that circulation patterns for fiction in public libraries can be used to identify core collections.

Fussler and Simon (1969) in their study recommended a combination of factors in determining titles to be weeded, including date of publication, language, and circulation history. Treuswell's (1965) measures and criteria for weeding based on circulation have generated much interest since their publication; Treuswell's techniques are either attacked or proclaimed as outstanding criteria for weeding. Turner (1980) presents a review of the Treuswell method that uses calculations based on the amount of time elapsed since the last circulation. Treuswell has authored a number of articles and the most significant are reviewed in Slote (1982, pp. 77–79).

Circulation use records are of much greater potential in libraries in which automated circulation systems have been put into operation, and statistics can be generated that will give the circulation history of specific titles more readily than was available under previous circulation systems.

Age

Age has been suggested as a criterion for weeding, but it must be very carefully applied, along with other factors. Age might be employed as a factor in the selection for storage, but even here potential use and circulation must be considered. Muller (1965) in her study indicated that age is a poor predictor of future or even current use. The criteria for monographs and serials will also be varied. Age as a factor can be applied to obsolete material that may be superseded by later works or subsequent editions if the historical need is not a factor. There will also be a wide variance in subjects; for example, between science and the humanities, and even between scientific subjects such as chemistry and mathematics or medicine and botany. Slote (1982) in a review of the literature on weeding concludes that "The age of the volume was found to be somewhat predictive of future use, but generally of little practical value. Basically, the rejection of a small number of older volumes—the classics, which circulate with patterns similar to those of newer books—causes the age of volumes to be an inferior predictor of the future use" (p. 65).

Weeding of Duplicate Titles

Agreement to weed duplicate titles may be the most easily reached decision. Titles that have had high circulation may be reduced in the number of copies retained after popularity has decreased. The need for varied editions may also not be necessary, except in a research library or in that part of a collection in which research depth is more necessary.

Condition

Condition of a title should also be a consideration. Titles that need extensive repair or that may be on brittle paper often can be more appropriately replaced with a reprint edition or by conversion to microform. Specific criteria must be developed to fit the circumstances and policies of each library collection. In her study, Seymour (1972) reviews differences in usage between serials and monographs, particularly noting that serials do not usually circulate, that in-house use is more difficult to determine, and that most use studies have concentrated on citations to articles as a measurement of use rather than circulation. Seymour concludes that "the most practical criteria would be a cut-off date before which all volumes of a serial would be stored or discarded" (p. 188), although noting there is some disagreement on this principle. Because most studies have been carried out on scientific periodicals, citation studies cannot be applied in the same way to all other disciplines.

Summary

As has been noted, all libraries do some deaccessioning by design or as a result of wear, theft, etc. The most important aspect in developing a deaccessioning or weeding program is a self-study of the needs and purpose of each particular library and the clientele it serves.

Streit (1982) summarizes the need for self-appraisal:

> First, the library should approach deaccession only when there is a clear sense of the library's goals and functions. The library should require itself to answer honestly the question of whether it indeed is a research institution and, if so, the type and level of research it supports. Second, the library's ability to make sound deaccession decisions must be based upon a thorough knowledge of its collections. It should measure the breadth and depth of affected materials against standard bibliographies, similar or related materials in other libraries, and, in a complementary fashion, against collateral holdings in its own collections. Third, the responsible library will query whether it is able to provide scholarly access and adequate physical and environmental care for its collections, especially those of research value. Fourth, the library ought to consider its cultural and intellectual role in the local community, keeping in mind that its holdings may be valued for their local association as well as their scholarly significance. (pp. 658–659)

Although Streit is speaking of research libraries and the possibility of deaccessioning through sales, his advice sets a firm base for the beginnings of decision making in planning any deaccession or weeding program.

Storage

At one time or another every library will have space problems, especially large research libraries. The president of Harvard University, Charles Eliot, is often credited with first recognizing the problem of continued growth and the need for storage. In his report for 1898–1899 (cited in Elkins, 1954), Eliot stated:

> One who watches the rapid accumulation of books in any large library must long for some means of dividing the books that are used from those that are not used, and for a more compact mode than the iron stacks supply of storing the books that are not used. Although the iron stack was a great improvement on any former method of shelving books in a large library, it still wastes much room, and access to the books that are wanted is made slower and more difficult by the presence on the shelves of a great number of books that are never wanted. (p. 300)

The past several decades have seen a tremendous increase in the production of books, and it is not at all unusual for larger libraries to add over 100,000 volumes per year. Downs (1961) reviewed the problem of ever increasing sizes of library collections in his article, "Crisis in Our University Libraries." Ellsworth (1969) summarized the problems and costs of library storage. His book is still useful, although the cost information must be updated if used. In selecting a storage facility, whether rental or new construction, all pertinent problems must be carefully reviewed in terms of the goals and services to be provided. Cooperative storage centers may be a solution for some libraries.

In a storage facility, compact shelving of some type will generally be used. Traditional shelving practices are inefficient in the use of floor space, whereas compacting may increase the capacity of books stored in an area up to 100%. An increase in the number of books stored can be achieved by shelving according to size, decreasing aisle widths, as well as the installation of mechanized systems that move along rails in order to provide access. Poole (1978) reviews a number of types of compact storage systems on the market.

What to Store

The most obvious material to be stored is that which will have the least use. This may sound simple, but the selection of material for storage can be highly complicated. Fussler and Simon (1969) and Trueswell (1965) suggest mechanized guidelines for selection of materials for storage. Other writers have developed similar models, but there is no general agreement on the best method. Using circulation data is most often suggested; that is, those books that have not circulated in the most recent 5 years would be the most likely candidates for placement into storage. Circulation, coupled with other data such as date of publication, language, subject, etc., should also be considered.

Serials and monographs differ in use, and different criteria should be applied. It is more costly to select monographs for storage than larger runs of serial titles and large monograph sets. The retirement program of Yale University (Ash, 1963) was based on broad types of materials, materials in specialized topics, serials that had ceased publication, little-used language materials, and other categories selected in subject groupings. Each library must carefully plan a program to build a storage selection program to best meet the needs of the library in terms of space and service to its patrons, just as it would develop a selection program for new acquisitions.

Storage Facilities

Just as in selecting books for storage, there are no standard or established criteria for the selection of storage space. Space may become available in an existing building by rearrangement of space or the installation of compact shelving. Some libraries have constructed storage facilities adjacent to or distant from central buildings. Such decisions to establish a storage facility are based on many factors, including the cost and availability of space, cost of transporting materials between more distant locations, etc. As an alternative to a new building, some libraries have leased storage facilities. The cost of such facilities may be a major factor, but leasing is an alternative to large expenditures for a new building, an annex, or a separate storage facility.

Cooperative storage is another alternative. The best known of such facilities are the Center for Research Libraries (formerly called the Midwest Interlibrary Center), the New England Depository Library, and the Hampshire Inter-Library Center. These facilities and others are reviewed by Line (1980).

As library networks have been established in recent years, there has been some movement toward establishing cooperative storage centers, but most efforts to date have centered on union lists, shared or cooperative acquisitions, cooperative processing, and open access to patrons, especially students and faculties of cooperating colleges and universities.

Converting to Microform

Almost all libraries will collect some microforms in the selection and acquisition processes. The amount of material available in microformat has increased year by year since the 1940s. In order to build research collections of retrospective serials, newspapers, and rare books, there is often no other practical alternative than to purchase in microform. Converting paper copy in existing collections presents other problems, and each library must study its needs and the specific costs relating to such conversion. Questions to be addressed include:

1. Space needs that might be freed in converting to a microformat
2. Condition of original, that is, brittle or acidic paper, etc.
3. Intrinsic value of original material, including value to specific collections of each individual library
4. Availability of commercial microforms

5. Availability of reprint editions
6. Availability in another library versus the need to have copy in house
7. Need to protect original paper copies from excessive use and thus substituting microform for patron use
8. Projected use and effect on hard copy

Many large research libraries have had preservation microfilming projects in operation for many years. The New York Public Library has been a leader in the field, with programs for filming in operation since the 1930s. Extensive preservation programs of converting brittle books to microfilm have also been operated by the Library of Congress. The *National Register of Microform Masters* has been published by the Library of Congress since 1965 and provides a listing of master negatives for both contributing libraries and commercial publishers. Newspapers are listed in another publication *Newspapers in Microform* and manuscripts in the *National Union Catalog of Manuscript Collections*.

Other guides include the *Guide to Microforms in Print*, which lists books, journals, government documents, and other archival collections available from commercial micropublishers. Additional guides, including *Guide to Reprints*, list reprint publications, including monographs, serials, and so forth. These sources should be checked before microfilming to avoid unnecessary duplication of effort. A number of cooperative ventures are underway in preservation microfilming, including a project by the Research Libraries Group (1983) to film deteriorating nineteenth century American imprints.

Computer-output microfilm (COM), the process of recording directly onto film from a computer, has greatly expanded the capacity and lowered the cost of producing data in microforms. Additional new technologies are being developed. The Library of Congress in 1982 awarded two contracts for the development of the optical disk for information preservation and management. Optical disk technology holds great promise for computerized mass storage, retrieval, and preservation of printed materials.

COOPERATIVE EFFORTS IN CONSERVATION

Following the studies made by W. J. Barrow and the attention called to the deterioration of paper printed in the first half of the twentieth century, the subject of paper deterioration became a topic at the June 18, 1960 meeting of the Association of Research Libraries (ARL) in Montreal, Canada. As a result of these discussions, a committee on the preservation of research library materials was established. Further discussions and studies were undertaken, and in 1962 a study was funded by the Council on Library Resources. A report was prepared under the direction of Gordon Williams and distributed to members of the Association of Research Libraries in 1964. One of the earliest attempts at a cooperative approach in looking at conservation and preservation problems, this report was endorsed by ARL in 1965 and published in the *Library Journal* in January 1966.

Haas (1972) summarized the report as follows:

> that the most practicable solution is a federally supported central agency that will assure the physical preservation for as long as possible of at least one example of every deteriorating record, and that will make copies of these records readily available to any library when required. Such an agency would: 1) undertake the centralized preservation of deteriorating records deposited by libraries; 2) coordinate its own preservation program with local programs of individual libraries to assure that all significant records are preserved while avoiding unwitting duplication; 3) assure the ready availability of microform or full-size photocopies of deteriorating materials to all libraries; and 4) itself preserve, in the interest of textual preservation, economy, and the ready availability of copies, all microform masters made at its expense or deposited by others, and coordinate the preservation of microform masters made by other agencies. (p. 276)

No major cooperative programs followed this study and report, but in 1970, the Association of Research Libraries received a grant from the U.S. Office of Education to further the study of preservation problems by individual libraries as well as libraries in cooperation. The final report (Haas, 1972) reviewed and incorporated many of the recommendations of the 1964 report but did not recommend a national preservation library. Haas detailed the need for continued research, education, training, and conservation efforts by individual libraries. Noting that the essence of the 1964 ARL report was for collective action, he detailed a number of recommendations for establishing a national consortium of research libraries to study and implement preservation programs. Although these reports stimulated study and movement in research and the establishment of individual preservation programs, no major national programs were established.

At the American Library Association conference in Chicago in 1976, the Library of Congress announced its plans for developing a national preservation program. A two-day conference was held at the Library of Congress on December 16–17, 1976 with 40 participants. Darling (1977) reviewed the conference and noted that Haas, a conference participant, enumerated the achievements that should be accomplished within 10 years:

> preservation master microfilm collection and a bibliographic system that routinely accommodates microforms; a cadre of trained conservators and a preservation-wise library profession; a cold storage facility to buy time for those things which cannot be treated immediately; public awareness of the importance of preservation—we have a matter of great public concern, but we don't have a concerned public; full cooperation among all affected parties and a free flow of information—this must not become a proprietary matter, for we are talking about the substance of civilization. The goal is not to preserve the resources of many individual libraries but rather to preserve, according to some yet-to-be-established plan, the substance of an indispensable part of the record of human achievement. (p. 449)

Other attempts at regional cooperation have resulted primarily in studies to determine the preservation problems within various regions. An example is the Western States Materials Conservation Project which, under a grant from the National Historical Publications Records Commission and other funding agencies, organized a planning conference in each of the 17 Western council states. Lowell (1980), the project director, stated the objectives of the project in these terms:

> 1) To form a cadre of conservation advocates in the West who are committed to, and are willing to work for, conservation solutions at the local, state, regional and national levels; 2) to identify library and archives conservation needs in the West, and the feasibility for a variety of actions to meet these needs; 3) to develop a coordinated, cooperative plan of action to serve as the framework for addressing conservation in the West during the 1980s; and 4) to begin an implementation process for that action. (p. 28)

All these conferences and studies are beginning to have an effect on the planning and implementation of preservation programs. The National Conservation Advisory Council's *Report of the Study Committee on Libraries and Archives* (1978) noted that the major obstacle to conservation programs is the cost during times of shrinking financial resources. The committee recommended the establishment of regional cooperative centers but cautioned that development should be formulated on stable funding and available trained and experienced conservators. The report recommended that regional centers should provide services in consultation on treatment, disaster recovery assistance, and consultation on environment and storage. The report concluded by recommending possible ways for sponsoring and governance, funding, physical facilities, standards, etc.

The best known cooperative center established to date is the New England Document Center in North Andover, Massachusetts. Cunha (1973), the center's first director, described its objectives as follows:

> to administer and supervise a workshop, necessary facilities and staff to restore, preserve and maintain the physical condition of books, prints, maps, broadsides, manuscripts, and similar documentary materials of historic, archival, or cultural interest. Whenever necessary for the accomplishment of this objective, the Center will investigate materials and equipment and conduct studies and tests in order to develop methods to protect, preserve, and maintain the integrity or improve the physical condition of such documentary materials; assist member institutions to carry out conservation programs; and render conservation services to them. (p. 231)

Following its establishment in 1974, the Research Libraries Group (RLG) appointed a preservation committee to study preservation programs. The committee was expanded with the reorganization of RLG in 1978 and has met to formulate cooperative preservation programs since 1980. The program goals are stated as follows:

> Through the RLG Preservation Program, members are seeking the most appropriate ways to divide and share the responsibility for preservation in order to make the most effective use of their aggregate human and fiscal resources. The goals of the program, which are mirrored in the formal charge to the Preservation Committee, are,
> 1. To develop a plan for sharing preservation responsibilities and thus to ensure continuing availability of research resources in all appropriate fields.
> 2. To develop a means to exchange information regularly about items preserved at member institutions.
> 3. To define policy issues governing preservation responsibilities of RLG members that correspond to their collecting responsibilities.
> 4. To outline systems development work required to use RLIN effectively for preservation purposes, e.g., information about preservation decisions, management reports, etc.
> 5. To evaluate available technologies related to preservation to determine RLG's potential role as a site for pilot projects, testing, or experimentation.
> 6. To identify special data bases or retrospective conversion projects that would expand coverage of information within RLIN and assist in supporting rational cooperative preservation policies.
> Underlying these objectives is the growing realization that the scale of preservation needs of most major research libraries is vast, and there are no inexpensive technological solutions. It is assumed that no single institution will be able to mount a program comprehensive enough to rehabilitate its entire collection. To ensure the wisest application of limited funds, the requirement for cooperation is clear. (Research Libraries Group, Inc., 1983, p. 7)

The Association of Research Libraries has also commenced programs in preservation, including surveys on preservation needs and the establishment of an assisted self-study program through its Office of Management Study.

Effective preservation programs are beginning to develop nationwide, but considering the massive problems and amounts of material to be treated, preservation must be considered only in its infancy. Only through cooperative programs, including research, consultation, bibliographic apparatus, training of specialists in all aspects of conservation, and the exchange of technology, can the libraries and archives of the nation hope to preserve the world's written cultural heritage.

HOW TO KEEP UP-TO-DATE

Preservation of library materials is presently a field that generates both interest and much research and in which development is occurring. A national preservation program officer was appointed in 1981 at the Library of Congress, and those in the field of preservation will look to the Library of Congress for leadership and direction. The National Preservation Program of the Library of Congress will sponsor programs over the next few years on various aspects of preservation. The Library of Congress preservation office is active in its publication program, and its research and techniques should be followed.

The preservation of library materials section of the American Library Association established in 1979 has an active program of meetings and its committees are studying preservation problems. The Association of Research Libraries' Office of Management Studies has expanded its interest in preservation programs, developed a self-study program, and is planning additional enhancements and programs. The Research Libraries Group has a permanent preservation committee that is making plans for cooperative programs in preservation. All interested in preservation should follow the activities of these organizations and their printed reports.

The literature of preservation has expanded rapidly in recent years with articles appearing in major library periodicals. Articles appear regularly in the periodicals issued by the American Library Association and in many journals published by various state associations as well as those produced by the commercial presses. The American Library Association quarterly, *Library Resources & Technical Services,* is now including an annual review on the state of preservation that includes a bibliography of the year's literature of preservation.

REFERENCES

American Library Association. Library Technology Project. *Protecting the library and its resources.* Chicago: American Library Association, 1963.

American Library Association. *Minimum specifications for Class "A" library binding.* Chicago: American Library Association, 1934.

American Library Association. *Standards for reinforced (pre-library bound) new books.* Chicago: American Library Association, 1939.

Ash, L. M. *Yale's selective book retirement program: Report of a three year project.* Hamden, Conn.: Archon Books, 1963.

Banks, P. N. Environmental standards for storage of books and manuscripts. *Library Journal,* 1974, *99,* 339–43.

Bohem, H. *Disaster prevention and disaster preparedness.* Berkeley: Office of the Assistant Vice President, Library Plans and Policies, Systemwide Administration, University of California, 1978.

Buchanan, S. The Stanford Library flood restoration project. *College and Research Libraries,* 1979, *40,* 539–48.

Church, R. W. (Ed.). *Deterioration of book stock: Causes and remedies.* Richmond, Va.: Virginia State Library, 1959.

Cunha, G. M. *Conservation of library materials, a manual and bibliography on the care, repair and restoration of library materials* (2nd ed., 2 vols.). Metuchen, N.J.: Scarecrow Press, Inc., 1971.

Cunha, G. M. National trends in cooperative approaches to conservation. *Pennsylvania Library Association (PLA) Bulletin,* 1973, *28,* 226–231.

Darling, P. W. Developing a preservation microfilming program. *Library Journal,* 1974, *99,* 2803–2809.

Darling, P. W. Housekeeping. In J. R. Russell (Ed.), *Preservation of library materials.* New York: Special Libraries Association, 1980.

Darling, P. W. Preservation: A national plan at last? *Library Journal,* 1977, *102,* 447–49.

Darling, P. W. *Preservation planning program: An assisted self-study manual for libraries.* Washington, D.C.: Association of Research Libraries, Office of Management Studies, 1982.

Daugherty, R. A., Gapen, K., Keller, N. J., & Miller, S. L. *Preliminary report on losses in libraries: A pilot opinion survey.* Columbus, Ohio: Ohio State University Libraries, 1977. (ERIC Document Reproduction Service No. ED 165 773)

Downs, R. B. Crisis in our university libraries. *College and Research Libraries,* 1961, *22,* 7–10.

Dureau, J. M. *Principles for the conservation and restoration of collections in libraries.* Paper presented at the conference of the International Federation of Library Associations and Institutions, Copenhagen, Denmark, 1979. (ERIC Document Reproduction Service No. ED 186 009)

Elkins, K. C. President Eliot and the storage of dead books. *Harvard Library Bulletin,* 1954, *8,* 299–312.

Ellsworth, R. E. *The economics of book storage in college and university libraries.* Metuchen, N.J.: Scarecrow Press, Inc., 1969.

Evans, G. E. Limits to growth or the need to weed. *California Librarian*, 1977, *38*, 8–16.

Fussler, H. H., & Simon, J. L. *Patterns in the use of books in large research libraries.* Chicago: University of Chicago Press, 1969.

Gallo, P. Problems in the use of insecticides on occupied premises. In G. Thompson (Ed.), *Recent advances in conservation, contributions to the Rome Conference, 1961.* London: Butterworths, 1963.

General Services Administration. *Protecting federal record centers and archives from fire.* Washington, D.C.: General Services Administration, 1977.

Gosnell, C. F. Insurance, library. In *Enclyclopedia of library and information science* (Vol. 12). New York: Marcel Dekker, Inc., N.Y., 1974.

Guide to microforms in print. Washington, D.C.: Microcard Editions, 1961–. Annual.

Guide to reprints. Washington, D.C.: Microcard Editions, 1967–. Annual.

Harris, C. Mass deacidification. *Library Journal*, 1979, *104*, 1423–1427.

Hass, W. J. *Preparation of detailed specifications for a national system for the preservation of library materials.* Washington, D.C.: Association of Research Libraries, 1972.

Jenkins, J. H. *Rare books and manuscript thefts: A security system for librarians, booksellers, and collectors.* New York: Antiquarian Booksellers Association of America, 1982.

Kelly, G. B. Mass deacidification with diethyl zinc. *Library Scene*, 1980, *9*(3), 6–7.

Kelly, G. B., & Williams, J. C. Mass deacidification with diethyl zinc, large scale trials. *AIC Preprints*, 1978, 81–92.

Knight, N. H. Theft detection systems for libraries revisited: An updated survey. *Library Technology Reports*, 1979, *15*, 221–410.

Library of Congress. Preservation Office. *Emergency procedures for salvaging flood or water damaged library materials.* 1972.

Library Resources & Technical Services (Vols. 1–). Chicago: American Library Association. Library Resources and Technical Services Division, Winter 1957–.

Line, M. B. Storage and deposit libraries. In *Encyclopedia of library and information science*, Vol. 29, pp. 101–133. New York: Marcel Dekker, 1980.

Lowell, H. P. Preparing for your library disaster. *Pacific Northwest Library Quarterly*, 1979, *44*, 1–6.

Lowell, H. P. Conservation planning in the west. *Library Scene*, 1980, *9*, 28–29.

Morrow, C. C. A conservaton policy statement for research libraries. *Occasional Papers* (No. 139). Urbana, Ill.: University of Illinois, Graduate School of Library Science, 1979.

Muller, E. Are new books read more than old ones? *Library Quarterly*, 1965, *35*, 166–172.

National Conservation Advisory Council. *Report of the study committee on libraries and archives.* Washington, D.C.: Author, 1978.

National Fire Protection Association. *Protection of library collections.* Boston: National Fire Protection Association, 1979.

National register of microform masters. Washington, D.C.: Library of Congress, 1965–. Irregular, then annual.

National union catalog of manuscript collections. Washington, D.C.: Library of Congress, 1962–. Annual.

Newspapers in microfilm. Published periodically by the Library of Congress. Companion volumes cover United States and foreign countries.

Patterson, R. H. Organizing for conservation: A model charge to a conservation committee. *Library Journal*, 1979, *104*, 1116–1119.

Plumbe, W. J. *The preservation of books in tropical and subtropical countries.* London: Oxford University Press, 1964.

Poole, F. G. *Thoughts on the conservation of library materials.* Paper presented at the Seminar on Library and Archives Conservation, Boston, 1972.

Poole, F. G. Toward a national preservation program: A working paper. Washington, D.C.: Library of Congress, 1976. (Reprinted in J. P. Baker, & M. C. Soroka (Eds.), *Library conservation: Preservation in perspective.* Stroudsburg, Pa.: Dowden, Hutchinson & Ross, 1978.)

Poole, F. G. Compact shelving. In Novak, G. (Ed.), *Running out of space—what are the alternatives?* Chicago: American Library Association, 1978.

Preparing for emergencies and disasters. Washington, D.C.: Systems and Procedures Exchange Center, Office of Management Studies, Association of Research Libraries, 1980. (SPEC Kit, No. 69)

The preservation of deteriorating books. *Library Journal,* 1966, *91,* 51–56.

Research Libraries Group, Inc. *RLG preservation manual.* Stanford, Calif.: Author, 1983.

Rogers, R. D., & Weber, D. C. *University library administration.* New York: Wilson, 1971.

Scott, B. A. Waging the war against crime in Florida's public libraries. *Library and Archival Security,* 1980, *3,* 27–30.

Seymour, C. A. Weeding the collection: A review of research on identifying obsolete stock. Part II. Serials. *Libri,* 1972, *22,* 183–189.

Shelley, K. L. The future of conservation in research libraries. *Journal of Academic Librarianship,* 1976, *1,* 15–18.

Slote, S. J. Identifying useful core collections: A study of weeding fiction in public libraries. *Library Quarterly,* 1971, *41,* 25–34.

Slote, S. J. *Weeding library collections—II* (2nd ed.). Littleton, Col.: Libraries Unlimited, Inc., 1982.

Smith, R. D. Paper impermanence as a consequence of pH and storage conditions. *Library Quarterly,* 1969, *39,* 153–195.

Smith, R. D. Progress in mass deacidification at the public archives. *Canadian Library Journal,* 1979, *36,* 325–334.

Spawn, W. After the water comes. *Pennsylvania Library Association Bulletin,* 1973, *28,* 243–251.

Streit, S. Research library deaccessioning: Practical considerations. *Wilson Library Bulletin,* 1982, *56,* 658–662.

Tauber, M. F. *Library binding manual: A handbook of useful procedures for the maintenance of library volumes.* Boston: Library Binding Institute, 1972.

Torrence, J. S. A justification of air-conditioning in libraries. *Journal of Librarianship,* 1975, *7,* 199–206.

Trelles, O. F. Protection of libraries. *Law Library Journal,* 1973, *66,* 241–258.

Trueswell, R. W. A quantitative measure of user circulation requirements and its possible effect on stack thinning and multiple copy determination. *American Documentation,* 1965, *16,* 20–25.

Turner, S. J. Trueswell's weeding techniques: The facts. *College & Research Libraries,* 1980, *41,* 134–38.

Weiss, D. Book theft and book mutilation in a large urban university library. *College & Research Libraries,* 1981, *48,* 341–347.

Weiss, D. A. Binding institute, library (Vol. 2). In E. Kent, & H. Lancour (Eds.), *Encyclopedia of library and information science.* New York: Marcel Dekker, 1969.

Weiss, H. B., & Carruthers, R. H. *Insect enemies of books*. New York: New York Public Library, 1945.
Wessel, C. J. Environmental factors affecting the permanence of library materials. *Library Quarterly*, 1970, *40*, 39–84.
Williams, J. C., & Kelly, G. B. Research on mass treatments in conservation. *American Institute for Conservation Bulletin*, 1974, *14*, 69–77.
W. J. Barrow Restoration Shop, Inc. The Barrow two-bath deacidification method. *American Archivist*, 1976, *39*, 161–164.

BIBLIOGRAPHY

Bahr, A. H. *Book theft and library security systems, 1978–79*. White Plains, N.Y.: Knowledge Information Industry Publishers, 1978.
Baker, J. P., & Soroka, M. C. *Library conservation: Preservation in perspective*. New York: Academic Press, 1978.
Banks, P. N. *Preservation of library materials*. Chicago: Newberry Library, 1978. (Reprinted from the *Encyclopedia of library and information science*. Vol. 23, 180–222. New York: Marcel Dekker, 1969.)
Basic preservation procedures. Washington, D.C.: Systems and Procedures Exchange Center, Office of Management Studies, Association of Research Libraries, 1981. (SPEC Kit, No. 70)
Belver, C. G., Servi, P. N., Anker, A. L., & Drott, M. C. The aging of scientific literature: A citation analysis. *Journal of Documentation*, 1979, *35*, 179–196.
Berger, P. Minor repairs in a small research library: The case for an in-house minor repairs workshop. *Library Journal*, 1979, *104*, 1311–1317.
Braham, W. A. A regional approach to conservation: The New England Document Conservation Center. *American Archivist*, 1977, *40*, 421–427.
Brenni, V. J. *Bookbinding: A guide to the literature*. Westport, Conn.: Greenwood Press, 1982.
Cassata, M. B. Storage of library material. In *Encyclopedia of library and information science* (Vol. 29). New York: Marcel Dekker, 1980.
Clark, A. S. Microforms as a substitute for the original in the collection development process. In R. B. Stuart, & G. B. Miller, Jr. (Eds.), *Collection development in libraries: A treatise* (Part B). Greenwich, Conn.: JAI Press, Inc., 1980.
Conger, L. The annex library at Princeton University: The development of a compact storage library. *College & Research Libraries*, 1970, *31*, 160–168.
Cunha, G. *What an institution can do to survey its conservation needs*. New York: New York Library Association, 1977.
Cunha, G. M. *Library conservation: 1980s and beyond* (2 vols.). Metuchen, N.J.: Scarecrow Press, Inc., 1982.
Cunha, G. M., & Cunha, D. G. *Library and archives conservation: 1980s and beyond* (2 vols.). Metuchen, N.J.: Scarecrow Press, Inc., 1983.
Darling, P. W. Developing a preservation microfilming program. *Library Journal*, 1974, *99*, 2803–2809.
Darling, P. W. Collection officer or collector: The preservation side of the development responsibility. In R. D. Stuart, & G. B. Miller (Eds.), *Collection development in libraries* (Part A). pp. 281–288. Greenwich, Conn.: JAI Press, 1980.

Darling, P. W. Creativity vs. despair: The challenge of preservation administration. *Library Trends*, 1981, *30*, 179–188.

Darling, P. W. *Preservation planning program: Resource notebook*. Washington, D.C.: Association of Research Libraries, 1982.

Darling, P. W., & Ogden, S. From problems perceived to programs in practice: The preservation of library resources in the U.S.A., 1956–1980. *Library Resources & Technical Services*, 1981, *25*, 9–29.

Davies, L. A., & Tueller, J. R. *Book drying in a space chamber*. Sunnyvale, Calif.: Lockheed Missiles and Space Company, Inc., 1980.

Dean, J. Binding and preparation of periodicals: Alternative structures and procedures. *Serials Review*, 1980, *6*, 87–90.

Dean, J. The role of the bookbinder in preservation. *Wilson Library Bulletin*, 1981, *56*, 182–186.

Deterioration and preservation of library materials. Proceedings of the 34th annual conference of the University of Chicago, Graduate Library School, 1969. In *The Library Quarterly*, 1970, *40*, 1–198.

Gabriel, M. R., & Ladd, D. P. *The microform revolution in libraries*. Greenwich, Conn.: JAI Press, Inc., 1980.

Gwinn, N. E. CLR and preservation. *College & Research Libraries*, 1981, *42*, 104–126.

Harrison, A. W., Collister, E. A., & Willis, R. E. *The conservation of archival and library materials: A resource guide to audiovisual aids*. Metuchen, N.J.: Scarecrow Press, Inc., 1982.

Henderson, K. L., & Henderson, W. T. (Eds.). *Conserving and preserving library materials*. Urbana–Champaign: University of Illinois, 1983.

Horton, C. *Cleaning and preserving bindings and related materials* (2nd ed.). Chicago: Library Technology Program, American Library Association, 1969.

Kirsh, K. C., & Rubenstein, A. H. Converting from hard copy to microfilm: An administrative experiment. *Collection Management*, 1978, *2*, 279–302.

Kyle, H. *Library materials preservation manual: Practical methods for preserving books, pamphlets and other printed materials*. Bronxville, N.Y.: Nicholas T. Smith, 1983.

Lawrence, G. S. A cost model for storage and weeding programs. *College & Research Libraries*, 1982, *42*, 139–147.

Library Binding Institute. *Standards for library binding* (7th ed.). Boston: Library Binding Institute, 1981.

Library of Congress. *A national preservation program. Proceedings of the planning conference*. Washington, D.C.: Library of Congress, Preservation Office, 1980.

Line, M. B. Half-life of periodical literature: Apparent and real obsolescence. *Journal of Documentation*, 1970, *26*, 53–54.

Morris, J. *Managing the library fire risk* (2nd ed.). Berkeley, Calif.: University of California, 1979.

Morrow, C. C. *Conservation treatment procedures: A manual of step-by-step procedures for the maintenance and repair of library materials*. Littleton, Col.: Libraries Unlimited, Inc., 1982.

Morrow, C. C., & Schoenly, S. B. *A conservation bibliography for librarians, archivists, and administrators*. Troy, N.Y.: Whitson Publishing Co., 1979.

Morrow, C. C., & Walker, G. *The preservation challenge: A guide to conserving library materials*. White Plains, N.Y. Knowledge Information Industries, 1983.

Myers, G. E. *Insurance manual for libraries*. Chicago: American Library Association, 1977.

Myers, J. N., & Bedford, D. D. (Eds.). *Disasters: Prevention and coping.* Proceedings of the Conference, May 21–22, 1980. Stanford, Calif.: Stanford University Libraries, 1981.

Novak, G. *Running out of space—what are the alternatives?* Chicago: American Library Association, 1978.

O'Niel, E. T. The effects of demand level on optimal size of journal collections. *Collection Management,* 1978, *2,* 205–216.

Orne, J. *Storage warehouses* (The State of the Library Art. Vol. 3, Part 3.). New Brunswick, N.J.: Graduate School of Library Science, Rutgers University, 1960.

Planning for preservation. Washington, D.C.: Systems and Procedures Exchange Center, Office of Management Studies, Association of Research Libraries, 1980. (SPEC Kit, No. 66)

Preparing for emergencies. Washington, D.C.: Systems and Procedures Exchange Center, Office of Management Studies, Association of Research Libraries, 1980. (SPEC Kit, No. 69)

Preservation of library materials. Washington, D.C.: Systems and Procedures Exchange Center, Office of Management Studies, Association of Research Libraries, 1977. (SPEC Kit, No. 35)

Preservation of library materials. In *Pennsylvania Library Association Bulletin,* 1973, *28,* 219–251.

Reed, M. J. P. Identification of storage candidates among monographs. *Collection Management,* 1978, *2,* 203–216.

Roberts, M. T., & Etherington, D. *Bookbinding and conservation of books: A dictionary of descriptive terminology.* Washington, D.C.: Library of Congress, 1982.

Romeo, L. J. Electronic theft detection systems: A survey conducted in 1976. Parts I–IV. *Library and Archival Security,* 1979, *2*(3–4), 1–78; 1980, *3*(1), 1–23; 1980, *3*(2), 1–16; 1980, *3*(3–4), 1–22.

Russell, J. R. (Ed.). *Preservation of library materials.* Proceedings of a seminar sponsored by the Library Binding Institute and the Princeton-Trenton Chapter of Special Libraries Association, Rutgers University, 1979. New York: Special Libraries Association, 1980.

Schefrin, R. A. The barriers to and barriers of library security. *Wilson Library Bulletin,* 1971, *45,* 870–878.

Seymour, C. A. Weeding the collection: A review of research on identifying obsolete stock (Part 1: Monographs). *Libri,* 1972, *22,* 137–148.

Stam, D. H. "Prove all things: Hold fast that which is good:" Deaccessioning and research libraries. *College & Research Libraries,* 1982, *43,* 5–13.

The Stanford Lockheed Meyer Library flood report. Stanford, Calif.: Stanford University, 1980.

Swartzburg, S. G. *Preserving library materials: A manual.* Metuchen, N.J.: Scarecrow Press, Inc., 1980.

Thompson, G. *The museum environment.* London: Butterworths, 1978.

Tomer, C. Identification, evaluation, and selection of books for preservation. *Collection Management,* 1979, *3,* 45–54.

Totten, H. L. The selection of library materials for storage: A state of the art. *Library Trends,* 1971, *19,* 341–351.

Walker, G. Library binding as a conservation measure. *Collection Management,* 1982, *4,* 55–71.

Waters, P. *Procedures for salvage of water damaged library materials* (2nd ed.). Washington, D.C.: Library of Congress, 1979.

Weeding of library collections. Proceedings of a meeting of the California Library
    Association Collection Development Libraries Meeting, October 1976. *California
    Librarian*, 1977, *38*, 5–49.
Wessel, C. J. Deterioration of library materials. In *Encyclopedia of library and infor-
    mation science* (Vol. 7). New York: Marcel Dekker, Inc., 1972.
Winger, H. W., & Smith, R. D. (Eds.). *Deterioration and preservation of library materi-
    als*. Chicago: University of Chicago Press, 1970.

7 Circulation Functions

Leslie A. Manning

INTRODUCTION

The purpose of this chapter is to provide an outline of the historical development of library circulation and to describe the functions that comprise circulation services. The management of circulation and automation will be discussed only briefly, and auxiliary functions such as stacks maintenance will not be covered. Additional information regarding the automation of circulation can be found in Chapter 3.

There seems to be no comprehensive definition of library circulation, but circulation services most often include patron registration, charge–discharge, and the controlling processes of renewals, recalls, holds, and notifications. Various additional lending operations, such as interlibrary loan activities and reserve book collections, are also part of circulation. The exact composition of circulation services varies from library to library, and significant variation occurs within even the same library over a period of time.

Definitions of technical services functions (Rochell, 1981; Tauber, 1954) include circulation services. Although there are numerous similarities among circulation functions and other technical services functions, in practice, many libraries have not placed circulation within the administrative structure of technical services. The increasing use of automation for circulation functions has highlighted those similarities. The recent development of integrated automated systems has led more libraries to place circulation into the same administrative unit with more traditional technical activities.

HISTORICAL DEVELOPMENT

Library administrators have been looking for inexpensive and accurate circulation systems since the mid-1800s. The service versus cost dilemma exists today, and it will probably continue to demand constant examination as long as libraries are faced with limited resources and increasing growth.

A century ago library circulation was a relatively simple matter. When a reader wanted to take a book from the library, he or she signed the "day book." The author, title, and date were also recorded. The ledger system, with separate pages for each registered patron and with a concise record of each borrower's transactions, was a later refinement. The disadvantage of both systems was the failure to conveniently indicate disposition of the books. A solution to this problem came in the form of wooden blocks. A block was put on the shelf in the space of the charged volume. On each block was a place for the name of the borrower. Libraries had, for the first time, a method of identifying both the borrowers and the books charged out.

Around the turn of the century, a new system came into use. The new system required permanent book cards, patron registration, and date-due slips. The initial implementation of this new system was attributed to the Newark (New Jersey) Public Library under the direction of John Cotton Dana (Greer, 1955). A 1961 study (George Fry and Associates, Inc.) indicated that 67.9% of the nonpublic libraries and 32.5% of the main branch libraries of public library systems were using some form of the Newark system. It has proven to be so effective and so adaptable that it is still in use. Attributes of the Newark system include accurate files conveniently located at the circulation desk by patron name, due date, and call number. It also provides opportunities to generate accurate statistical reports, to accommodate different loan periods, and to allow several tasks to be simultaneously completed. A major problem with the Newark system is the relatively labor intensive nature of the operations. One of the interesting features of the system is the emphasis on mechanical manipulation of circulation information through the use of book cards, patron registration cards, stamps, etc. Also, it set the stage for associating patron information to items through the loan transaction and the eventual use of transaction numbers.

For the last 100 years or so, ingenious librarians and library equipment manufacturers have designed circulation systems using the latest technology such as multi-part forms, elaborate photographic systems, punch cards, punch tape, and literally anything else that seemed to offer a cost-effective circulation system. In obvious frustration, one author (George Fry and Associates, Inc., 1961) finally suggested that the ultimate answer to the circulation problem might reside in disposable copies of library materials, which would obviate the need for circulation systems.

Since the mid-1960s the use of an electronic circulation system has become a reality in many libraries. The advantages of speed, the ability to manage large amounts of data, and the long-term trends of increasing computer power and decreasing cost have attracted libraries to automated circulation. The situation now seems so promising that library automation extends far beyond just the circulation functions into more integrated systems for cataloging, acquisitions, public access catalogs, decision support systems, and virtually all other library operations.

FUNCTIONS

Patron Registration

An obvious first step in any circulation system is to register the patrons or borrowers. This procedure, while time-consuming and somewhat expensive, is necessary for several reasons. First, it is necessary to establish the potential borrower as a legitimate member of the library's clientele. Registration identifies the borrower as a member of the community in the case of public libraries or as an enrolled student, faculty, or staff member in the typical academic environment. This identification is necessary for the accomplishment of the notification process associated with holds, recalls, fines, and overdue materials. However, patron registration need not stop here; it also serves as an excellent opportunity to communicate library policy and procedure. Patron registration has long been recognized as the initial contact point with the public. As such, a good impression is essential. The final purpose of patron registration is to obtain an accurate statistical description of the patron population, which plays an important role in the budget preparations and program development.

Maintenance of an accurate patron registration file is extremely important in today's highly mobile society. The United States has historically been a nation on the move. The average American family relocates as often as once every 5 years, and the patron registration file must be updated accordingly. In academic libraries in which current enrollment in school is the criterion for borrowing privileges, patron maintenance is an issue every semester.

Charge and Discharge Functions

The *A.L.A. Glossary of Library Terms* (Thompson, 1943, p. 29) defines circulation as "the activity of a library in lending books to borrowers and keeping the records of the loans." Clearly this definition is too narrow in the present context, but it does seem to illustrate the importance of the charging and discharging functions.

As a minimum requirement, circulation systems should accomplish the following: (1) identify the books charged out, (2) identify the borrowers, (3) get the materials returned, and (4) provide adequate statistical information (George Fry and Associates, Inc., 1961). The characteristics of a viable circulation system are accuracy, simplicity, economy, and compatibility with other components in the greater perspective of the library system. Attainment of such characteristics involves compromise; there is no single circulation system that is perfect for every library. The specific details, such as loan periods or maximum number of books that can be loaned to a patron, are established by individual policy.

Controlling Processes

There are several additional circulation functions that are closely related to the charge functions. These are referred to as controlling processes because they further regulate the loan periods of circulated items. These subfunctions include renewals, holds or reserves, recalls, fines, and notifications. The simplest and most straightforward of these subfunctions is the renewal activity. *Renewal* represents the extension of the loan period by recharging the same item to the same patron. Complications might occur if the item has been requested by another patron through the hold or recall procedure.

The *hold* procedure is sometimes referred to as the reserve procedure in public libraries. With this procedure, library materials that are currently borrowed by one patron but wanted by another can be identified and held or reserved upon request. The patron who wants a book that is circulating to another borrower initiates a request for a hold on the book. A record is then made at the circulation desk that serves to identify the patron making the request, the book in question, and often a period of time during which the patron can wait for the book. The next step occurs upon the return of the book. The circulation attendant, alerted from the charge record that the book is now "on hold" for another patron, segregates the book and takes necessary steps to notify the requesting patron that the book is available and being held. This is a simplified example of an activity that can be more complicated if multiple copies, multiple branches, or multiple patrons are involved. Information regarding holds for specific titles can also be used as an effective selection tool.

Another important controlling activity concerns circulation *recalls*. Libraries often allow patrons to renew books on the condition that the item will be promptly returned if another patron later needs to use it. The recall activity consists of calling books back into the library so that they can be loaned to the other patron. Thus a request for a hold or reserve initiates a recall of a renewed book. Once again, this relatively simple activity can become very complicated, either by the number of recall requests that are received, by the geographical distances, or by the time delays between the recall request and the actual return of the book.

In order to encourage quick compliance to recall requests, as well as to ensure prompt return of loaned materials, libraries often impose a system of fines. The *fines* activity is also closely related to the charge and discharge activities. Depending on individual library policy, fines may be imposed after a grace period. The fines themselves vary in amounts, and they can be accumulated in a number of different ways. The two most common are straight line (accumulation of a fixed amount per day), and sliding scale (accumulation of decreasing or increasing daily amounts). Fines are normally accumulated up to a certain amount per book and then stay at that maximum amount. As is the case with holds and recalls, the fines function can become complex, particularly when a library has separate loan periods for different patron types, media types, branch locations, etc.

The controlling activities of recall and fines as well as the function of notifying patrons of overdue materials is dependent upon the library's ability to send notices to the patrons. The proper functioning of the *notification* process is dependent on accurately maintained patron registration files, clearly defined policies regarding loan periods and fines, and patron response to the notice itself.

Interlibrary Loan

Because no library contains all books and most contain only very selected collections, the need arises to obtain copies of materials that are not part of the library's collection. The solution to this problem resides in the cooperative efforts between libraries called interlibrary loan. Interlibrary loan allows all those libraries that are willing to cooperate and accept standard conventions to serve as one large geographically scattered library whose collection is accessible to all users. This cooperative process is frequently part of the responsibility of the circulation department.

Interlibrary loan is perhaps the oldest form of cooperation among libraries. The first draft of a national code and guidelines regarding interlibrary loan was presented and discussed at the 1912 ALA annual conference. The codes have been regularly revised since that date, with the latest revision in 1980 (Interlibrary Loan Committee, RASD, ALA). The national interlibrary loan code provides a nationally recognized code to govern and regulate requests between libraries that have no other cooperative agreements. The code recognized that libraries participating in the cooperative effort have numerous obligations to each other. The borrowing library is subject to the restrictions of the lending library. The lending library is encouraged to be as generous as local circumstance will allow. The model interlibrary loan code recognizes the need for cooperative agreements that are apart from the national code for regional, state, local, or special groups. The model provides guidelines for specialized loan agreements that complement the national code while providing for more flexibility.

Interlibrary loan operations in a library can be divided into two basic groups: those associated with borrowing materials from another library and those associated with lending materials to another library. Both of these activities represent a more involved variation of the complete range of activities that comprise the general circulation functions. This is due to the presence of a third party, the other library.

The borrowing activity is initiated when a user requests materials that can only be obtained outside the local library's resources. The interlibrary loan staff then verifies the bibliographic citation and identifies other libraries that own the desired materials through the use of bibliographic union lists, book catalogs, and bibliographical utilities. The accuracy of this step is essential to procuring the correct item and future cooperation. Requests on standard forms are then sent to a library that owns the material. After receipt of the requested book, the user is notified of its arrival and the item is charged out to him. At the end of the loan period, the user returns the item to the library, and it in turn is sent back to the owning (lending) library. These borrowing activities are further complicated in practice when materials cannot be correctly verified, fees must be paid, or more than one lending library must be contacted.

The lending activities for the interlibrary loan function are initiated upon receipt of a request from a borrowing library. The first step involves verification of ownership and availability of the requested item. Once the item is located, it is sent to the requesting (borrowing) library. The final step consists of ensuring prompt return of the item. Lending activities are certainly more difficult if the requested item cannot be located or if the materials are not returned from the borrowing library.

Interlibrary loan has been greatly enhanced with the growth of national computerized bibliographic databases. Although the initial impetus of the databases was cooperative cataloging, their advantage to interlibrary loan operations was immediately obvious. This use of the databases led the bibliographical utilities to develop interlibrary loan subsystems that have increased not only the speed but also the volume of interlibrary lending. Automated interlibrary loan subsystems are also redistributing the lending burden from just the large research libraries to all member libraries.

Charging fees for lending is a major issue. Interlibrary loan activities are increasing rapidly due to participation in bibliographic utilities and decreasing book budgets. Libraries that lend more materials than they borrow (net lenders) have frequently provided this service to other libraries without charge. The changing economic picture and the increasing volume of activity have led more and more of the net lenders to charge for lending services. Local, state, and regional cooperative groups, recognizing the value and expense of lending service, are developing compensation programs for net lenders.

Reserves Collection

The circulation departments of school and academic libraries sometimes take on the added responsibility of organizing and maintaining a reserve book collection. The reserve book collection is usually a separate, closed collection of materials designated by faculty as required reading for courses. The materials have limited loan periods, and generally there are relatively high fines to assure greater access by the large numbers of students who must use them. This collection changes each term as courses and requirements change. The reserve book collection concept should not be confused with the "reserve" request or hold procedure that was discussed earlier in this chapter.

The activities performed in organizing a reserve collection begin with the notification from the faculty that specific materials are required reading for their courses. The circulation staff then collects the specified items, marks them as reserve materials, and generates the necessary files. The files or lists that provide access to the collection include an author file, title file, call number file, course number–name file, and a listing by faculty member's name. Further, the items on reserve must be noted in the regular circulation files or in the card catalog to minimize the confusion of patrons who may not know that certain items are in the reserve collection. The reserve collection procedure becomes problematic when required materials are not owned by the library, multiple copies are needed, or requested items are already in circulation. At the end of each term, materials that are no longer needed in the reserve collection are returned to their permanent stacks location, the necessary records are updated, and the process outlined above begins again.

MANAGING CIRCULATION

Library circulation is a necessary ongoing activity. As the environment of the library changes, the circulation operations must also adapt. Choosing an appropriate charging system is a periodic consideration. Even when the "final" determination is to retain the existing system and maintain the status quo for just a few more years, the library administration has the benefit, through the review process, of knowing exactly what the marketplace is offering and how new products affect the costs and services of the library. As long as the environment continues to change, librarians will have to review their systems.

One of the most practical and popular methods for reviewing circulation systems is the cost-benefit study. Briefly stated, it identifies the relative costs of systems and attempts to balance these costs against the relative advantages of each choice. A detailed systems study for manual circulation operations is contained in the *Study of Circulation Control Systems* (George Fry and Associates, 1961). A cost–benefit study for automated circulation systems is somewhat more complex. Capital equipment, labor, and material are weighed against such benefits as turn-around time, patron satisfaction with better selection and collection maintenance, operational efficiency, and statistical information.

During the past 20 years there have been numerous studies and texts on the subject of systems analysis of circulation (Lubans, 1975; Dougherty and Heinritz, 1966). As with librarianship, systems analysis is a relatively dynamic area of research and study. For example, one very new approach is structure systems analysis and design (De-Marco, 1978). Although this technique is developing in the computer software industry, librarianship can certainly borrow from its more useful attributes and procedures.

LITERATURE OF CIRCULATION

Library Literature by H. W. Wilson Company and *Information Science Abstracts* by Documentation Abstracts, Inc. provide access to journal articles, theses, research reports, and monographs on various aspects of circulation. Articles on circulation are printed in a broad range of library journals, including those dealing with automation, reference services, and technical services. Most current journal articles on circulation are found in the titles on library automation that are discussed in Chapter 3. The literature lacks a current, comprehensive text on circulation policy, administration, and operations.

SUMMARY

As we have seen, the functional components of library circulation systems are not standardized. Rather, they are conditional on the library's environment. The circulation system evolves gradually and requires constant review and analysis. The functions for circulating materials are complex and detailed. Further, circulation is a major public relations activity because all patrons directly interact with the system. Few areas in the library require more skill in interpersonal communication or attention to detail.

REFERENCES

DeMarco, T. *Structured analysis and system specification.* New York: Yourdon, 1978.

Dougherty, R. M., & Heinritz, F. J. *Scientific management of library operations.* New York: Scarecrow Press, 1966.

George Fry and Associates, Inc. *Study of circulation control systems.* Chicago: Library Technology Project of the American Library Association, 1961.

Greer, H. T. *Charging systems.* Chicago: American Library Association, 1955.

Information Science Abstracts (Vols. 1–). Philadelphia: Documentation Abstracts, Inc., March 1966–.

Interlibrary Loan Committee, Reference and Adult Services Division, ALA. *Interlibrary loan codes, 1980: International lending principles and guidelines, 1978.* Chicago: American Library Association, 1980.

Library Literature. New York: H. W. Wilson, 1933–.

Lubans, J. Jr., & Chapman, E. A. *Reader in library systems analysis.* Englewood, Col.: Microcard Editions Books, 1975.

Rochell, C. *Wheeler and Goldhor's practical administration of public libraries.* (Rev. ed.). New York: Harper & Row, 1981.

Tauber, M. F. *Technical services in libraries.* New York: Columbia University Press, 1954.

Thompson, E. H. *A.L.A. Glossary of library terms with a selection of terms in related fields.* Chicago: American Library Association, 1943.

BIBLIOGRAPHY

Bahr, A. H. *Automated library circulation systems, 1979–80* (2nd ed.). White Plains, N.Y.: Knowledge Industry Publications, 1979.

Bloomberg, M. *Introduction to public services for library technicians* (2nd ed.). Littleton, Col.: Libraries Unlimited, 1977.

Boss, R. W., & McQueen, J. Automated circulation control systems. *Library Technology Reports,* 1982, *18,* 123–267.

Buckland, M. K. *Book availability and the library user.* New York: Pergamon Press, Inc., 1978.

Burgess, T. K. A cost effectiveness model for comparing various circulation systems. *Journal of Library Automation,* 1973, *6,* 75–86.

Burkhalter, B. R. (Ed.). *Case studies in systems analysis in a university library.* Metuchen, N.Y.: Scarecrow Press, Inc., 1968.

Fasana, P. J. *A computer based system for reserve activities in a university library.* New York: Columbia University, 1969. (ERIC Documentation Reproduction Service No. ED 035 431)

Freedman, M. J. Circulation systems past and present. *Journal of Library Automation,* 1981, *14,* 278–285.

Hunt, D. H. (Ed.). Charging systems. *Drexel Library Quarterly,* 1965, *1,* (3), 1–37.

Jestes, E. C. Manual versus automated circulation: A comparison of operating costs in a university library. *Journal of Academic Librarianship,* 1980, *6,* 144–150.

Magrill, R. M., & Rinehart, C. *Library technical services: A selected, annotated bibliography.* Westport, Conn.: Greenwood Press, 1977.

Mansfield, J. W. Human factors of queuing: A library circulation model. *Journal of Academic Librarianship*, 1981, *6*, 342–344.

Martin, J. R. Automation and the service attitudes of ARL circulation managers. *Journal of Library Automation*, 1981, *14*, 190–194.

Matthews, J. R. *Choosing an automated library system: A planning guide.* Chicago: American Library Association, 1980.

Mosley, I. J. Cost effectiveness analysis of the automation of a circulation system. *Journal of Library Automation*, 1977, *10*, 240–254.

Stevens, N. D. Library networks and resource sharing in the United States: An historical and philosophical overview. *American Society for Information Science Journal*, 1980, *31*, 405–412.

Thomson, S. K. *Interlibrary loan procedure manual.* Chicago: American Library Association, 1970.

Index